IFIP Advances in Information and Communication Technology

528

Editor-in-Chief

Kai Rannenberg, *Goethe University Frankfurt, Germany*

IFIP – The International Federation for Information Processing

IFIP was founded in 1960 under the auspices of UNESCO, following the first World Computer Congress held in Paris the previous year. A federation for societies working in information processing, IFIP's aim is two-fold: to support information processing in the countries of its members and to encourage technology transfer to developing nations. As its mission statement clearly states:

> *IFIP is the global non-profit federation of societies of ICT professionals that aims at achieving a worldwide professional and socially responsible development and application of information and communication technologies.*

IFIP is a non-profit-making organization, run almost solely by 2500 volunteers. It operates through a number of technical committees and working groups, which organize events and publications. IFIP's events range from large international open conferences to working conferences and local seminars.

The flagship event is the IFIP World Computer Congress, at which both invited and contributed papers are presented. Contributed papers are rigorously refereed and the rejection rate is high.

As with the Congress, participation in the open conferences is open to all and papers may be invited or submitted. Again, submitted papers are stringently refereed.

The working conferences are structured differently. They are usually run by a working group and attendance is generally smaller and occasionally by invitation only. Their purpose is to create an atmosphere conducive to innovation and development. Refereeing is also rigorous and papers are subjected to extensive group discussion.

Publications arising from IFIP events vary. The papers presented at the IFIP World Computer Congress and at open conferences are published as conference proceedings, while the results of the working conferences are often published as collections of selected and edited papers.

IFIP distinguishes three types of institutional membership: Country Representative Members, Members at Large, and Associate Members. The type of organization that can apply for membership is a wide variety and includes national or international societies of individual computer scientists/ICT professionals, associations or federations of such societies, government institutions/government related organizations, national or international research institutes or consortia, universities, academies of sciences, companies, national or international associations or federations of companies.

More information about this series at http://www.springer.com/series/6102

Nurit Gal-Oz · Peter R. Lewis (Eds.)

Trust
Management XII

12th IFIP WG 11.11 International Conference, IFIPTM 2018
Toronto, ON, Canada, July 10–13, 2018
Proceedings

Springer

Editors
Nurit Gal-Oz
Sapir Academic College
D.N. Hof Ashkelon
Israel

Peter R. Lewis
Aston University
Birmingham
UK

ISSN 1868-4238   ISSN 1868-422X (electronic)
IFIP Advances in Information and Communication Technology
ISBN 978-3-030-07006-9   ISBN 978-3-319-95276-5 (eBook)
https://doi.org/10.1007/978-3-319-95276-5

Printed on acid-free paper

This Springer imprint is published by the registered company Springer International Publishing AG
part of Springer Nature
The registered company address is: Gewerbestrasse 11, 6330 Cham, Switzerland

Preface

The 12th edition of IFIPTM, the IFIP WG11.11 International Conference on Trust Management held in Toronto, Canada, continued the tradition of a technological scientific gathering that focuses on trust, an essential component of any resilient society.

Since 2007, IFIPTM conferences have provided a global platform for the reporting of research, development, policy, and practice in areas related to trust, security, and privacy. IFIPTM 2018 invited research in areas concerning trust from a broad perspective including trust and reputation models, privacy issues, social and behavioral models of trust, economic and sociological trust, trust building in large-scale systems, the relationship between trust and security, trust under attacks, and trustworthiness of adaptive systems.

The program of the conference features both theoretical research papers and reports of real-world case studies. This year we have received 22 submissions from 14 different countries and were able to accept seven full papers and three short papers. Our 33 Program Committee members produced a total of 90 reviews and were engaged in an effective discussion process. The selected papers represent the broad topical areas of the call for papers.

We are happy to include in these proceedings the paper accompanying the keynote by Theo Dimitrakos, holder of the William Winsborough Commemorative Address and Award 2018. The objective of the award is to publicly recognize an individual who has significantly contributed to the development of computational trust or trust management, especially achievements with an international perspective. The award is given in memory of Professor William Winsborough, who taught at the University of Texas at San Antonio, in recognition of his leadership in the field of trust and trust management. Theo was honored for his contribution to the scientific growth and shaping of the area with a series of relevant papers in the first decade of this millennium. He also contributed to the creation of the scientific communities through the iTrust project and conference and subsequent IFIP WG 11.11 creation and management for several years. From both a scientific and organizational perspective, Theo helped to establish the trust management field. His keynote paper discusses security controls-oriented reference architecture, an approach that extends commonly used security architecture methodologies by placing particular emphasis on how security controls are specified, refined, implemented, traced, and assessed throughout the security design and development life-cycle.

We would like to express our thanks to everyone who contributed to the organization of IFIPTM this year. We thank the general chairs, Stephen Marsh and Jeremy Pitt, for their great efforts in organizing the conference and making it an exciting event. We thank the other chairs on the committee, Sheikh Mahbub Habib, Tosan Atele-williams, Anirban Basu, Christian Damsgaard Jensen, Saghar Behrooz, and

Kelvin Ellison, who provided continual and unstinting support during the entire endeavor. Finally, we are indebted to the entire Program Committee for their commitment and enthusiasm in all phases of the reviewing process, and for the quality and insight of their reviews.

July 2018   Nurit Gal-Oz
                                                                                         Peter Lewis

Organization

Program Committee

Anirban Basu	KDDI Research, Inc.
David Chadwick	University of Kent, UK
Theo Dimitrakos	European Security Competence Center, Huawei Technologies
Natasha Dwyer	Victoria University, Australia
Benedikt Eberhardinger	University of Augsburg, Germany
Rino Falcone	Institute of Cognitive Sciences and Technologies-CNR
Hui Fang	Shanghai University of Finance and Economics, China
Carmen Fernández-Gago	University of Malaga, Spain
Simone Fischer-Hübner	Karlstad University, Sweden
Sara Foresti	Università degli Studi di Milano, Italy
Lenzini Gabriele	University of Luxembourg, Luxembourg
Nurit Gal-Oz	Sapir Academic College, Israel
Dieter Gollmann	Hamburg University of Technology, Germany
Stefanos Gritzalis	University of the Aegean, Greece
Ehud Gudes	Ben-Gurion University, Israel
Sheikh Mahbub Habib	TU Darmstadt, Germany
Peter Herrmann	Norwegian University of Science and Technology, Norway
Roslan Ismail	Tenaga National University, Malaysia
Christian D. Jensen	Technical University of Denmark
Yuecel Karabulut	Oracle, USA
Peter Lewis	Aston University, UK
Yang Liu	Nanyang Technological University, Singapore
Stephen Marsh	University of Ontario Institute of Technology, Canada
Sjouke Mauw	University of Luxembourg, Luxembourg
Weizhi Meng	Technical University of Denmark, Denmark
Tim Muller	University of Oxford, UK
Yuko Murayama	Tsuda College, Japan
Masakatsu Nishigaki	Shizuoka University, Japan
Mehrdad Nojoumian	Florida Atlantic University, USA
Günther Pernul	Universität Regensburg, Germany
Jeremy Pitt	Imperial College London, UK
Pierangela Samarati	University of Milan, Italy
Ketil Stoelen	SINTEF, Norway
Tim Storer	University of Glasgow, UK
Claire Vishik	Intel Corporation, UK
Shouhuai Xu	University of Texas at San Antonio, USA
Jie Zhang	Nanyang Technological University, Singapore

Additional Reviewers

Alexopoulos, Nikolaos
Böhm, Fabian
Drogkaris, Prokopios
Gadyatskaya, Olga
Groll, Sebastian
Kaporis, Alexis
Karyda, Maria
Nguyen, Phu
Omerovic, Aida
Puchta, Alexander
Skjuve, Marita

Contents

How to Develop a Security Controls Oriented Reference Architecture for Cloud, IoT and SDN/NFV Platforms

Theo Dimitrakos[1,2(✉)]

[1] School of Computing, University of Kent, Canterbury, UK
t.dimitrakos@kent.ac.uk
[2] CSPL, Huawei Technologies Duesseldorf GmbH, Düsseldorf, Germany
theo.dimitrakos@huawei.com

Abstract. In this paper we present a security architecture style and approach named *Security Controls Oriented Reference (SCORE) Architecture.* The SCORE Architecture extends commonly used security architecture methodologies by placing particular emphasis on how security controls are specified, refined, implemented, traced and assessed throughout the security design and development life-cycle. It encompasses experience of over 30 years in secure systems design and development and it has been applied in practice for developing security capabilities for on top of advanced Cloud, NFV and IoT platforms.

Keywords: Security controls · Reference architecture · Security risk
Systems design

1 Introduction

Modernization represents the changes that every organization must face as the generations of technology, skills and expectations are inevitably replaced by the next ones. Telecom Service Providers (TSP), Cloud Service Providers (CSP) and Enterprises alike prepare for the inevitable impact that Cloud Computing, Software Defined Networks (SDN) with Network Function Virtualization (NFV) and the Internet of Things (IoT) have on how to conduct business and compete.

Cloud, SDN/NFV and IoT are delivery models for technology enabled services that drive greater agility, speed and cost savings. Although used in different scope, they all provide on-demand access via a network to an elastic pool of interconnected computing assets (e.g. devices, services, applications, frameworks, platforms, servers, storage, and networks) that can be rapidly provisioned and released with minimal service provider interaction and scaled as needed to enable pay per use. They enable faster delivery of services and on premise cost savings they to optimise the time from idea to solution. They also depend on complex supply networks and ecosystems with shared responsibility models for their delivery and operation. Enterprises will typically consume applications, compute services or devices offered and sometimes also operated by multiple providers. TSP and CSP will often deliver and operate platforms that are developed by many different vendors and whose operations and maintenance (O&M) often involves one or more third parties. In a platform provider, different product lines focus on but interdependent products and services that are later integrated into a Cloud, NFV or IoT platforms. Reference architectures and shared responsibility models are essential tools to govern and align such complex development, integration and O&M ecosystems.

An architectural style [1, 2] is a named collection of architectural design decisions that can be applied to a specific information system and operation context in order constrain and guide architectural design decisions in that context and elicit beneficial qualities in the resulting system. A reference architecture (RA) provides a method and template solution for developing an architecture for a particular domain. It also provides a common set of concepts which stress commonality. It is an architecture where the structures and respective elements and relations provide templates for concrete architectures in a particular domain or in a family of software systems.

A security reference architecture (SRA) for Cloud, NFV or IoT platforms is a RA that focuses on: *(a)* the specification of common security capabilities that are fulfilled by security services and the design of blue-prints for such services; and *(b)* the specification of security requirements that need to be fulfilled by the platform and the design of platform enhancements to fulfill these requirements (leveraging where appropriate the security services). It is not the design of a final solution but a baseline that enables aligning platform development and optimizing service delivery and business operation. SRAs for Cloud, NFV and IoT platforms and services are important for a variety of reasons including the following:

- Provide a reference model for security architecture and security policy to those who have a project to produce or use NFV deployments on public or private cloud infrastructures or inter-cloud software-defined overlay network services that enable IoT.
- Enable effective communication of technical solutions, security impact and development strategy to the senior management of a provider and their customers
- Offer guidance for mission-specific product designs that work together.
- Combine knowledge from TSP and CSP with experts from the Cloud, NfV and SDN security communities (e.g. in ETSI, IETF, CSA, ISF).
- Capture relevant security standards and where appropriate align with them.

In this paper we present a security architecture style and approach named Security Controls Oriented Reference (SCORE) Architecture, which extends commonly used security architecture methodologies by placing particular emphasis on how security controls are specified, refined, implemented, traced and assessed throughout the security design and development lifecycle.

The motivation for SCORE Architecture has been to build into the platform design and development processes the ability to: *(1)* explain in a structured how security and compliance requirements are satisfied by the system design and implementation; *(2)* continuously assess if security and compliance requirements are met to a satisfactory degree; *(3)* ensure the mechanisms satisfying these requirements offer a sufficient level of assurance; *(4)* ensure clear methods of collecting evidence about the ICT system's conformance to these requirements.

2 Basic Concepts

The key concepts used in the SCORE Architecture approach are the summarized in Fig. 1 and detailed in the subsequent sections.

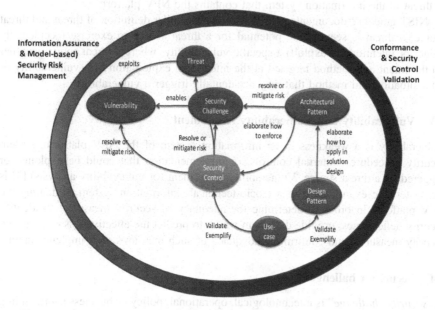

Fig. 1. Overview of the main concepts used in the SCORE Architecture approach.

2.1 Information Assurance, Risk, Continuous Monitoring and Validation

Information Assurance (IA) [3, 4] is about assuring information and managing risks related to the use, processing, storage and transmission of information and data and to the systems and processes used for this purposes. Security risk management [5–7] provides an overall framework guiding the selection of security controls in relation a security (impact/risk) classification. When combined with continuous monitoring [8], evidence-based validation of security control implementation, regular controls update and risk re-assessment, it enables risk-based decision-making and adaptation for security adaptation, and resilience through tailoring and enhancing of security controls and validating the correctness and effectiveness of their implementation.

2.2 Security Threats and Threat Assessment

We define security threat as any circumstance or event with the potential to adversely impact organizational operations of the carrier or enterprise (including mission, functions, image or reputation), organizational assets, individuals, other organizations, or the nations served by the carrier through the NFV platform via unauthorized access, destruction, disclosure, modification of information, and/or denial of service. Typically, a threat source realizes a threat by exploiting some vulnerability. A threat may also be enabled by a security challenge either by means of directly enabling some vulnerability or by means of enabling a threat source to exploit another vulnerability of the system that is not directly caused by the security challenge.

Adapting [4], we define Threat Assessment as the formal description and evaluation of threat to the information system that contains the NFV platform.

NIST guidance documents [9, 10] also offer a similar definition of threat and threat source: a threat is seen as the potential for a threat source to exercise (accidentally trigger or intentionally exploit) a specific vulnerability, where a threat source is either (1) the intent and method targeted at the intentional exploitation of a vulnerability or (2) a situation and method that may accidentally trigger a vulnerability.

2.3 Vulnerability and Vulnerability Assessment

Vulnerability is a weakness in an information system of the NFV platform, system security procedures, internal controls, or implementation that could be exploited or triggered by a threat source. Vulnerability assessment (or vulnerability analysis) [4] is the systematic examination of a (socio-technical) information system containing the NFV platform in order to determine the adequacy of security measures, to identify security deficiencies, provide data from which to predict the effectiveness of proposed security measures, and confirm the adequacy of such measures after implementation.

2.4 Security Challenges

A "*security challenge*" is a technological, operational, policy or business shortcoming, unresolved technical issue, design, implementation choice or operational complexity that may possibly give rise to vulnerabilities or enable a threat actor to exploit vulnerabilities. Security challenge may often be the security side-effects of a desired and necessary functionality of the system.

One can argue that the effects of security challenges may be split into threats and vulnerabilities and therefore reduce or remove the need for capturing and recording security challenges. However our experience with applying security architecture best practice is that threats and vulnerabilities resulting from security challenges have complex interdependences and characteristic causality which may result in implicit but distinct semantic differences compared to a similar vulnerability caused by external factors. Security challenges for systems conforming to the ETSI NFV Reference Architecture implemented on top of a Cloud (IaaS) NFVI are provided in [13, 14]. These are consistent with, and more comprehensive than, previous security challenges and requirements elicited by ETSI [15] and CSA [16, 17].

2.5 Security Requirements

A security requirement is a requirement levied on the information system and organization that contains or operates the NFV platform. It is derived from mission or business needs, regulation, legislation, directives, organizational policies, standards, threat analyses, risk management advisories, guidance and procedures in order to ensure the confidentiality/privacy, integrity, accountability and availability of information (including data and software) that is being processed, stored or transmitted.

2.6 Security Controls and Security Control Assessment

Security controls are the safeguards/countermeasures prescribed for information systems or organizations that are designed to: protect the confidentiality/privacy, integrity, accountability and availability of information that is processed, stored and transmitted by those systems/organizations; and to satisfy a set of defined security requirements [11]. A security control resolves or mitigates the risk associated with some threat either by correcting an existing vulnerability or by preventing a security challenge enable vulnerabilities or by preventing vulnerability exploitation by a threat source. A security control must come together with metrics for assessing the level of assurance of its implementation.

A *Security Control Baseline* [5] is the set of minimum security controls that provides a starting point for the *"security controls tailoring"* process [11]: *(i)* identifying and designating common controls; *(ii)* applying scoping considerations on the applicability and implementation of baseline controls; *(iii)* selecting compensating security controls; *(iv)* assigning specific values to organization-defined security control parameters; *(v)* supplementing baselines with additional security controls or control enhancements; and *(vi)* providing additional specification information for control implementation. Security controls may also be enhanced as part of tailoring in order to: *(a)* build in additional, but related, functionality to the control; *(b)* increase the strength of the control; or *(c)* add assurance to the control.

Security Control Inheritance [4] means that an information system receives protection from security controls (or portions of security controls) that are developed, implemented, assessed, authorized, and monitored by entities other than those responsible for the system or application; entities either internal or external to the organization where the system or application resides.

Security Control Assessment is the testing or evaluation of security controls to determine the extent to which the controls are implemented correctly, operating as intended and producing the desired outcome with respect to meeting the security requirements for an information system or organization [4].

2.7 Architectural and Design Patterns

An architectural pattern is a rigorous description in a specific architectural style that solves and delineates some essential cohesive elements of a system architecture. The functionality described by an architectural pattern is sometimes referred to in the literature as a Common Capability [18].

A design pattern elaborates how to apply the architectural pattern into a specific information system or product implementation and how to collect the corresponding evidence to asses both conformance to the architectural pattern and the fulfillment of the corresponding security controls. Different system or solution architectures may implement the same patterns [19].

Architectural and design patterns should be used to elaborate how security controls are realized and enforced and what is the required evidence to fulfill the level of assurance of the control implementation. It should then also capture dependences between security controls, trace their relationship to security challenges and security requirements and evidence how a collection of security controls resolve or mitigate corresponding threats and vulnerabilities. Use-cases should be used as the preferred means of explaining by means of exemplar scenarios how threats and vulnerabilities are resolved or mitigated via the application of security controls as realized by the corresponding architectural patterns.

3   SCORE Architecture Process

A simplified overview of the architecture development process used in the SCORE Architecture approach is described in Fig. 2: In this section we elaborate each stage of this process.

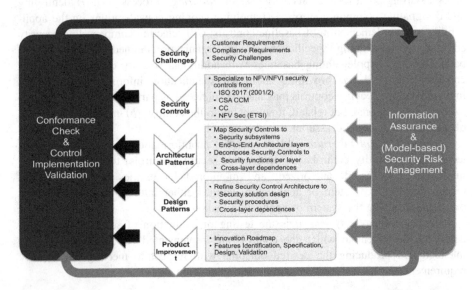

Fig. 2. Simplified overview of the process that underpins the SCORE Architecture

3.1   Information Assurance: A Security Risk Management

Risk Management and *Information Assurance* are continuous governance processes that govern the assessment and impact analysis of threats, vulnerabilities and security challenges and the selection, adaptation and refinement ("tailoring") of security controls as well as risk associated with the sufficiency of the selected security control implementations. Security risk management and information assurance are enacted during and in between these sequentially linked steps and they may trigger iteration from any sequentially linked design and development stage to any preceding stage.

The SCORE Architecture recommends that NCSS/NIST Risk Management Framework (RMF) [20] enhanced with the guidance of ENISA publications "Cloud Computing Risk Assessment" [21] and "Cloud Computing Information Assurance" [22]. The following Fig. 3 summarizes the risk management steps.

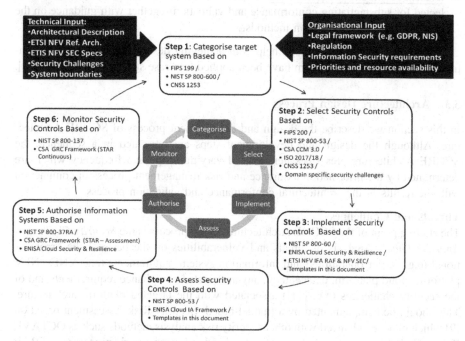

Fig. 3. Extending NIST RMF in accordance to the SCORE Architecture framework

3.2 Architectural Conformance and Implementation Validation

Typically the implementation of security controls is validated by internal and third party security auditors and certification authorities. However, in order to improve security and privacy by design through continuous improvement and alignment between control definition and implementation, SCORE Architecture recommends that *architectural conformance and implementation validation* is enacted as a continuous process complementing risk management and information assurance. First the conformance of the design and implementation of a control to the specification of the control is ensured, then once implementation is approved the conformance of the implementation with the design and architecture patterns is assured in addition to the validation of the implementation. The SCORE Architecture requires that every control comes together with:

– Conformance guidance: qualitative information and metrics on how to assess conformance of the control architecture. Each architectural pattern contains criteria that must be met by the conformant design patterns.

- Validation metrics and requirements: test-cases, metrics, validation criteria and qualitative guidance that help validate the correctness of the implementation of a control. This may be similar to what certification bodies and auditors would require when assessing the system.
- Evidence collection requirements: a classification of the data that need to be collected for substantiating conformance and validation together with guidance on the preferred evidence collection methods.

Additional techniques that can help with achieving design conformance are mentioned in [22] and some of them have been applied to a case study on CryptoDB [23].

3.3 Architecture Design Process

In this section we describe the design and development process of SCORE Architecture. Although the design and development steps are presented in a sequence, the SCORE Architecture prescribes iterations of varying scope and frequency which are determined by the information assurance and risk management process in conjunction with the results of the architectural conformance and validation process.

Threats and Challenges

The starting point of the SCORE Architecture design process is the *Security Challenges Analysis Phase*. Analysis of threats and vulnerabilities on the basis of the organizational (e.g. carrier operations) and information system requirements (e.g. VNFs, NFV platform, cloud platform, datacenters), any anticipated compliance requirements and of the security challenges (e.g. [11]) associated with the targeted platform architecture. This should be complemented by a (model-based) Security Risk Assessment based on [9] which may be enhanced with other security risk analysis methods such as OCTAVE [24] or COBRA for assessing security risk related to human centric processes or FRAP [25] and m CORAS [26, 27] for assessing information system or product/platform risks. Risk and impact should be classified so as to enable a base line of control for each risk acceptance and impact level and also be traced by to the associated threats, vulnerabilities and organizational or compliance requirements.

Security Controls

An important stage of the SCORE Architecture process is the elicitation and specification of the specific security controls for the system being architected. The security controls underpin the risk management process and provide a reference for the information assurance process. They also scope and steer the development of security architectural patterns and consequently design patterns and their imprint must be traceable and measurable (or assessable) in every step from information system design to the targeted application and platform implementations. The elicitation and specification of security controls typically includes the following steps: *(1)* Security control catalog selection; *(2)* Security categorization; *(3)* Security control base-line determination; *(4)* Security control tailoring.

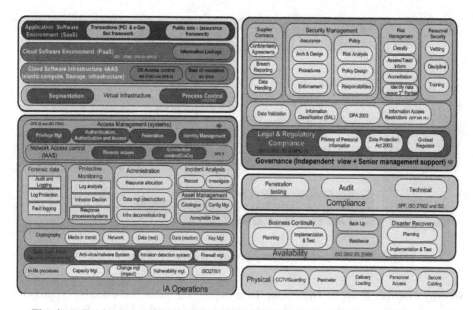

Fig. 4. Indicative categorization for a catalog (repository) of relevant security controls

Security Control Repository and Catalog Selection: Defining the security controls catalog form a repository of security controls. For Cloud, IoT and NFV platforms, SCORE Architecture recommends a base-line for the security controls repository (Fig. 4) based on ISO/IEC 27017 extending ISO/IEC 27001 and 27002 complemented with CSA Cloud Controls Matrix including their reference to the scope of applicability of each control. Figure 4: summarizes an indicative collection and classification of relevant security controls based on CSAISO/IEC 27001 and 27017/27018

Security Categorization: Determining the criticality and sensitivity of the information to be processed, stored, or transmitted by the target platform including the corresponding Operation and Maintenance (O&M) processes. *FIPS Publication 199* [28] offers commonly referenced security categorization. SCORE Architecture the following formula in for describing impact, where the acceptable values for potential impact are *low, moderate,* or *high.* This formula extends [28] with additional security objectives relating to privacy and accountability in order to accommodate recent regulations in Europe relating to the implementation of GDPR [28] and NIS directive [29]:

Security_Category = {(confidentiality, impact), (privacy, impact), (integrity, impact), (accountability, impact), (availability, impact)}.

Following the security categorization, security controls are then selected as countermeasures to the potential adverse impact described in the results of the security classification. Figure 5 summarizes the security control selection and tailoring process described in this section and the corresponding documentation extending [16, 31].

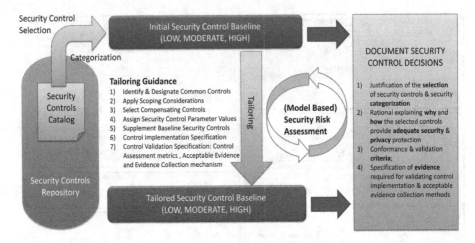

Fig. 5. Summary of the security controls selection and documentation

Security Controls Baseline Definition: Determining the most cost-effective, appropriate set of security controls, which if implemented and determined to be effective, would mitigate security risk while complying with security requirements and security challenges defined in the previous phase. To assist organizations in making the appropriate selection of security controls, NIST defines the concept of *baseline controls* [11]. Baseline controls are the starting point for the security control selection process. Furthermore [11] in Appendix D defines three security control base-lines in accordance with FIPS Publication 199 and FIPS Publication 200.

The security controls must be carefully reviewed and revised periodically to reflect experience gained from using the controls, directives and regulations, changing security requirements and new or emerging threats, vulnerabilities, and attack methods as well as new security challenges resulting from the emergence of new technologies. Also security controls catalogs may be specialized for different regions to reflect differences in legislation.

Once the applicable security controls baseline has been selected, the controls in the baseline need to be tailored.

Security Controls Tailoring: To modify appropriately and align the controls more closely with the specific conditions of the targeted system and its intended context of operation. Security controls must not be removed at any stage from the baseline to serve operation convenience. The following tailoring activities must be approved by authorizing officials in coordination with selected organizational officials:

- Identifying and designating common controls in initial security control baselines;
- Applying scoping considerations to the remaining baseline security controls;
- Selecting compensating security controls, if needed;
- Assigning specific values to organization-defined security control parameters via explicit assignment and selection statements;

- Supplementing baselines with additional security controls and control enhancements, if needed – see [11, 31] for details and references to examples of recommended supplementary security controls;
- Providing additional specification information for control implementation, if needed.

Every security control from a baseline must be accounted for either by the organizations consuming or operating the service or by the product or platform owner. Each of these actors must determine which controls are implemented solely by the actor, which correspond to shared responsibility and which are implemented by another of these actors.

Documenting Security Controls: It is necessary to document all relevant decisions take during the security control selection process. Such documentation provides a very important input in assessing the security of a system in relation to the potential mission or business impact. This documentation together with supporting evidence about the correctness and conformance of the security control implementations provides valuable information for information assurance, architectural improvements, change or revision and compliance assessment or accreditation. It also constitutes a reference document for NFV platform providers, VNF developers, Cloud IaaS providers, carriers and enterprises understanding how to implement shared or common controls and control overlays.

Architectural and Design Patterns Definition

This phase of SCORE Architecture starts by mapping security controls to the different layers and components of the target system. In this mapping, security controls provide the common technical requirements for the elicitation of common capabilities which are documented by means of architectural patterns. Detailed examples of how to elicit common technical requirements and identify common capabilities for cloud platforms are provided in [18]. An illustrative high level overview of such a mapping is provided in Fig. 6.

In addition to defining common (security) capabilities and their architectural or design patterns, conformance and traceability must be assured and maintained. SCORE Architecture provides templates for architectural and design patterns that ensure:

(1) Specifying which security controls are satisfied by the pattern;
(2) Explain how the requirements, description, intend and dependences are met by the pattern for each referenced security control;
(3) Specifying criteria, metrics and preferred conformance validation methods for ensuring conformance of subsequent design patterns to the architectural pattern;
(4) Specifying criteria, metrics and preferred methods for validating the implementation of the architectural or design pattern and for collecting evidence that is suitable to support such validation.

The dependences to other design patterns – including those describing relevant information models as well the application of relevant policies and procedures – must be specified explicitly. Typically design pattern dependences inherit and extend architectural pattern dependences. The implementation results in interdependent

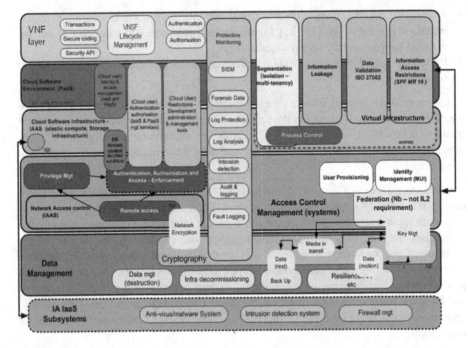

Fig. 6. Mapping security controls into subsystems of the NFV/Cloud platform layers

sub-system. It is therefore very important to ensure traceability of dependences and validate it as part of architectural conformance. Furthermore, technical use-cases (decomposing and refining the generic use-cases used for common capabilities and architectural patterns) should be used in order to describe the functionalities and usage scenarios of the corresponding design patterns. It is recommended that refinement of architectural pattern to design pattern is aligned with and informed by the refinement of general use-case through to technical use-cases and its decomposition to several sub-use cases.

Product Improvement

The SCORE Architecture also includes guidelines for product improvement that are consistent with system engineering methods such as IPD, ISC and Agile. These guidelines comprise:

- Guidance on (product) features identification, specification, design, validation including (1) design specialization; (2) prioritization of technical requirements and templates to assist this prioritization; (3) GAP analysis against the prioritized requirements and templates to assist this analysis; (4) Change impact assessment and (5) change management; (6) Time-line definition
- Guidance on defining an innovation roadmap and a product improvement time-line in order to guide future enhancements and identified shortcomings. SCORE provides templates to assist innovation roadmap creation and maintenance.

4 Conclusion

In this paper I presented a method for developing reference security architectures for distributed information systems such Cloud, IoT and NFV platforms. This approach reflects over 20 years of research and incorporates methodologies developed through analysis and experimentation in [17] (where 100 organizations conducted 25 experiments in Enterprise use of Cloud Computing) with model-based risk analysis (e.g. [26, 27]) and guidance from NIST, ENISA, ETSI, ISO and CSA. In its current form, the SCORE Architecture approach has been used for developing reference architectures of innovative security capabilities for intrusion prevention and data protection in multi-provider clouds in the context of EIT Digital High Impact Initiative on Trusted Cloud in cooperation where BT, TIM and Huawei participated. It has also been validated in additional use-cases with KDDI Research and it is currently being used by security researchers in Huawei for developing security reference architectures for NFV and Hybrid Cloud platforms.

References

1. Taylor, R.N., Medvidović, N.N., Dashofy, E.M.: Software Architecture: Foundations. Theory and Practice, Wiley, Hoboken (2009)
2. Shaw, M., Garlan, D.: Software Architecture: Perspectives on an Emerging Discipline. Prentice Hall, Upper Saddle River (1996)
3. Kissel, R.: Glossary of Key Information Security Terms (NISTIR 7298 Revision 2). NIST (National Institute of Standards and Technology) (2013)
4. CNSS: National Information Assurance (IA) Glossary. CNSS Instruction No. 4009. National Security Agency (NSA) (2003)
5. FIPS: Minimum Security Requirements for Federal Information and Information Systems (FIPS 200). Federal Information Processing Standards (2006)
6. NIST: Guide for Applying the Risk Management Framework (RMF) to Federal Information Systems: a Security Life Cycle Approach. National Institute of Standards and Technology (2010, updated)
7. NIST: Risk Management Framework for Information Systems and Organizations: A System Life Cycle Approach for Security and Privacy (Discussion Draft) (2017)
8. Dempsey, K., Chawla, N.S., Johnson, A., Johnston, R., Jones, A.C., Orebaugh, A., Scholl, M., Stine, K.: Information Security Continuous Monitoring (ISCM) for Federal Information Systems and Organizations. National Institute of Standards and Technology (2011)
9. Joint Task Force Transformation Initiative: Guide for Conducting Risk Assessments (NIST SP 800-30r1). National Institute of Standards and Technology (2012)
10. Stoneburner, G., Goguen, A., Feringa, A.: Risk Management Guide for Information Technology Systems. NIST - National Institute of Standards and Technology (2002)
11. Joint Task Force: Security and Privacy Controls for Federal Information Systems and Organizations. National Institute of Standards and Technology (2013)
12. ETSI: Network Functions Virtualisation (NFV); Architectural Framework. The European Telecommunications Standards Institute (2013)
13. Dimitrakos, T.: Security Challenges and Guidance for Protecting NFV on Cloud IaaS. ETSI NFV Security Week (2017). https://docbox.etsi.org/workshop/2017/201706_SECURITYWEEK/05_NFVSECURITY

14. Dimitrakos, T.: Towards a security reference architecture for Network Function Virtualisation: security challenges and security controls. In: NECS (2017)
15. ETSI: Network Functions Virtualisation (NFV), NFV Security, Security and Trust Guidance. The European Telecommunications Standards Institute (2014)
16. CSA: Network Function Virtualization. CSA (2016)
17. CSA: Best Practices for Mitigating Risks in Virtualized Environments. CSA (2015)
18. Dimitrakos, T.: Service Oriented Infrastructures and Cloud Service Platforms for the Enterprise: A Selection of Common Capabilities Validated in Real-Life Business Trials. Springer, Heidelberg (2009). https://doi.org/10.1007/978-3-642-04086-3. (Ed. by, T. Dimitrakos, J. Martrat, S. Wesner)
19. Taylor, R.N., Medvidovic, N., Dashofy, E.M.: Software Architecture: Foundations, Theory, and Practice. Wiley, Hoboken (2009)
20. NIST: Risk Management Framework (RMF) Overview, 30 November 2016
21. ENISA: Cloud Computing Benefits, Risks and Recommendations for Information Security. European Network and Information Security Agency (2009)
22. ENISA: Cloud Computing: Information Assurance Framework. The European Network and Information Security Agency (2009)
23. Abi-Antoun, M., Barnes, J.M.: Analyzing security architectures. In: IEEE/ACM International Conference on Automated Software Engineering (ASE 2010) (2010)
24. Caralli, R.A., Stevens, J.F., Young, L.R., Wilson, W.R.: Introducing OCTAVE Allegro: improving the information security risk assessment process. Software Engineering Institute CMU/SEI Report Number: CMU/SEI-2007-TR-012 (2007)
25. Peltier, T.R.: Information Security Risk Analysis, 3rd edn. CRC Press, Boca Raton (2010)
26. Fredriksen, R., et al.: The CORAS framework for a model-based risk management process. In: Anderson, S., Felici, M., Bologna, S. (eds.) SAFECOMP 2002. LNCS, vol. 2434, pp. 94–105. Springer, Heidelberg (2002). https://doi.org/10.1007/3-540-45732-1_11
27. Lund, M.S., Solhaug, B., Stolen, K.: Model-Driven Risk Analysis - The CORAS Approach. Springer, Heidelberg (2011). https://doi.org/10.1007/978-3-642-12323-8
28. The European Parliament and the Council of the European Union, Regulation (EU) 2016/679. Off. J. Eur. Union (2016)
29. The European Parliament and the Council of the European Union, "Directive (EU) 2016/1148. Off. J. Eur. Union (2016)
30. Stine, K., Kissel, R., Barker, W.C., Fahlsing, J., Gulick, J.: Volume I: Guide for Mapping Types of Information and Information Systems to Security Categories. National Institute of Standards and Technology (2008)
31. Cloud Security Alliance (CSA): Cloud Controls Matrix, 9 January 2017. https://cloudsecurityalliance.org/group/cloud-controls-matrix/
32. Software Engineering Institute: Architecture Conformance. https://www.sei.cmu.edu/architecture/research/previousresearch/conformance.cfm

Continuous User Authentication Using Smartwatch Motion Sensor Data

Neamah Al-Naffakh[1,2(✉)], Nathan Clarke[1,3(✉)], and Fudong Li[1(✉)]

[1] Centre for Security, Communications and Network Research,
Plymouth University, Plymouth, UK
{Neamah.Al-Naffakh,NClarke,FudongLi}@plymouth.ac.uk
[2] Computer Science and Mathematics College, Kufa University, Najaf, Iraq
[3] Security Research Institute, Edith Cowan University, Perth, WA, Australia

Abstract. Smartwatches, which contain an accelerometer and gyroscope, have recently been used to implement gait/activity-based biometrics. However, many research questions have not been addressed in the prior work such as the training and test data was collected in the same day from a limited dataset, using unrealistic activities (e.g., punch) and/or the authors did not carry out any particular study to identify the most discriminative features. This paper aims to highlight the impact of these factors on the biometric performance. The acceleration and gyroscope data of the gait and game activity was captured from 60 users over multiple days, which resulted in a totally of 24 h of the user's movement. Segment-based approach was used to divide the time-series acceleration and gyroscope data. When the cross-day evaluation was applied, the best obtained EER was 0.69%, and 4.54% for the walking and game activities respectively. The EERs were significantly reduced into 0.05% and 2.35% for the above activities by introducing the majority voting schema. These results were obtained by utilizing a novel feature selection process in which the system minimizing the number of features and maximizing the discriminative information. The results have shown that smartwatch-based activity recognition has significant potential to recognize individuals in a continuous and user friendly approach.

Keywords: Biometrics · Mobile authentication · Gait biometrics
Accelerometer · Smartwatch authentication · Activity recognition
Neural network · User authentication

1 Introduction

Activity recognition studies that used the acceleration (Acc) and gyroscope (Gyr) data to identify the user's identity based on their physical activities (e.g., normal walking and typing) attracted a lot of research. However, a large amount of the prior art captured the user's movement data by using costly specialized devices (i.e., attaching a wearable sensor to different positions around the human body such as hip, waist, and lower leg) [1–3]. Furthermore, these devices require a comprehensive set-up that reduce the usefulness of their performance and increases the cost of implementation into a potential real-world system. Although the applications of activity recognition are

N. Gal-Oz and P. R. Lewis (Eds.): IFIPTM 2018, IFIP AICT 528, pp. 15–28, 2018.
https://doi.org/10.1007/978-3-319-95276-5_2

greatly expanded by utilizing the potential of smartphone sensors (i.e., Acc and Gyr), it is widely understood that smartphones suffer from several issues to produce a consistent and reliable biometric signal in real life. For example, the problem of orientations (i.e., screen rotations) and off-body carry (e.g., when the device is carried in a handbag), making the collected data less accurate or unusable. These limitations can be addressed by alternative techniques such as smartwatches, which contain the requisite sensors such as Acc Gyr, due to their fixed contact with individuals (i.e., either on left or right wrist). As a result, these devices have the ability to capture more accurate personal data than smartphones do.

Traditional user authentication approaches on smartphones and smartwatches such as password and PIN-based authentication are considered significantly intrusive which impact their usability and subsequently security [4–6]. For example, Microsoft conducted a comprehensive study and showed that 72% of participants disabled their login credentials (i.e., PIN code) because of its intrusive implementation [7]. Moreover, PIN-based authentication technique is susceptible to several types of attacks such as brute force and shoulder surfing [8]. Given that smartwatches are usually connected with a smartphone via Bluetooth, implicit and continuous authentication to secure information on both devices from unauthorized access is essential. Activity recognition using smartwatches offers several advantages over traditional authentication techniques. For instance, it is reliable (i.e., nearly impossible to imitate), convenient for a user (i.e., does not require explicit user interaction with a sensor during authentication), and provides transparent and continuous user authentication as long as the user's hand moves [6]. To this end, this paper explores the use of smartwatches for transparent authentication based upon gait and game activities. The main contributions of this study are demonstrated as follows:

- To the best of the author's knowledge, this is the biggest dataset for smartwatch-based gait authentication, which contains gait data of 60 users over multiple days
- The novel feature selection method utilised a dynamic feature vector for each user and successfully reduced the feature vector size with better performance.
- Identifying the optimal source sensor for the authentication task.
- Highlighting the impact of Majority schema on the system accuracy.
- Vastly superior results were achieved that outperform the prior accelerometer – based studies.

The rest of the paper is organized as follows: Sect. 2 reviews the state of the art in transparent and continuous authentication that specifically uses accelerometer and gyroscope sensors. Data collection, feature extraction, the experimental procedure, and results are outlined in Sects. 3 and 4. Section 5 presents the conclusions and future research directions.

2 Related Work

Behavioural biometrics systems aim to authenticate individuals transparently based upon their activities (e.g., gait, keystroke, and handwriting). Apart from the traditional authentication approaches (i.e., PIN and passwords), a significant amount of studies have recently explored the use of built in smartphones sensors in order to improve the level of security as well as offer continuous and unobtrusive authentication. For example, Zhen et al. [9] proposed to verify users based upon their keystroke while other studies involved gait [16–20], activity [11–14], typing [33, 34], and arm movement [15, 23, 25]. The use of sensor data, specifically the Acc and Gyr data, attracting an enormous amount of attention. Whilst previous research in activity recognition has focused on body worn sensors or using the smartphone sensors (i.e. Acc and Gyr), little attention is given to the use of smartwatches – which tend to be sensor-rich highly personal technologies. Moreover, given that smartwatches are usually worn in a fixed position (i.e. right or left wrist), they offer the opportunity to collect the user's motion data in a more effective and reliable fashion than smartphones could. A comprehensive analysis of the prior studies on activity and gait recognition using smartphones and smartwatches sensors is summarized in Table 1.

Although the presented studies in Table 1 provide important insight in the domain of sensor-based activity recognition, they suffer from several issues such as data collection methodology. In most evaluations a relatively small dataset was used and frequently obtained on the same day (SD), which is not a realistic evaluation as such data does not show the variability of the human behaviour over the time and might be overlap across a large population. Most research claim a system resilient to the cross-day (CD) problem either trains on data from trials that are also used to test (thus not making it a true cross-day system) or has a high error rate, preventing the system being used practically. The lack of realistic data underpins a significant barrier in applying activity recognition in practice. Therefore, this study presents a realistic scenario (in terms of the data collection) by training and testing the user's movement data over multiple days. Moreover, the most effective device (i.e., smartwatches) is used to collect the user's motion signal, and hence design an effective transparent and continuous user authentication system for both smartphones/smartwatches.

With respect to features, cycle and segment-based approaches are used in order to pre-process the raw Acc and Gyr data and then extract several statistical and cepstral coefficient features from the segmented data (e.g., standard deviation, Variance, and Mel Frequency Cepstral Coefficients). While the cycle-based approach offers a precise manner of generating samples from the testing data by detecting steps and splitting the data accordingly, most recent studies showed that the fundamental performance of using cycle extraction method was low (At best 14.4% of EER). The high error rate of using this method was highlighted by several studies [4–6, 18] such as smartphones not being securely fastened to the user, cheap sensors, cycles are not guaranteed to be the same length, and rounding errors. In contrast, more promising results (i.e., EERs ranging from 1.4% to 8.24%) were reported by applying the segment-based approach to the raw data [19, 22].

To predict the user's identity, several studies utilized the standard classification methods (e.g. Euclidean Distance and Dynamic Time Warping metrics) to create a single reference template and is later tested based upon the similarity between the template and the test data. While this approach works well for certain biometric modalities (e.g., fingerprint or facial recognition), it does not seem to be the most effective type of system

Table 1. Comprehensive analysis on gait authentication using mobile and smartwatch sensors.

Study	Approach	Features type	Classification methods	Accuracy %	Users	Duration	Device	System type
[10]	S	TD	NN	91.7 (CCR)	29	SD	M	G
[11]	S	TD&FD	KNN	93.3 (CCR)	28	SD	M	AR
[12]	S	TD	SVM	92 (TP) 1 (FP)	315	SD	M	AR
[13]	S	TD	RF	5.6 (EER)	57	CD	M	AR
[14]	S	TD&FD	SVM	85 (CCR)	5	SD	M	AR
[15]	S	TD	EUC	5 (EER)	22	SD	M	GES
[16]	C	TD	DTW	29.4 (EER)	48	CD	M	G
[17]	C	TD	DTW	21.7 (EER)	48	CD	M	G
[18]	S	FD	HMM	6.15 (EER)	48	CD	M	G
[19]	S	FD	KNN	8.24 (EER)	36	CD	M	G
[20]	C	TD	GMM UBM	14.4 (EER)	35	CD	M	G
[21]	S	TD	RF	10 (FRR), 0 (FAR)	20	SD	SW	AR
[22]	S	TD	RF	1.4 (EER)	59	SD	SW	G
[23]	S	TD	DTW	3.3 (EER)	26	CD	SW	GES
[24]	S	TD	SVM	88.5 (CCR)	13	SD	SW&M	G
[25]	S	TD & FD	KNN	88.4(TP), 1.3 (FP)	10	SD	SW	GES
[26]	S	TD	RF	8.8 (EER)	15	SD	SW	GES
[27]	S	TD	RF	93.3 (CCR)	17	SD	SW	AR
[28]	S	TD&FD	KNN	95 (CCR)	40	SD	SW	G
[29]	S	TD	RF	4 (EER)	18	CD	M + SW	G
[30]	S	TD	KNN	2.9 (EER)	15	SD	SW	G
[31]	S	TD	SVM	0.65 (EER)	20	SD	M + SW	G
[32]	C	TD	DTW	30 (FRR), 15 (FAR)	5	CD	SW	GES
[33]	S	TD	Man	4.27 (EER)	10	SD	SW	GES
[34]	S	TD	SVM	6.56 (EER)	20	CD	SW	GES
[35]	S	FD	EUC	13.3 (EER)	29	SD	M + SW	GES
[36]	S	TD	SVM	4 (EER)	20	CD	SW	GES
[37]	S	TD&FD	SVM	92.8 (TP), 0.4 (FP)	30	SD	SW	AR
[38]	S	TD	KNN	5 (EER)	20	CD	SW	G

Legend: C: Cycle-based; S: Segment-based; TD: Time Domain; FD: Frequency Domain; DTW: Dynamic Time Warping; HMM: Hidden Markov Model; SVM: Support Vector Machine; KNN: k-nearest neighbors; RF: Random Forest; NN Neural Network; EUC: Euclidean Distance; Man: Manhattan Distance; GMM-UBM: Gaussian Mixture Model-Universal Background Model; KRR: Kernel Ridge Regression; EER: Equal Error Rate; CCR: Correct Classification Rate; TP: True Positive; FP: False Positive; FRR: False Rejection Rate; FAR: False Acceptance Rate; M: Mobile; SW Smartwatch AR: Activity Recognition; G: Gait; GES: Gesture; SD: Same Day; CD: Cross Day.

for activity recognition or other behavioural biometric techniques. This is because the user's behaviour can change over time and be affected by other factors (e.g., mood and health). Therefore, this paper applied more complex algorithms (e.g., Neural Networks) to train and test the user's reference template.

3 Experimental Methodology

In order to overcome some of the shortcomings of prior work, this paper will explore the following research questions:

1- How does the accuracy vary across same and cross-day evaluation methodologies?
2- Which sensor can provide a more consistent and reliable motion data for recognizing individuals?
3- What impact do features have upon performance?
4- What is the impact of applying the Majority voting schema on the system performance?

To address these questions, the following experiments were conducted:

- Same & Cross day evaluation, accelerometer Vs gyroscope sensor (research questions 1 and 2)
- Dynamic feature selection (research question 3)
- Majority Voting Schema (research question 4).

3.1 Data Collection

This section describes the procedure for collecting the data and transforming it into a form suitable for traditional machine learning classification algorithms. As mentioned earlier in Sect. 2, the data collection methodology is definitely an issue for most gait and activity recognition related studies (e.g., the user's motion data was collected by placing a smartphone in a fixed position, using small dataset that was frequently captured on the same day). Therefore, it is important to select the most appropriate technology to capture the movement data and ensure the population sample being used as large and significantly reliable as possible. To achieve that, this study utilized the Microsoft Band to collect 24 hours of the movement data from 60 users; to the best of the author's knowledge, this is the largest dataset within this domain. During the data collection, the Acc and Gyr signal were sampled at 32 Hz. As soon as the data was collected by the smartwatch, it was sent to a smartphone residing in the user's pocket via Bluetooth. For all 60 users, each was asked to follow a predefined scenario. Aiming to study the practicality of such a system, the scenario included two simple and realistic activities that reflect the user's daily activities (i.e., normal walk, and playing Game). Each user completed six sessions for each activity over multiple days (a single session contained two minutes of the user's motion data); each of the three sessions were provided on different days within a time frame of 3 weeks. For the gait activity, users were required to walk on a predefined route on flat ground and encouraged to walk in their own natural and comfortable manner. For a more realistic scenario, the user had to stop in order to open a door, and take multiple turns. Moreover, no other variables, such as type of footwear or clothing, were controlled. In the game activity, users were asked to sit and playing a simple game on the touch screen of their smartphone. Once the data collection was completed, the signal processing phase was undertaken - a brief description of the steps are

- Time interpolation: Due to the limited accuracy of the sensors in the Microsoft Band, the smartwatch was not able to record data at a fixed sample rate. Therefore, time interpolation was required to make sure that the time period between two successive data points was always equal.
- Filtering: a low pass filter was applied in order to enhance the accuracy of the signal. This was carried out with several settings (i.e., 10, 20, and 30) and through experimentation the cut-off frequency of 20 Hz achieved the best accuracy (examples of the filtering are shown in Fig. 1).
- Segmentation: the tri-axial raw format for both Acc and Gyr signals were segmented into 10 seconds segments by using a sliding window approach with no overlapping. Therefore, in total 72 samples for each activity and each user over multiple days were gathered.

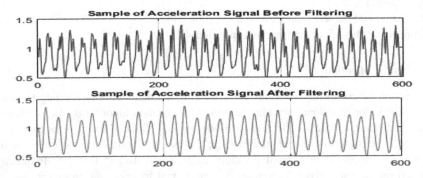

Fig. 1. The acceleration signal before and after filtering

3.2 Feature Extraction

As illustrated earlier, the raw Acc and Gyr signals are segmented into 10 seconds of time-series data and hence represented by a fixed set of features. In total, 88 of the time domain features were extracted based upon prior work identified in gait and activity recognition studies [10–20]. These features are the same regardless of whether the sample is being generated from Acc and Gyr sensor data. Since most features are generated on a per-axis basis and each sensor has 3 axes, most features are represented by a vector of three values. Details of these features (e.g., what they are and how they are calculated) are presented in Table 2.

The feature selection step has become the focus of many research studies in the area of authentication in order to reduce the potentially large dimensionality of input data, with the resultant effect of enhancing performance and reducing the computational complexity of the classifier. Subsequently making it easier to manipulate and calculate feature vectors on processing and battery limited digital devices. This study utilised a dynamic feature vector that contains distinctive features for each user. For example, the reference template of user 1 could be created by using features 1, 2, 3, and 7 while features 3, 4, 5, and 7 might be used to form the reference template of user 2. This is

Table 2. List of the extracted time domain features

Features	NF	Description
Interquartile range	3	The range in the middle of the data. It is the difference between the upper and lower quartiles in the segment
Skewness	3	A measure of the symmetry of distributions around the mean value of the segment
Kurtosis	3	A measure of the shape of the curve for the segment data
Percentile 25,50	6	The percentile rank is measured using the following formula: $R = (P/100) * (N + 1)$. Where R represents the rank order of the values, P: percentile rank, and N is the total number of data points
Correlation coefficients	3	The relationship between two axes is calculated. The Correlation Coefficients is measured between X and Y axes, X and Z axes, and Y and Z axes
Difference	3	The difference between the maximum and minimum of the values in the segment
Median	3	The median values of the data points in the segment
Root mean square	3	The square root of the mean squared
Maximum	3	The largest 4 values are calculated and averaged.
Minimum	3	The smallest 4 values are calculated and averaged
Average	3	The mean of the values in the segment
Standard deviation	3	The Standard Deviation of the values in the segment
Average absolute difference	3	Average absolute distance of all values in the segment from the mean value over the number of data point
Time between peaks	3	During the user's walking, repetitive peaks are generated in the signal. Thus, the time between consecutive peaks was calculated and averaged
Peaks occurrence	3	Determines how many peaks are in the segment
Variance	3	The second-order moment of the data
Cosine similarity	3	All pairwise cosine similarity measurements between axes
Covariance	3	All pairwise covariances between axes
Binned distribution	30	Relative histogram distribution in linear spaced bins between the minimum and the maximum acceleration in the segment. Ten bins are used for each axis
Average resultant acceleration	1	For each value in the segment of x, y, and z axes, the square roots of the sum of the values of each axis squared over the segment size are calculated

Legend: **NF** stands for the number of generated features.

achieved by calculating the mean and standard deviation (STD) for each feature individually for all users and then compares the authorized user's results against impostors to select the feature set with the minimal overlap. In other words, for each feature, a score is calculated based upon the following condition:

- If the mean of imposter's activity is not within the range of the mean +/- STD of genuine, add 1 to the total score.
- Dynamically select the features according to their score order from high to low. The highest means less overlap between imposters and the genuine user as shown in Fig. 2.

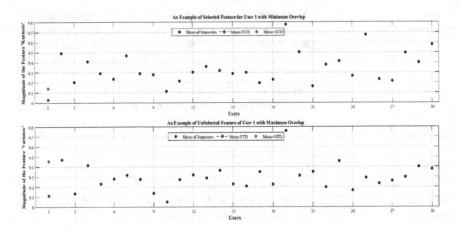

Fig. 2. The effect of the dynamic feature selection approach

3.3 Experimental Procedure

Biometric authentication or verification is a binary classification problem, where the aim is to determine if a system can identify a user correctly (a "genuine" user) or as an imposter. The reference and testing templates were created under two different scenarios (i.e., SD, and CD). In the SD scenario, the dataset was divided into two parts: 60% was used to train the classifier while the remaining 40% was utilised to evaluate the performance. To test the system under the CD scenario, the data from the first day was used for training and the second day data was employed for testing. A Feedforward Multi-layer Perceptron (FF MLP) neural network was used as the default classifier for the walking and game activities due to its reliable performance [6, 10]. For each experiment, four different FF MLP neural network training size were evaluated (i.e., 10, 15, 20, and 25) with an average of repeating each of them 10 times. All the presented results in this study were based on using FF MLP neural network of size 10 as it showed the lowest EER.

4   Results

After research questions of the prior art were identified and presented in the previous section, details of the results for the two evaluation scenarios (SD and CD), the two different smartwatch sensors (i.e., Acc and Gyr), are presented in the following subsections. The results are first presented for "single-sample mode" and then using the majority voting scheme.

4.1 Single Day vs Cross Day Evaluation

A well-known serious criticism of the prior gait/activity-based biometrics is the data collection strategy, which the training and test data captured during a single session—on a single day. This contradicts the notion that the only more reliable test comes from multi-day testing. This maxim holds because performance on single day datasets does little to test how resistant the system is to the variability of human gait over the time. In cases when the CD scenario is considered, the evaluation of most studies is often either done improperly (e.g., mixes the training and test data from multiple days [18, 19]) or the results are very poor [16, 17, 20, 32]. Table 3 demonstrates that the performance of using SD scenario is overly optimistic (i.e., EERs of 0.15% and 3.73% for the Acc and Gyr respectively). While the EERs are increased to 0.93% (for Acc) and 8.29% (for Gyr) under the CD test, this is a more realistic evaluation scenario as it avoids training the user's model every day.

Although sensor based-authentication systems could be implemented using accelerometers and/or gyroscopes as the source triaxial (three axes) sensor, the results clearly indicate that the gyroscope is not as effective as the accelerometer for authentication, which is consistent with what other researchers have found [4–6, 22, 27]. For example, the gait activity reported EERs of 0.15% and 0.93% for the SD and CD scenarios respectively, compared to 3.73% and 8.29% EER's by using the Gyr data of both scenarios respectively.

Table 3. The EER (%) of SD and CD using the Acc and Gyr sensors of walking activity

Activity type	Evaluation scenario	Sensor type	All features
Walking	SD	Acc	0.15
Walking	CD	Acc	0.93
Walking	SD	Gyr	3.73
Walking	CD	Gyr	8.29

Further experiments were conducted and the results presented in Table 4 in order to highlight the impact of selecting the most discriminative features subset for classification. The proposed feature selection approach successfully discarded some irrelevant and/or redundant features and improved the system accuracy. Impressive results were achieved by using the SD scenario for the walking activity (an EER of only 0.13% compared to EERs of 1.4%, 2.9%, and 0.65% [22, 30, 31]). By using a small feature subset of only 20 features, the proposed system can still precisely recognize the users with an EER of 0.78%.

As regards of the game activity, the reported results can be directly compared with the prior art [15, 26, 33, 35] that reported EERs in the range of 4.27%–13.3% (against to 0.89% in this study). Although the EERs of both activities are increased to 0.69% and 4.54% by applying the CD scenario, these results still managed to produce a high level of security and better than the previous accelerometer-based studies that achieved EERs ranging from 5.6% [13] to 29.4% [16].

Table 4. The EER (%) of the SD and CD test for the walking and game activities

Activity Type	Evaluation Scenario	Sensors	10 Features	20 Features	30 Features	40 Features	50 Features	60 Features	70 Features	80 Features	88 Features
Walking	SD	Acc	1.13	0.78	0.24	0.26	0.27	**0.13**	0.20	0.16	0.15
Walking	CD	Acc	4.68	2.39	1.43	0.9	0.84	0.83	**0.69**	0.77	0.93
Walking	SD	Gyr	6.6	4.88	3.63	3.74	**3.12**	3.58	3.48	3.43	3.73
Walking	CD	Gyr	11.09	9.76	8.62	8.49	8.94	8.53	8.42	**7.97**	8.29
Game	SD	Acc	2.40	1.76	1.38	1.18	**0.89**	1.20	1.14	1.20	1.33
Game	CD	Acc	4.97	4.82	4.83	4.79	4.62	**4.54**	5.17	5.80	5.61
Game	SD	Gyr	8.7	7.18	**6.12**	6.74	6.53	6.67	6.44	6.91	7.11
Game	CD	Gyr	12.88	11.08	10.40	**9.96**	10.21	10.33	10.09	**10.20**	10.82

Table 4 shows that the walking activity contains high levels of distinguished information, hence surpasses the results of the game activity. This most probably due to that more movement data can be obtained when users are walking (compared to a limited motion while playing a game on the touch screen of smartphones). As expected, the results demonstrate that biometric performance is degraded under the more realistic evaluation scenario (i.e., CD scenario), but that smartwatch-based biometrics is still highly recommended and viable to be used at least as a complementary mechanism to password-based authentication.

4.2 The Impact of the Proposed Dynamic Feature Vector

As mentioned earlier, it is clear that the proposed feature selection method was capable of reducing the number of features and has a positive impact on the system performance. With respect to the feature subset size, the reported EERs in Table 4 show that the SD test for both activities, requires less features than the CD (i.e., 60 and 50 features for the walking and game activities respectively). This could be explained because the user's arm pattern could be vary or be inconsistent over the time, hence more features are required for individual to be identified. Moreover, the selected feature subset fixed for all users (i.e., the size of the user's reference template of each activity was same for all users such as 60 features). Therefore, creating a dynamic feature vector size for each user independently might greatly reduce the EER (see Fig. 3). As shown in Fig. 3, reducing the number of features of the NW activity from 70 to 40 features decreased the EER for the majority of users or remains similar (apart from users 10, 16 18, 19, 24, 25, 30, 31, and 48 that negatively affect the overall system accuracy). Surprisingly, the EER was even better for some of the users (e.g., 3, 6, 10, 17, 20, 29, 37, 38, 40, 44, 47, 50, and 51). Therefore, the creation of dynamic feature vector size might offer better accuracy/error rates.

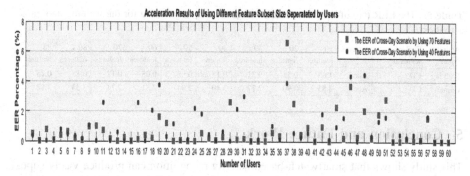

Fig. 3. The EER of using the walking activity and utilizing different feature subset size separated by users

4.3 Majority Voting Schema

So far all the presented results were based upon classifying single sample in order to calculate the EER. Although the findings in Table 4 yield good results, it was interesting to find out the possibility of reducing the amount of the rejected samples of a genuine user. Several studies [17–19, 22] have investigated the use of majority and quorum voting schemas in order to make a decision. The former is a scheme which accepts a user as genuine if a half or more of the user's test samples are positive; The biometric decision is then based upon merging multiple classification output to a single one. The latter is a method that authenticates a user as genuine if a requisite number of the user's samples are positive.

Although quorum voting usually yields greater performance, the majority voting appears to be more resilient to error given the higher threshold for classification. Quorum, while lowering the level of accuracy required to verifying a user, may result in a high false acceptance rate. This failure to identify imposters can be explained by the extremely low proportions of correct classifications required to accepting a user as genuine. Although this may be acceptable for systems more concerned with usability, such permissiveness will most likely render the system impractical for most uses. Majority voting, while requiring the system to be more discriminative, offers a greater level of security and thus is more likely to offer a suitable balance between usability and security. Ultimately, conscious decisions must be made to create a system that does not appear to the end user as too demanding without compromising the security. Therefore, this study utilized the majority voting rather than the quorum voting schema.

As shown in Table 5, the majority voting scheme yields significant improvement on the system performance. At best, the EERs of the walking and game activities were 0.05% and 2.53% respectively (compared to 0.69% and 4.54% of EERs when a single-sample evaluation was used). It is also interesting to notice that only 10 features were required for the game activity to produce the lowest EER. This might be explained because the user's arm pattern for this particular activity was consistent hence, less features was required to verify the legitimate user.

Table 5. The EER (%) of the CD scenario using the majority voting for the walking and game activities

Activity type	Evaluation scenario	Sensors	10 features	20 features	30 features	40 features	50 features	60 features	70 features	80 features	88 features
Walking	CD	Acc	1.68	0.51	0.21	0.15	0.08	**0.05**	0.12	0.18	0.15
Game	CD	Acc	**2.53**	2.90	2.77	3.40	2.94	2.81	2.74	3.33	3.12

5   Conclusion and Future Work

This study shows that smartwatch-based activity recognition can produce vastly superior results when evaluated properly by using the realistic CD scenario. It does show that the results do improve when authentication decisions are made using the majority voting schema rather than single 10 seconds sample of data. This paper shows that the proposed feature selection approach has a positive effect on the system accuracy with a reduction of 32% of the whole features. For example, 60 features were used for the walking activity rather than 88 features in order to produce the lowest EER. It is also examined the effect of using the CD scenario on the system performance. Overall, this study serves as an endorsement for smartwatch-based activity recognition.

Future work will explore the impact of the dynamic feature vector size for each user, applying a sensor fusion approach to combine the smartwatch accelerometer and gyroscope data, and testing different segment sizes (e.g., 7 and 5 seconds). Additionally, whilst this study utilized cross-day data collection, collecting real life data (i.e., users do not need to perform certain activities, but merely wear the smartwatch for a prolonged period) will enable a real-world evaluation of the approach. The challenge then becomes being able to identify which activity a user is doing –in order to be able to select the appropriate classifier to utilise. As such, future research will also focus upon developing a context-aware approach to predict the activity.

References

1. Gafurov, D., Helkala, K., Søndrol, T.: Biometric gait authentication using accelerometer sensor. J. Comput. **I**(7), 51–59 (2006)
2. Gafurov, D., Snekkenes, E., Bours, P.: Spoof attacks on gait authentication system. IEEE Trans. Forensics Secur. **2**(3), 491–502 (2007)
3. Nowlan, M.F.: Human Identification via Gait Recognition Using Accelerometer Gyro Forces. CPSC-536-Networked Embedded Systems and Sensor Networks, Professor Savvides, Fall 2009, p. 8 (2009). 2. Related Work and Human Gait
4. Al-Naffakh, N., Clarke, N., Dowland, P., Li, F.: Activity recognition using wearable computing. In: Proceedings of the 11th International Conference for Internet Technology and Secured Transactions (ICITST-2016), Barcelona, pp. 189–195 (2016)
5. Al-Naffakh, N., Clarke, N., Haskell-Dowland, P., Li, F.: A comprehensive evaluation of feature selection for gait recognition using smartwatches. Int. J. Inf. Secur. Res. (IJISR) **6**(3), 1–10 (2016)

6. Al-Naffakh, N., Clarke, N., Li, F., Haskell-Dowland, P.: Unobtrusive gait recognition using smartwatches. In: The International Conference of the Biometrics Special Interest Group (BIOSIG), pp. 1–8 (2017)
7. Hamblen, M.: Mobile phone security no-brainer: use a device passcode (2013). http://www.computerworld.com/article/2497183/mobile-security/mobile-phone-security-no-brainer–use-a-device-passcode.html. Accessed 01 Mar 2018
8. Kim, I.: Keypad against brute force attacks on smartphones. IET Inf. Secur. 6(2), 71 (2012). http://digital-library.theiet.org/content/journals/10.1049/iet-ifs.2010.0212
9. Zheng, N., Bai, K., Huang, H., Wang, H.: You are how you touch: user verification on smartphones via tapping behaviour. Technical report, College of William & Mary, Williamsburg, VA, USA, December 2012
10. Kwapisz, J.R., Weiss, G.M., Moore, S.A.: Activity recognition using cell phone accelerometers. ACM SIGKDD Explor. Newslett. 12(2), 74 (2011)
11. Kumar, R., Phoha, V.V., Serwadda, A.: Continuous authentication of smartphone users by fusing typing, swiping, and phone movement patterns. In: 2016 IEEE (BTAS-2016) (2016)
12. Gascon, H., Uellenbeck, S., Wolf, C., Rieck, K.: Continuous authentication on mobile devices by analysis of typing motion behavior. Presented at Proceedings of GI Conference Sicherheit (Sicherheit, Schutz und Verlsslichkeit) (2014)
13. Kumar, R., Kundu, P.P., Shukla, D., Phoha, V.V.: Continuous User Authentication via Unlabeled Phone Movement Patterns. arXiv preprint arXiv:1708.04399 (2017)
14. Heng, X., Wang, Z., Wang, J.: Human activity recognition based on transformed accelerometer data from a mobile phone. Int. J. Commun. Syst. 29(13), 1981–1991 (2014)
15. Okumura, F., Kubota, A., Hatori, Y., Matsuot, K., Hashimotot, M., Koiket, A.: A study on biometric authentication based on arm sweep action with acceleration sensor. In: International Symposium on Intelligent Signal Processing and Communications, ISPACS 2006, Tottori, Japan (2006)
16. Muaaz, M., Nickel, C.: Influence of different walking speeds and surfaces on accelerometer-based biometric gait recognition. In: 35th International Conference on Telecommunications and Signal Processing (TSP), pp. 508–512 (2012)
17. Nickel, C., Derawi, M.O., Bours, P., Busch, C.: Scenario test of accelerometer-based biometric gait recognition. In: The Third International Workshop on Security and Communication Networks, IWSCN 2011, pp. 15–21 (2011)
18. Nickel, C., Busch, C.: Classifying accelerometer data via hidden Markov models to authenticate people by the way they walk. In: 2011 Carnahan Conference on Security Technology, vol. 28, no. 10, pp. 1–6 (2011)
19. Nickel, C., Wirtl, T., Busch, C.: Authentication of smartphone users based on the way they walk using k-NN algorithm. In: IIH-MSP Conference, Greece, pp. 16–20 (2012)
20. Muaaz, M., Mayrhofer, R.: Accelerometer based Gait recognition using adapted Gaussian mixture models. In: Proceedings of the 14th International Conference on Advances in Mobile Computing and Multimedia, pp. 288–291 (2016)
21. Mare, S., Molina-Markham, A., Cornelius, C., Peterson, R., Kotz, D.: ZEBRA: zero-effort bilateral recurring authentication. In: Security and Privacy (SP) (2014)
22. Johnston, A.H., Weiss, G.M.: Smartwatch-based biometric gait recognition. In: Biometrics Theory, Applications and Systems (BTAS), Arlington, VA, USA (2015)
23. Yang, J., Li, Y., Xie, M.: MotionAuth: motion-based authentication for wrist worn smart devices. In: The IEEE International Conference on Pervasive Computing and Communication Workshops (PerComWorkshops), pp. 550–555 (2015)

24. Ramos, F., Moreira, A., Costa, A., Perkusich, A.: Combining smartphone and smartwatch sensor data in activity recognition approaches: an experimental evaluation. In: The 28th International Conference on Software Engineering and Knowledge Engineering, USA, pp. 267–272 (2016)
25. Davidson, S., Smith, D., Yang, C., Cheah, S.: Smartwatch User Identification as a Means of Authentication, Department of Computer Science and Engineering Std. (2016)
26. Kamoi, H., Ohtsuki, T.: Biometrie authentication using hand movement information from wrist-worn PPG sensors. In: Proceedings of IEEE 27th Annual International Symposium Personal Indoor Mobile Radio Communications (PIMRC), Valencia, Spain, pp. 1–5 (2016)
27. Weiss, G.M., Timko, J.L., Gallagher, C.M., Yoneda, K., Schreiber, A.J.: Smartwatch-based activity recognition: a machine learning approach. In: IEEE-EMBS International Conference on Biomedical and Health Informatics (BHI), pp. 426–429 (2016)
28. Kumar, R., Phoha, V.V., Raina, R.: Authenticating users through their arm movement patterns. arXiv preprint arXiv:1603.02211 (2016)
29. Babins, S., Manar, M., Nitesh, S.: Walk-Unlock: Zero-Interaction Authentication Protected with Multi-Modal Gait Biometrics. arXiv preprint arXiv:1605.00766 (2016)
30. Cola, G., Avvenuti, M., Musso, F.: Gait-based authentication using a wrist-worn device. In: Proceedings of the 13th International Conference on Mobile and Ubiquitous Systems: Computing, Networking and Services, Hiroshima, Japan, pp. 208–217 (2016)
31. Dong, J., Cai, Z.: User authentication using motion sensor data from both wearables and smartphones. In: The Chinese Conference on Biometric Recognition, pp. 756–764 (2016)
32. Lewis, A., Li, Y., Xie, M.: Real time motion-based authentication for smartwatch. In: The IEEE International Conference on Communications and Network Security (CNS), Philadelphia, PA, USA (2016)
33. Wang, Z., Shen, C., Chen, Y.: Handwaving authentication: unlocking your smartwatch through handwaving biometrics. In: Zhou, J., et al. (eds.) CCBR 2017. LNCS, vol. 10568, pp. 545–553. Springer, Cham (2017). https://doi.org/10.1007/978-3-319-69923-3_59
34. Griswold-Steiner, I., Matovu, R., Serwadda, A.: HandwritingWatcher: a mechanism for smartwatch-driven handwriting authentication. In: The IEEE International Joint Conference on Biometrics (IJCB 2017), USA (2017)
35. Findling, R., Muaaz, M., Hintze, D., Mayrhofer, R.: ShakeUnlock: securely transfer authentication states between mobile devices. IEEE Trans. Mob. Comput. 16(4), 1163–1175 (2017)
36. Lianga, C.G., Xu, X.Y., Yu, J.D.: User-authentication on wearable devices based on punch gesture biometrics. In: The International Conference on Information Science and Technology, IST 2017 (2017)
37. Zeng, Y., Pande, A., Zhu, J., Mohapatra, P.: WearIA: wearable device implicit authentication based on activity information. In: The International Conference on a World of Wireless, Mobile and Multimedia Networks (WoWMoM), Macau, China, pp. 1–9 (2017)
38. Xu, W., Shen, Y., Zhang, Y., Bergmann, N., Hu, W.: Gait-watch: a context-aware authentication system for smart watch based on gait recognition. In: Proceedings of 2nd International Conference Internet Things Design Implement, Pittsburgh, PA, USA, pp. 59–70 (2017)

Privacy Policy Annotation
for Semi-automated Analysis:
A Cost-Effective Approach

Dhiren A. Audich$^{(\boxtimes)}$, Rozita Dara, and Blair Nonnecke

University of Guelph, 50 Stone Road, Guelph, ON N1G 2W1, Canada
{daudich,drozita,nonnecke}@uoguelph.ca

Abstract. Privacy policies go largely unread as they are not standardized, often written in jargon, and frequently long. Several attempts have been made to simplify and improve readability with varying degrees of success. This paper looks at keyword extraction, comparing human extraction to natural language algorithms as a first step in building a taxonomy for creating an ontology (a key tool in improving access and usability of privacy policies).

In this paper, we present two alternatives to using costly domain experts are used to perform keyword extraction: trained participants (non-domain experts) read and extracted keywords from online privacy policies; and second, supervised and unsupervised learning algorithms extracted keywords. Results show that supervised learning algorithm outperform unsupervised learning algorithms over a large corpus of 631 policies, and that trained participants outperform the algorithms, but at a much higher cost.

1 Introduction

A 2015 Pew Research Centre survey found that 91% of American adults either agree or strongly agree that they have lost control of how their private information is collected and used [1]. The collection of personally identifiable information (PII) by online service providers is often justified with claims of creating a more user-centric web experience. However, PII is sold and shared frequently with third parties that use it to profile users and track them across domains. While users are increasingly concerned about their privacy online [2] they scarcely understand the implications of PII sharing [3].

Privacy policies are the only means of informing users and mitigating their fears over privacy loss, and by law, companies have to disclose the gathering, processing, and sharing of PII in their privacy policies [4–7]. Unfortunately, most policies are often lengthy, difficult and time-consuming to read, and as a result are infrequently read [2,8–10]. The demotivating nature and the difficulty of reading privacy policies amounts to a lack of transparency. Failing to provide usable privacy policies prevents users from making informed decisions and can

Published by Springer International Publishing AG 2018. All Rights Reserved
N. Gal-Oz and P. R. Lewis (Eds.): IFIPTM 2018, IFIP AICT 528, pp. 29–44, 2018.
https://doi.org/10.1007/978-3-319-95276-5_3

lead them to accept terms of use jeopardizing their privacy and PII. Recently, Cranor et al. showed through their analysis of 75 policies that most policies do not provide enough transparency about data collection for the users to make informed privacy decisions [11].

In addition to length and readability, privacy policies also differ from one another by their content of legal and technical jargon, and coverage [8, 9, 12]. While it is true that FIPPs (Fair Information Practice Principles) and OECD (Organization for Economic Co-operation and Development) offer general guidelines for writing privacy policies, they only provide a conceptual framework; a qualitative review of policies reveals that language and structure being used differs between policies and economic zones (E.U., U.S.A, Canada) [9, 13]. There is also an inconsistent amount of jargon used between policies, and policies of organizations in the E.U. tend to have supplementary information that tends to be absent from American and Canadian policies [11, 12, 14]. Boilerplate language is mostly the norm for cookie policies.

To improve readability and semi-automate their evaluation, attempts to introduce a standard structure to privacy policies has met with limited success. For example, the preeminent Platform for Privacy Preferences (P3P) [15, 16] failed due to poor adoption and issues related to validating policies [17]. In response to user concerns, several prominent online service providers started using privacy enhancing technologies (PET), e.g., opt-out mechanisms, anonymisation of personal data, and layered policies [18, 19]. Without these becoming a common standard, opaque and verbose policies are still the norm.

Given the widespread deployment of privacy policies and their importance to users, we propose to semi-automate the evaluation of policies and support their reading through the use of intelligent reasoning. By combining intelligent reasoning with natural language processing (NLP) techniques we hope to reduce the time needed for users to find key information in policies by highlighting sections directly related to users' privacy concerns.

The first step to constructing an intelligent reasoning system would be to conduct contextual analysis of privacy policies, for comprehension, and capture it in a taxonomy, a hierarchical representation of privacy policy concepts. In other words, the taxonomy would capture the vocabulary of privacy policies. There are two main ways to capture vocabularies: manually and automatically. Manually capturing the vocabulary involves reading and knowing domain text which would involve hours of manual labour that can be costly. An easier approach would be to use NLP techniques to automatically extract keywords for taxonomy creation [20, 21]. This requires fewer man hours compared to the manual methods; hence, is cheaper. Presently, no taxonomy exists for the online privacy policy domain. Hence, the ultimate objective of this research is to create and validate a taxonomy with the aid of NLP algorithms and then further by subject matter experts. This paper focuses only on the keyword and keyphrase extraction part of this larger process.

Keyword and keyphrase extraction forms the backbone of topic modelling and information retrieval systems. In this paper, NLP was used to extract keywords and keyphrases from hundreds of policies. In addition, we employed trained participants to extract keywords and phrases from a much smaller subset of policies, with the intent of comparing the manual extraction to that of the NLP. The overall goal of evaluating automatic keyword extraction algorithms was to examine which algorithm performs best against human annotators for the domain of online privacy policies. The best of these would then be chosen to become part of a larger process to enrich domain-expert curated taxonomy which would then be used to construct an ontology.

Our research confirms that whilst automatic keyword and keyphrase extraction remains a difficult task, supervised learning algorithms perform marginally better against unsupervised algorithms. Furthermore, trained annotators, collectively, can cheaply out-perform domain experts; their combined output being further used to improve the training set for the supervised learning algorithm.

The remainder of this paper is structured as follows: Sect. 2 discusses related work; Sect. 3 describes previous work on which the current research is built on; Sect. 4 presents motivation and describes methodology; Sect. 5 presents our investigation with training non-domain experts for the task of keyword and keyphrase extraction; Sect. 6 presents our investigation after working a supervised learning algorithm for the task of keyword and keyphrase extraction; Sect. 7 discusses the implication and avenues for future work; we conclude our work in Sect. 8.

2   Related Work

In a previous study, Wilson et al. [12] created the OPP-115 corpus, a corpus of 115 manually annotated privacy policies with 23,000 *data practices*. A *data practice* is roughly defined as a purpose or consequence of collecting, storing, or generating data about a user. In the study, the 10 domain experts (privacy experts, public policy experts, and legal scholars) used a custom designed web-based tool to annotate practices and assign various attributes to them for classification purposes. Each policy took an average of 72 min to annotate. Whilst this approach produced a high quality and nuanced data set, it is costly to expand and maintain such a knowledge base both in time and money. Automation and crowdsourcing could reduce the cost of creating and maintaining such a data set, and still maintain a reasonable amount of quality.

In the research conducted by Ramnath et al., the researchers proposed combining machine learning and crowdsourcing (for validation) to semi-automate the extraction of key privacy practices [22]. Through their preliminary study they were able to show that non-domain experts were able to find an answer to their privacy concern relatively quickly ($\sim$45 s per question) when they were only shown relevant paragraphs that were mostly likely to contain an answer to the question. They also found that answers to privacy concerns were usually concentrated rather than scattered all over the policy. This is an important find because it means that if users were directed to relevant sections in the policy they would be able to address their privacy concerns relatively quickly instead of reading the entire policy. Additionally, Pan and Zinkhan have showed that when users are presented with a short and straightforward policy, they are more inclined to read it [23].

In a more recent user study conducted by Wilson et al. [24], the quality of crowdsourced answering of privacy concerns was tested against domain experts with particular emphasis on highlighted text. The researchers found that highlighting relevant text had no negative impact on accuracy of answers. They also found out that users tend not to be biased by the highlights and are still likely to read the surrounding text to gain context and answer privacy concerning questions. They also found an 80% agreement rate between the crowdsourced workers and the domain experts for the same questions [24]. Similarly, Mysore Sathyendra et al. showed through their study that it was possible to highlight and extract opt-out practices from privacy policy using keywords and classification algorithms with reasonable accuracy; of the various models tested, best model used a logistic regression classification algorithm with a manually crafted feature set and achieved an F1 score of 59% [25].

The general drawback of crowdsourcing, especially with respect to privacy policies, is that it relies on non-expert users to read policies to provide data. Since most users are not motivated to reading policies to begin with, it would take a long time to crowdsource enough data to be useful. However, what is clear is that highlighting relevant text with appropriate keywords can still provide some feedback to the concerned users that are inclined to read shorter policies.

3   Background

Keyword/keyphrases extraction remains a difficult task; the state-of-the-art performance of keyword extraction algorithms hovers around 20–30% [26]. Keyword (or keyphrase) extraction has been historically used to recognize key topics and concepts in documents. This task involves identifying and ranking candidate keywords based on the relatedness to the document. Keyword extraction algorithms utilize various techniques to perform their task: statistical learning, part-of-speech (POS) tagging, lexical and syntactic feature extraction. Generally, they work in two steps:

1. Identifying candidate keywords/keyphrases from the document using heuristics.
2. Recognizing if the chosen candidate keywords/keyphrases are correct or not using supervised and unsupervised methods.

3.1   Supervised Learning vs. Unsupervised Learning

Machine learning can be divided into two broad types: supervised and unsupervised learning. The majority of the machine learning techniques involve supervised learning algorithms which rely on a tagged corpus for training a model to learn features (keywords) from the text. After sufficient training, the model is then applied on similar corpus to extract keywords. The keyword assignments made over the training data set forms the reference, also known as controlled vocabulary, and treated as classes used in a classification problem. Some examples of supervised learning algorithms include, K-nearest neighbour (k-NN) [27,28], Naive Bayes (NB) [29], GenEx [30], and Support Vector Machines (SVM) [31].

Since creating a tagged corpus is a very time consuming task, unsupervised learning algorithms are used which do not require any training set for the training of models. They instead rely on linguistic and statistical features of the text. The task is framed as a ranking or clustering problem.

3.2   Per Policy Keyword Extraction Fares Best

Our previous research [32] used five unsupervised learning algorithms to extract keywords for the purpose of identifying key concepts with the goal of generating a taxonomy for the online privacy policy domain. The research was conducted in two experiments. In the first, the algorithms were evaluated over a smaller corpus where a set of manually extracted terms by the researcher was used as the baseline. Researcher's manually extracted terms are also used in Experiment I (Sect. 5) as the baseline. Second, the algorithms were evaluated over a larger corpus where the results from the best performing algorithm from the first experiment was held as the baseline. While the algorithm Term-Frequency Inverse Document Frequency (TF-IDF) achieved an F_1-score of 27% over a small corpus (21 policies), over a large corpora (631 policies) algorithms evaluating single documents individually, such as AlchemyAPI[1] and TextRank [33], performed the best.

Results from both experiments suffered from four major types of errors. *Overgeneration* errors are a type of precision error where the algorithm incorrectly identifies a candidate term as a keyword because one of its sub-words appears frequently in a document or corpus. *Redundancy* errors are a type of precision error where the algorithm correctly identifies a keyword simultaneously identifying another keyword that is semantically similar, e.g. 'account use' and 'account usage'. *Infrequency* errors occur when a candidate term is not selected due to its low frequency of appearance in a document or a corpus. *Evaluation* errors are a type of recall error that occur when a candidate term is not identified as a keyword despite it being semantically similar to a baseline keyword. Since the unsupervised algorithms focus on the task of ranking and/or clustering based on semantic and lexical analysis, these errors are a result of language used in the privacy policies which tends to be inconsistent between policies.

The alternative to unsupervised learning algorithms are supervised learning algorithms in which a model is first trained on a set of manually extracted terms, and thus the task becomes one of classification, i.e., whether a candidate keyword should be classified as a document keyword or not. In case of privacy policies, we expect the results to improve because training a model would reduce

---

[1] http://www.alchemyapi.com/products/alchemylanguage/keyword-extraction.

various errors that occurred with unsupervised learning. For example, since the keywords are first being extracted manually; if the terms are infrequent, the trained model would learn this bias reducing infrequency errors. In this paper we employ a supervised learning algorithm to test our hypothesis.

4   Study Design

The primary objective of this experiment was to test whether a supervised learning algorithm could outperform the unsupervised learning algorithms used in our previous study. As such, choosing an effective supervised challenger was key. To compare unsupervised algorithms, a supervised learning algorithm, KEA, was investigated. KEA is an effective supervised learning algorithm utilizing a Naive Bayes algorithm for training learning models [34]. It is a simple and well-known algorithm that is has been often used as a baseline throughout the literature [35–40].

KEA works in two phases: training and model creation, and extraction. In the training phase, candidate keyphrases are selected both from the training documents and the corpus, features (attributes) are calculated, and keyphrases determined. Candidate keyphrase selection works in three phases: text pre-processing, identifying the candidate keyphrases, and stemming and case-folding. Features that are calculated are, TF-IDF and first occurrence (the first time the term occurs in a document), which are then discretized for the machine learning scheme. Finally, the keyphrase are determined from the discretized values using the Naive Bayes technique [41]. In the extraction phase, the candidate keyphrase selection is repeated on the documents to calculate feature values. Then the Naive Bayes algorithm is used along with the values calculated in the model to determine if a candidate keyphrase is a keyphrase or not.

The study was broadly broken up into two parts: Experiment I examines manual extraction by trained non-domain experts, while Experiment II compares supervised and unsupervised techniques.

5   Experiment I: Manual Keyword Extraction

5.1   Participants

Four participants were selected for this experiment. Since this was a preliminary study conducted to test if non-experts can be trained enough to extract important keywords, we thought that 4 participants was enough. All had a graduate level education in Computer Science with varying knowledge of online privacy and were male with a mean age of 33.65 (range 22–60). None had a research background in privacy and they rarely read website privacy policies.

5.2   Procedure

The participants were briefed on intelligent reasoning systems and taxonomies to ensure they understood the basic concepts and how their keywords would be used. A set of criteria for manual extraction was then provided with examples to help participants select the appropriate keywords and keyphrases as illustrated in Table 1). In order to have some time limit, it was estimated that it took less than 2 h to read and annotate 5 policies. Hence, the participants were given 2 h to read 5 privacy policies (a subset of the 21 privacy policies used for the training model; see Table 2), and highlight terms (unigrams, bigrams, trigrams, etc.) they thought were important: concepts, themes, and terms; pertaining to the online privacy domain and as outlined in the criterion. The 5 policies selected were from different industry sectors; intended for a diverse audience; and conformed to the laws of multiple countries; they included: Google, Facebook, UEFA, Royal Bank of Canada, and Wal-Mart (including policy for California). Over a 2 h period, each participant was presented with the privacy policies in a different order to reduce the possibility of an ordering bias.

Participants used an open source program called 'Skim'[2] for annotation. A Python script was then used to extract all of the highlighted keywords and store the results in a comma separated values (CSV) file for further analysis.

Table 1. Criteria for manually extracting key terms.

Concept	Examples
Legal terms	*Online Privacy Protection Act, non-disclosure agreement*
Legal organizations (government, regulatory, commercial, and computing organizations)	*federal trade commission*
Acronyms of legal organizations and acts	*FTC, COPPA*
Legal entities that can be used to define an organization or an individual	*personal information, address, account id, internet protocol address*
Data sharing	*3rd party cookies, aggregate information, google analytics*
Hosting	*backup storage, servers*
Web & tech related terms	*ad data, cookies, analytics, tracking cookies*
Legal actions and legal processes	*tracking, surveillance*
Mobile privacy	*geo-location, device identification*

To ensure consistency of key term extraction across the data sets, the following post-processing steps were taken to normalize the text:

---

[2] https://sourceforge.net/projects/skim-app/.

Table 2. Breakdown of the 21 privacy policy corpus for Experiment I.

Domain	No. of websites selected
Healthcare	1
Insurance	2
Banking & Financial	5
E-commerce	3
File sharing	1
Search engines	2
Social networking	3
EU specific	3
Cloud hosting	1
Total	21

1. All of the terms were first converted to lowercase.
2. Non-printable characters (as defined by the `string.printable` set in Python3) were removed; and the remaining special characters that were not caught by previous filters (*@#), as well as other ASCII based characters from the `string.punctuation` set in Python3 were removed.
3. Tokenized numbers were also removed as they do not tend to add value to the taxonomy e.g. '1945'.
4. The standard Porter Stemming Algorithm [42] was used from the NLTK[3] library to consolidate inflected word forms to their root.
5. Finally, duplicates were removed from the resulting sets.

5.3   Results

First, the data collected from all of the participants were compared to the data set generated by the primary researcher. The results are shown in Table 3.

It must be noted that participant 3 only completed 3 of the 5 policies because he found reading some policies quite challenging and hence taking longer to read. He also reported to initially having trouble understanding the task. Despite this, participant 3 was not dropped because we were mostly interested in the quality of the keywords rather than completion of task specifically. Furthermore, our analysis is mostly based on individual work, and despite the third participant failing to complete the task we wanted to highlight that they were still able to achieve results about half as good as the researcher.

In general, participants reported that policies were repetitive and often vaguely described their intent with regard to collecting personal information. When asked to state which privacy policy was most clear and readable, Facebook was described as the most transparent with UEFA being the least. The highest F_1-*score* was 59% with a mean of 51.75%.

---

[3] http://www.nltk.org/.

Table 3. Results from manual keyword extraction by participants.

	Researcher	1	2	3	4
Terms	560	581	650	353	504
Precision		49%	55%	59%	56%
Recall		51%	64%	37%	51%
F_1-score		50%	59%	45%	53%
JSC		0.67	0.58	0.71	0.64

In order to test the collective efficacy of the annotations, the researcher's data set was compared with the combined data set of all of the participants. The results are reported in Table 4.

Table 4. Comparing performance of manual extraction primary researcher vs. combined data set generated by participants.

	Researcher	Participants
Terms	560	1038
Precision		40%
Recall		75%
F_1-score		52%
JSC		0.65

Finally, all five data sets were compared to each other by holding one of the data set as the baseline and comparing it with the rest. The results are reported in Table 5. The mean of all of the values was 52.1%, which agreed with the previous analysis in Table 4. This was significantly higher than the 20–30% performance of most state-of-the-art keyword extraction algorithms.

Table 5. Comparing F_1-scores between participants' and researcher's data sets.

	Researcher	P1	P2	P3	P4
Researcher	–	50%	59%	45%	53%
P1	50%	–	56%	46%	52%
P2	59%	56%	–	50%	58%
P3	45%	46%	50%	–	55%
P4	53%	52%	58%	55%	–

6   Experiment II: Supervised Learning

For this experiment, a corpus of 631 privacy policies as developed by the Data Management and Privacy Governance Lab at the University of Guelph was used to evaluate the supervised learning algorithm- KEA. This is the same corpus that was used to evaluate unsupervised learning algorithms in the previous paper.

6.1   Part I

In the first part of the experiment, a set of 21 policies were used for manual extraction of keywords which in turn were used to train the learning model for KEA. The 21 policies were qualitatively determined to ensure diversity. They were selected based on the their: length, transparency, comprehension (level of difficulty), intended geographic audience (U.S., E.U, Canada), industry sectors (healthcare, e-commerce, etc.), and the most visited websites[4]. A breakdown of these policies is summarized in Table 2. An overview of Experiment II Part I is shown in Fig. 1.

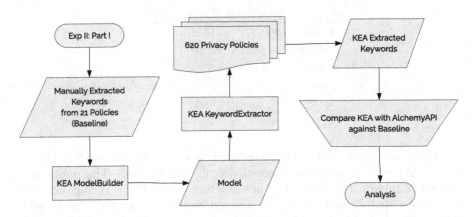

Fig. 1. Experiment II Part I: testing KEA against manual extraction and AlchemyAPI.

Results. Once a model was trained over the manually extracted set of keywords, KEA was then run over the entire corpus. Results from the algorithm were then compared with the results from unsupervised algorithms (see Table 6). Initial results showed that the supervised algorithm performed better than the unsupervised ones but not significantly.

6.2   Part II

To demonstrate that KEA performs well over smaller training sets, and better when results across multiple annotators are combined, in the second part of

---

[4] As listed under: https://en.wikipedia.org/wiki/List_of_most_popular_websites.

Table 6. Comparing performance of unsupervised vs. supervised learning algorithms for keyword extraction

	AlchemyAPI	KEA
Terms	12635	10798
Precision	3%	4%
Recall	44%	47%
F_1-score	5%	7%
JSC	0.97	0.97

the experiment, the model was trained on the annotation for only the 5 policies chosen for Experiment I (Sect. 5). The trained model was then tasked with extracting keywords and keyphrases from the rest of the corpora (626 policies). This was done for all the participants and the results were compared against each other; reported in Table 7.

Table 7. Comparing F_1-scores between participants' and researcher's generated data sets from KEA.

	Researcher	P1	P2	P3	P4
Researcher	–	62%	70%	64%	72%
P1	62%	–	71%	75%	72%
P2	70%	71%	–	67%	79%
P3	64%	75%	67%	–	67%
P4	72%	72%	79%	67%	–

Since the training set only contained 5 privacy policies with roughly half of the terms present amongst all of the participants, the training set did not contain enough variance to train distinctly different models. The obvious exception being participant 3 who only annotated 3 policies.

Table 8. Comparing performance of keyword extraction from KEA based on primary researcher vs. combined data set generated by participants.

	Researcher	Participants
Terms	30261	49377
Precision		57%
Recall		93%
F_1-score		71%
JSC		0.45

Once again, participants' data sets were combined and compared against the researcher's data set of generated keywords to see if the accuracy rose with more number of annotators; the results are presented in Table 8. The combined data set achieves a score of F_1-*score* of 71%. One reason why the scores are different for the combined data sets (Table 4) is due to the smaller training set for the third participant. With less labelled data to train with, the training algorithm could overgeneralize what is not considered a keyword and hence ignore a large number of candidate keywords.

7   Discussion and Future Work

The mean F_1-*score* of 52% in Experiment I (Table 3) demonstrates an important aspect of keyword extraction with privacy policies- keyword extraction with privacy policies is a hard task. While 52% is a score better than the 20–30% performance of most state-of-the-art keyword extraction algorithms, a qualitative analysis of the annotated keywords/keyphrases by the participants suggests that despite having a concrete set of rules, examples, and training, participant's understanding of the technical terms and the text can still result in a diverse and non-overlapping set of terms. What one participant considers an important concept is not shared by a peer. This was mostly true for the more ambiguous and less technical parts of the policies, while technical details were easily picked up by all participants. Since all of the participants had a background in Computer Science, technical details would be easy to comprehend and more transparent to them. However, this might not be the case if the participant had no technical background; then, everything would have been equally less transparent. When written ambiguously privacy policies are difficult to comprehend.

In Part I of Experiment II it was found that the supervised learning algorithm improved the F_1-*score* of keywords being extracted. This is important for two primary reasons: quality and cost. One of the most time consuming tasks involved in generating a taxonomy is capturing major important themes and concepts of the target domain. This is where keyword extraction plays an important role in reducing the time taken to capture all of the themes and concepts. In this case, instead of reading a large number of privacy policies to identify all of the important themes and concepts, supervised learning promises to be a viable alternative. The generated keywords act as candidate terms that can be used to enrich a taxonomy, thus reducing the cost and time of reading a large number of privacy policies as well as improving the quality of the taxonomy by including terms that might have been covered in text that might not have been read due to resource restrictions.

Furthermore, the diversity of keywords/keyphrases found, in Experiment I, between participants can be used to improve the training data for supervised learning. The training data in Experiment II Part I was generated by a single researcher, it might be useful for another researcher or domain expert to read a set of non-overlapping policies and generate another set of training data. This would not only validate the current training data but also create more labelled data to train the model on. It would also prove helpful to review the candidate terms generated by participants in the first experiment and enrich the present training data, i.e., carefully merge all of the data sets to create a more comprehensive data set that captures all relevant keywords/keyphrases including the ones that might have been missed by individuals within the group.

Part II of the second experiment showed that if non-domain experts are given sufficient training, a supervised learning algorithm trained with their labelled data set could result in a trainings model that is able to extract most of the keywords and keyphrases that are being extracted with the help of training model, and built with labelled data from domain experts. Hence, it is possible to reduce cost and train non-experts and extract keywords and keyphrases with reasonable success.

Currently, privacy policies are heterogeneous as there are no laws/guidelines that mandate a certain structure, concepts, or terminology. This makes finding, identifying and understanding relevant information a time consuming task. By utilizing an intelligent reasoning system and mapping important concepts, ideas, and themes our work helps to identify important sections in an unstructured privacy policy; thus, resulting in less time needed to find important information in policies improving transparency and making polices more usable. It could further be used to introduce structure in future policies.

8 Conclusion

In this paper, we extended our previous work on keyword and keyphrase extraction over the domain of online privacy policies. In Experiment I, the difficulty of extracting keywords from privacy policies was demonstrated and the challenges associated with this task was discussed. In Experiment II we applied a supervised algorithm for keyword extraction, and demonstrated its superior performance over unsupervised algorithms applied to the same corpus of 631 online privacy policies. Our results confirm that using natural language processing techniques for keyword and keyphrase retrieval from privacy policies remains a challenging task.

Our preliminary results will guide further research in the field of online privacy and machine learning, and making policies more transparent and usable. We intend to improve our training set by having other domain experts (researchers and lawyers) identify key concepts, ideas, and themes in a non-overlapping set of privacy policies. In addition, it will be useful to compare how trained supervised algorithms perform against domain experts. Our research forms the first step in creating a context aware system for real-time privacy policy evaluation.

References

1. Madden, M., Rainie, L.: Americans Attitudes About Privacy, Security and Surveillance, May 2015. Available: http://www.pewinternet.org/2015/05/20/americans-attitudes-about-privacy-security-and-surveillance/. Accessed 10 June 2016

2. Jensen, C., Potts, C.: Privacy policies as decision-making tools: an evaluation of online privacy notices. In: 2004 Conference on Human Factors in Computing Systems, vol. 6, no. 1, pp. 471–478 (2004)
3. Winkler, S., Zeadally, S.: Privacy policy analysis of popular web platforms. IEEE Technol. Soc. Mag. **35**(2), 75–85 (2016)
4. Privacy Online: Fair Information Practices in the Electronic Marketplace, May 2000. http://1.usa.gov/1XeBiuY. Accessed 10 June 2016
5. Council Regulation 2016/679 of 27 April 2016 on the protection of natural persons with regard to the processing of personal data and on the free movement of such data, and repealing Directive 95/46/EC (General Data Protection Regulation) [2016] OJ L119/I, April 2016. http://eur-lex.europa.eu/legal-content/EN/TXT/PDF/?uri=CELEX:32016R0679&from=EN. Accessed 10 June 2016
6. Personal Information Protection and Electronic Documents Act, April 2000. http://laws-lois.justice.gc.ca/eng/acts/P-8.6/index.html. Accessed 10 June 2016
7. Digital Privacy Act, June 2015. http://laws-lois.justice.gc.ca/eng/annualstatutes/2015_32/page-1.html. Accessed 10 June 2016
8. McDonald, A.M., Cranor, L.F.: Cost of reading privacy policies. ISJLP **4**, 543 (2008)
9. McDonald, A.M., Reeder, R.W., Kelley, P.G., Cranor, L.F.: A comparative study of online privacy policies and formats. In: Goldberg, I., Atallah, M.J. (eds.) PETS 2009. LNCS, vol. 5672, pp. 37–55. Springer, Heidelberg (2009). https://doi.org/10.1007/978-3-642-03168-7_3
10. Milne, G.R., Culnan, M.J.: Strategies for reducing online privacy risks: why consumers read (or don't read) online privacy notices. J. Interact. Mark. **18**(3), 15–29 (2004)
11. Cranor, L.F., Hoke, C., Leon, P.G., Au, A.: Are they worth reading-an in-depth analysis of online trackers' privacy policies. I/S: J. Law Policy Inf. Soc. **11**, 325 (2015)
12. Wilson, S., Schaub, F., Dara, A.A., Liu, F., Cherivirala, S., Leon, P.G., Andersen, M.S., Zimmeck, S., Sathyendra, K.M., Russell, N.C., Norton, T.B., Hovy, E., Reidenberg, J., Sadeh, N.: The creation and analysis of a website privacy policy corpus. In: Proceedings of the 54th Annual Meeting of the Association for Computational Linguistics (Volume 1: Long Papers), vol. 1, pp. 1330–1340 (2016)
13. Sadeh, N., Acquisti, R., Breaux, T.D., Cranor, L.F., Mcdonalda, A.M., Reidenbergb, J.R., Smith, N.A., Liu, F., Russellb, N.C., Schaub, F., et al.: The usable privacy policy project: combining crowdsourcing, machine learning and natural language processing to semi-automatically answer those privacy questions users care about (2013)
14. Sun, Y.: Automatic Evaluation of Privacy Policy (2012)
15. Cranor, L.F., Langheinrich, M., Marchiori, M.: A P3P preference exchange language 1.0 (APPEL1. 0). W3C working draft, vol. 15 (2002)
16. Cranor, L.F.: P3P: making privacy policies more useful. IEEE Secur. Priv. **1**(6), 50–55 (2003)
17. Lämmel, R., Pek, E.: Understanding privacy policies. Empir. Softw. Eng. **18**(2), 310–374 (2013)
18. Ten steps to develop a multilayered privacy notice, February 2006. https://www.huntonprivacyblog.com/wp-content/uploads/sites/18/2012/07/Centre-10-Steps-to-Multilayered-Privacy-Notice.pdf. Accessed 10 June 2016

19. Munur, M., Branam, S., Mrkobrad, M.: Best practices in drafting plain-language and layered privacy policies, September 2012. https://iapp.org/news/a/2012-09-13-best-practices-in-drafting-plain-language-and-layered-privacy/. Accessed 10 June 2016

20. Cimiano, P., Völker, J.: Text2Onto. In: Montoyo, A., Muñoz, R., Métais, E. (eds.) NLDB 2005. LNCS, vol. 3513, pp. 227–238. Springer, Heidelberg (2005). https://doi.org/10.1007/11428817_21

21. Velardi, P., Fabriani, P., Missikoff, M.: Using text processing techniques to automatically enrich a domain ontology. In: Proceedings of the International Conference on Formal Ontology in Information Systems-Volume 2001, pp. 270–284. ACM (2001)

22. Ramanath, R., Schaub, F., Wilson, S., Liu, F., Sadeh, N., Smith, N.A.: Identifying relevant text fragments to help crowdsource privacy policy annotations. In: Second AAAI Conference on Human Computation and Crowdsourcing (2014)

23. Pan, Y., Zinkhan, G.M.: Exploring the impact of online privacy disclosures on consumer trust. J. Retail. 82(4), 331–338 (2006)

24. Wilson, S., Schaub, F., Ramanath, R., Sadeh, N., Liu, F., Smith, N.A., Liu, F.: Crowdsourcing annotations for websites' privacy policies: can it really work? In: Proceedings of the 25th International Conference on World Wide Web, pp. 133–143. International World Wide Web Conferences Steering Committee (2016)

25. Sathyendra, K.M., Schaub, F., Wilson, S., Sadeh, N.: Automatic extraction of opt-out choices from privacy policies. In: 2016 AAAI Fall Symposium Series (2016)

26. Kim, S.N., Medelyan, O., Kan, M.-Y., Baldwin, T.: SemEval-2010 Task 5: automatic keyphrase extraction from scientific articles. In: Proceedings of the 5th International Workshop on Semantic Evaluation, ser. SemEval 2010, pp. 21–26. Association for Computational Linguistics, Stroudsburg (2010)

27. Yeung, C.-M.A., Gibbins, N., Shadbolt, N.: A k-nearest-neighbour method for classifying web search results with data in Folksonomies. In: Proceedings of the 2008 IEEE/WIC/ACM International Conference on Web Intelligence and Intelligent Agent Technology - Volume 01, ser. WI-IAT 2008, pp. 70–76. IEEE Computer Society, Washington, D.C. (2008)

28. Tan, S.: Neighbor-weighted K-nearest neighbor for unbalanced text corpus. Expert Syst. Appl. 28(4), 667–671 (2005)

29. Frank, E., Paynter, G.W., Witten, I.H., Gutwin, C., Nevill-Manning, C.G.: Domain-specific keyphrase extraction. In: 16th International Joint Conference on Artificial Intelligence (IJCAI 1999), vol. 2, pp. 668–673. Morgan Kaufmann Publishers Inc., San Francisco (1999)

30. Turney, P.D.: Learning algorithms for keyphrase extraction. Inf. Retr. 2(4), 303–336 (2000)

31. Zhang, K., Xu, H., Tang, J., Li, J.: Keyword extraction using support vector machine. In: Yu, J.X., Kitsuregawa, M., Leong, H.V. (eds.) WAIM 2006. LNCS, vol. 4016, pp. 85–96. Springer, Heidelberg (2006). https://doi.org/10.1007/11775300_8

32. Audich, D.A., Dara, R., Nonnecke, B.: Extracting keyword and keyphrase from online privacy policies. In: 2016 Eleventh International Conference on Digital Information Management (ICDIM), pp. 127–132, September 2016

33. Mihalcea, R., Tarau, P.: TextRank: bringing order into texts. In: Proceedings of the 2004 Conference on Empirical Methods in Natural Language Processing. Association for Computational Linguistics (2004)

34. Witten, I.H., Paynter, G.W., Frank, E., Gutwin, C., Nevill-Manning, C.G.: KEA: practical automatic keyphrase extraction. In: Proceedings of the Fourth ACM Conference on Digital libraries, pp. 254–255. ACM (1999)

35. Kim, S.N., Kan, M.-Y.: Re-examining automatic keyphrase extraction approaches in scientific articles. In: Proceedings of the Workshop on Multiword Expressions: Identification, Interpretation, Disambiguation and Applications, pp. 9–16. Association for Computational Linguistics (2009)
36. Siddiqi, S., Sharan, A.: Keyword and keyphrase extraction techniques: a literature review. Int. J. Comput. Appl. **109**(2), 18–23 (2015)
37. Kim, S.N., Baldwin, T.: Extracting keywords from multi-party live chats. In: Proceedings of the 26th Pacific Asia Conference on Language, Information, and Computation, pp. 199–208 (2012)
38. Grineva, M., Grinev, M., Lizorkin, D.: Extracting key terms from noisy and multi-theme documents. In: Proceedings of the 18th International Conference on World Wide Web, pp. 661–670. ACM (2009)
39. Yih, W.-T., Goodman, J., Carvalho, V.R.: Finding advertising keywords on web pages. In: Proceedings of the 15th International Conference on World Wide Web, pp. 213–222. ACM (2006)
40. Hasan, K.S., Ng, V.: Automatic keyphrase extraction: a survey of the state of the art. In: ACL, vol. 1, pp. 1262–1273 (2014)
41. Lewis, D.D.: Naive (Bayes) at forty: the independence assumption in information retrieval. In: Nédellec, C., Rouveirol, C. (eds.) ECML 1998. LNCS, vol. 1398, pp. 4–15. Springer, Heidelberg (1998). https://doi.org/10.1007/BFb0026666
42. Porter, M.F.: An algorithm for suffix stripping. Program **14**(3), 130–137 (1980)

The Impact of Competence and Benevolence in a Computational Model of Trust

Ameneh Deljoo[1], Tom van Engers[2(✉)], Leon Gommans[1,3(✉)],
and Cees de Laat[1(✉)]

[1] Informatics Institute, University of Amsterdam, Amsterdam, The Netherlands
{a.deljoo,delaat}@uva.nl
[2] Leibniz Center for Law, University of Amsterdam, Amsterdam, The Netherlands
vanengers@uva.nl
[3] Air France-KLM, Amsterdam, The Netherlands
Leon.Gommans@KLM.com

Abstract. Trust is a fundamental element of any social network. However, despite numerous studies on trust, few have conducted studies across disciplines to provide a complete picture of the different dimensions of trustworthiness, such as integrity, competence and benevolence. In this paper, we focus on two of these dimensions, competence and benevolence. We propose techniques to evaluate the competence of the trustee in specific situations and infer the benevolence of the tustee towards the trustor when the trust evaluation is made. Moreover, we evaluate both competence and benevolence on the perceived trustworthiness of the trustee, taking into consideration the development of the relationship between the trustor and the trustee over time. We identified different stages in this relationship development and use them to evaluate trustworthiness of trustee in the absence of evidence that could be used to evaluate trustworthiness. Finally, we set an experimental scenario implemented as an agent-based model to evaluate our approach. The results obtained from these experiments show that the proposed techniques can improve the reliability of the estimation of the trustworthiness of the agents.

Keywords: Computational trust · Social trust · Benevolence
Competence · Agent based modeling

1 Introduction

Trust is considered a fundamental basis in social societies. The social networks, however, evolve over time therefore, we need a sophisticated method that enables an agent to select the trusted peer to interact with. Trust has both a backward looking as well as a forward looking dimension, i.e. one expects certain behavior

Published by Springer International Publishing AG 2018. All Rights Reserved
N. Gal-Oz and P. R. Lewis (Eds.): IFIPTM 2018, IFIP AICT 528, pp. 45–57, 2018.
https://doi.org/10.1007/978-3-319-95276-5_4

in the future based upon pastime experiences. Since one can never be sure that the conditions in the past are exactly the same as they are now (e.g., intentions of agents may change over time one may have to trust someone that had no experience with etc.), the estimation of trustworthiness is predominant to assess trust between each peer in such network. An agent-based model (ABM) of such societies requires a computational model of trust.

Trust is a concept that will always need contextualization. It is something completely different to trust that someone will pay his debts, not commit a crime or is able to solve a complex mathematical calculation. In our pursuit for a computational model of trust that can be used in ABMs that allow us to study (non-)compliance in societies we focus on the trustworthiness of an individual in performing a certain task in a given situation, taking into account the agent's competence in the matter, his overall integrity, and the stage of his relationships with the trustor. In order to better estimate the trustworthiness of trustees, it is important to consider these three dimensions individually, and to combine them in a dynamic way by taking into consideration the situation and the development of the relationship. However, the majority of the computational trust approaches presented in literature [1] estimates the trustworthiness of agents as one single factors rather than distinguishing these three trustees' factors. In this paper, we present a computational trust approach grounded on the trust model presented by Marsh [2]. We will show that the resulting computational trust model is able to capture the competence and benevolence of the trustee. To estimate the trustee's benevolence and competence, we use the evidence available to the trustee by considering different situations. Our approach combines the estimated competence of the trustee with the estimated benevolence into one single trustworthiness score. This score reflects the development of the relationship between trustor and trustee at the time of the assessment take into consideration. To estimate the competence of the trustee, we introduce three different stages of relationships between trustor and trustee. The results we obtain and present in this paper are very encouraging, as they show that there is a clear benefit in considering different stage of relationships between trustee and trustor in the described situations. The benevolence enhanced trust models allowed for a more accurate estimation of the trustees' trustworthiness than the original computational trust models [3]. The remainder of the paper is organized as follows. Section 2 highlights the trust model and its antecedents. Then, Sect. 3 introduces our social computational model with its components. Section 4 deals with the simulation and results of the proposed solutions. Related work is covered by Sect. 5. Finally, Sect. 6 concludes the paper.

2   Trust

Trust is an essential part of social interaction. Trust is a broad concept studied in areas such as sociology and psychology [4]. The concept of trust has received ample attention from various disciplines, and although prior research has put forth diverse interpretations of trust, a common core emerges.

Trust antecedents framework, illustrated in Fig. 1, was proposed by Mayer *et al.* [4]. Following Mayer *et al.* [4] we use the following trust definition: "Trust is the willingness of a party to be vulnerable to the actions of another party based on the expectation that the other will perform a particular action important to the trustor, irrespective of the ability to monitor or control other party [4]". Specifically, trust is a decision of the trustor regarding the perceived trustworthiness of a trustee. Four trust factors are generic and important during the trust evaluation, namely competence, benevolence and integrity of the trustee, and the trust propensity of the trustor. The decision to trust means that the trustor is willing to take any possible risk caused by the trustee or environment, no matter whether s/he has the competence to monitor or control the trustee or environment. Building on this definition, we define inter-organizational trust as the expectation held by one firm that another will not exploit its vulnerabilities when faced with the opportunity to do so [4–6]. This expectation is confirmed when parties:

- demonstrate competence relate to the potential ability of the evaluated entity to do a given task,
- act accordingly to fulfill the commitments even when acting on them is not in self-interest and accept the consequences, and
- do good and act out of kindness even if unforeseen contingencies arise.

Our definition thus bases inter-organizational trust on three related components: competence, integrity, and benevolence, which have been proposed by Mayer *et al.* [4]. Computational trust is considered as an enabler of technology in virtual societies, and the estimation of trustworthiness is paramount to assess the trust that a trustor agent has on a given trustee. An individual is more or less trustworthy in performing a task in a given situation depending on his competence in the matter, his overall integrity, and the stage of his relationships with the trustor. Therefore, in order to better estimate the trustworthiness of agents, it is important to consider these three dimensions individually, and to combine them in a dynamic way, by taking into consideration the situation and the development of the relationship. However, the majority of the computational trust approaches presented in literature estimate the trustworthiness of agents as a block and do not distinguish between these trustees' attributions.

Proposition 1. Close and long-term relationships have a direct impact on the competence and benevolence of partners.

In following, we present a computational trust approach grounded on multidisciplinary literature on trust that is able to capture the competence and benevolence of the agent under evaluation. This framework has been implemented with ABM.

3   Computational Trust Model

In this section, we introduce the social computational trust model. Our aim is to define a mechanism for estimating trustworthiness of a trustee that can be used by the trustor to evaluate trust and make decisions about the future relationship with the trustee. Extracting trustworthiness of trustee based on Mayer *et al.*'s model [4] has been only implemented by few scholars such as [3,7]. Most of these computational trust approaches estimate the trustees' trustworthiness using individual items of evidence about these trustees' behavior in the past interactions, either with the trustor or with third party agents [8–10]. However, none of these approaches is able to estimate the benevolence of the trustee. We claim that understanding the benevolence and competence of the trustee towards the trustor at the moment of the trust decision is fundamental for being able to accurately estimate the latter's trustworthiness. With this in mind, we present the main hypothesis of this work as follows;

Hypothesis 1. The extraction of benevolence-competence based on the information from the set of evidence on the trustee under evaluation and its use in adequate stages of the relationship between trustor and trustee shows that trustee's trustworthiness improves by increasing the number of interactions between trustor and trustee.

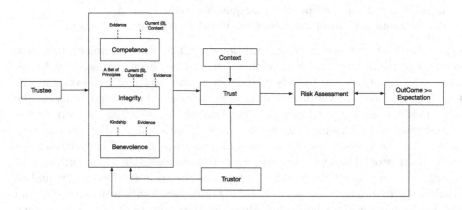

Fig. 1. Trust framework and its antecedents.

3.1   Basic Notation

Our generic computational trust model is applied to environments where trustor agents select the best trustees to interact with, having the posterior establishment of dyadic agreements between partners. We define the society of agents by A, where x and y represent as trustor and trustee respectively and $x, y \in A$. We represent $T_{(x,y)}$ as the amount of trust x has upon y based on the realization of a given task $t \in T$ with respect to the situation s_i, where $T = \{t_1, t_2, \ldots, t_m\}$ is the set of all possible m tasks in the society and $s_i = \{s_1, s_2, \ldots, s_i\}$ is the set of all possible situations in the society. These set of tasks bring duties for the trustee that need to be fulfilled. As we mentioned before, context plays an important role in our model. In order to characterize and describe the situation leading to an agreement, we consider the definition of context as including four main types of context: identity, time, location, and activity [11]. Urbano *et al.* [3] identified eight dimensions of context $\{d_1, d_2, \ldots, d_8\}^1$, where dimensions d_1 and d_2 represent the agents trustor and the trustee, respectively; d_3 and d_4 represent the time and the location of agreement; and d_5, d_6, d_7 and d_8 identify and characterize the type of the task, its complexity, deadline, and outcome of its realization, respectively. We adapt the Urbano *et al.* [3] context definition in this paper. For the simplicity, we assume that all agreements performed in the society of agents refer to the same type of task t (d_5), although tasks have different degrees of complexity (d_6) and deadlines (d_7). In this paper, we only consider four dimensions of context, which are d_1, d_2, d_5 and d_8. We exclude time, complexity and deadlines from our formalization. They will be addressed in a future publication.

Urbano *et al.* considered three different outcomes (d_8) is defined by $O = \{FD, FDD, V\}$, where FD (fulfill duty) means the trustor considers that the trustee performed whatever matter he had to perform on time, FDD (fulfill duty with delay) means the trustee was presented with an unexpected delay in the performance of the task (or duty), and V (violation) means the trustee did not perform the given task. Considering $O = \{FD, FDD, V\}$, possible values for this function are $val(FDD) = 1.0$, $val(FD) = 0.5$, and $val(V) = 0.5$.

Finally, the set of all the existed evidence on given trustee is represented by $E_{*,y} = \{e_i \in \varepsilon : v_2^{e_i} = y\}$, where ε represents all evidence available on trustee from the all the trustee's direct neighbor. Following, $E_{(x,y)}$ shows all the evidence about the direct interactions between trustor and trustee $E_{(x,y)} = \{e_i \in \varepsilon : v_1^{e_i} = x, v_2^{e_i} = y\}$.

3.2   Our Social Computational Trust Model

The benevolence-competence based computational model of trust that we present in this paper is a part of a larger framework of social trust based on Mayer's trust model. It integrates three distinct functions: the competence evaluation function ($Com_{(x,y)} : s_i \times Ex_{(*,y)} \in [0,1]$), the benevolence evaluation function ($Ben_{(x,y)} : E_{(x,y)} \in [0,1]$), and the trustworthiness evaluation function ($TW_{(x,y)} \in [0,1]$) in the set of situations s_i. We describe each of these functions in the following subsections. We illustrated the computational model in Fig. 2.

Benevolence Function. Benevolence is considered as a key element of trust and an antecedent of trustworthiness by several scholars (e.g. [12,13]). The estimated value of the benevolence of trustor x toward trustee y, $Ben_{(x,y)}$, is derived from the direct interactions (i.e. $E_{(x,y)}$) between trustee and trustor in the situations s_i. The output of the benevolence evaluation function $Ben_{(x,y)}$, defined in $[0,1]$, is

---

1 Dimensions are defined based on the scenarios.

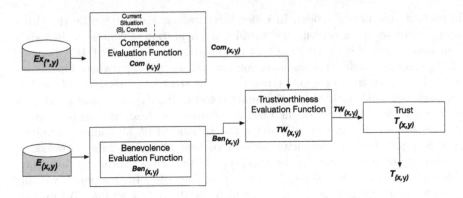

Fig. 2. Our benevolence-competence computational model of trust.

$$Ben_{(x,y)} = \frac{1}{|S|} \sum_{E_{(x,y)}} (val(E_{(x,y)})). \tag{1}$$

Where S is the set of situations, in which x has interactions with y.

Competence Function. The competence evaluation function $Com_{(x,y)}$ esti-mates the general ability of the trustee under evaluation in performing a given task t in a specific situation s. This function takes all the evidence available on the trustee under evaluation $Ex_{(*,y)}$ as input. The output of the competence evaluation function is the estimated competence of the agent, $Com_{(x,y)}$, defined in $[0,1]$. Competence, as risk, involves an agent making a judgment about the trustee's ability to perform the given task. We consider three different possible situations to evaluate trustee's ability.

1. There is no evidence available from the trustee. To judge the trustee's com-petence, the trustor will calculate the risk of trusting a stranger and decide based on the risk as

$$Risk = \frac{Cost \times (1 - Pr)}{benefit \times Pr}, \tag{2}$$

   where Pr is the probability of performing the task by the given trustee.
2. Situation β: there are some evidence but not for the considered context. In this situation, the trustor collects all the evidence from other agents and evaluates the competence of trustee based on them as

$$Com = \frac{1}{|N|} \sum_{\beta \in N} (val(E_{*,y}) \times \widehat{T}_x(y, \beta)), \tag{3}$$

where $\widehat{T}_x(y, \beta)$ denotes the basic trust that x has on y and β is the set of all situations in which x has interactions with y. The basic trust y calculated as $1 / |N| \sum_{\beta \in N} T_{(x,y)}$. N denotes as the set of situations similar to the present situation (s_i) in which x has interactions with y.

3. Situation α: there is related evidence about the agent in this context or similar situation.

$$Com = \frac{1}{|N|} \sum_{\alpha \in N} (val(E_{*,y})), \qquad (4)$$

where α is the set of all situations in which x has interactions with y. These three situations (no evidence available, β and α) are assumed to help an individual to make the decision. In this paper, we assume that trustor and trustee collaborate in the similar context (i.e. situation α).

Function $TW_{(x,y)}$. The trustworthiness evaluation function $TW_{(x,y)}$ takes into consideration the perception of the competence and benevolence of the trustee (Algorithm 1). We assume the same weight to the competence and benevolence dimension, this weight when both trustor and trustee are practically strangers ($W_{(x,y)} = 0$), and progressively increasing the weight of these to dimension as the partners get to know each other better, this weight becomes one when partners are considered to be closed (Proposition 1). In the Algorithm 1 $N_{(x,y)}$ represents the number of interactions between x and y, (line 1), and defined a minimum number of interactions ($N_{ben} = 2$) between trustor x and trustee y. $N_{(x,y)}$ used to combin the estimated value of the trustee's benevolence as returned by $F(Ben_{(x,y)})$ (line 2) with the estimated value of its competence as returned by $F(Com_{(x,y)})$ (line 3). Finally, the estimated value of the trustee's trustworthiness $TW_{(x,y)}$ is computed as a sum of $Com_{(x,y)}$ and $Ben_{(x,y)}$ (line 4).

Algorithm 1. Calculate $TW_{(x,y)}$

Require: $E_{(*,y)}$: the set of all evidence about trustee y.
Require: $N_{ben} = 2$: minimum interaction between trustee and trustor.
Ensure: $E_{(x,y)} \notin E_{(*,y)}$
1: $N_{(x,y)} \leftarrow |E_{(x,y)}|$
2: $Ben_{(x,y)} \leftarrow F(Ben_{(x,y)})$
3: $Com_{(x,y)} \leftarrow F(Com_{(x,y)})$
4: $TW_{(x,y)} = Com_{(x,y)} + Ben_{(x,y)}$
5: **return** $TW_{(x,y)}$

---

4   Simulation Setup

In this set of experiments, we want to test **Hypothesis 1**, which we reformulated as follows: The extraction of benevolence-competence based on the information from the set of evidence on the trustee under evaluation and its use in adequate stages of the relationship between trustor and trustee shows that trustee's trustworthiness improves by increasing the number of interactions between trustor and trustee.

The experiments were conducted in Jadex [14] environment. We set up a social network, shown in Fig. 3 to represent our network. We setup a collaborative network of organizations. This social network represents a collaborative network of organizations like the ones we study in our SARNET research project where service providers collaborate and act on behalf of partners, acts that may harm the individual interests, all in order to protect the collaborative network against cyber attacks. Each node represents an autonomous organization that needs to trust other parties and share sensitive information with them. For the simplicity, we assumed that there is only one task being negotiated by all nodes which mitigates an attack and shares the attack information with other parties[2].

We define four different situations: s_1 provides a specific number of samples within 24 h, s_2 provides a specific type of resource (e.g. allocating resources), s_3 blocks a link, and s_4 monitors a specific traffic.

This model starts after the establishment of an agreement between the trustor and the selected trustee, thus excluding the selection process itself. It focuses on both types of agents' decision concerning the fulfillment of the established agreement: the trustees may opt to fulfill the agreement (the trustors will report the outcome FDD) or to delay its realization. Accordingly, the trustors may respond to a delay by either retaliating, denouncing the breach (reporting outcome V) or forgiving the contingency (reporting outcome FD).

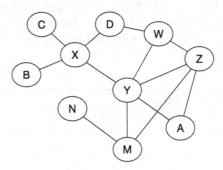

Fig. 3. Social network schema.

4.1   Result

Our result consists of two parts. First, we calculate benevolence of agent y by considering all the evidence (i.e. direct interactions) that x has on y. Second, evaluate the competence of agent given trustees a, z and y in four mentioned situations from the trustor's x view. Hence, we perform four different types of situations simultaneously, each with six agents. We assume that agents are honest and there is no conflict on the evidence and message are encrypted (the interminable agents cannot manipulate the message). In order to compare all approaches, we measure and average the number of agreements with outcomes

---

[2] The technical details and code of this research can be found in http://delaat.net/sarnet/index.html.

FD, FDD and V. We are able to calculate the benevolence and competence of each trustor by Eqs. 1 and 4. To calculate the $Ben_{(x,y)}$, we extract all the evidence that x has on y. We perform the simulation for 20, 50 and 100 rounds of interactions. We also consider that each agent can freely fulfill duty, fulfill duty with delay and violate the agreement. We have summarized the result in Table 1 (including mean M and standard deviation SD).

Table 1. $Ben_{(x,y)}$ evaluation for the number of rounds

No. of rounds →	20	50	100
$Ben_{(x,y)}$	*0.22*	0.31	**0.86**
SD	*0.113*	0.105	**0.081**
M	*0.762*	0.777	**0.810**

To evaluate the competence function, we select three agents a, z and y from the set of agents and calculate the competence of these three agents from trustor' x view. Agent x will collect (collecting the evidence is done by sending a query to each agent and asking its opinion) all the available evidence from the neighbour's of a, z and y which are reported in Table 2. The simulation has been perform for four different situations and three different rounds. As result, we compared mean (M) and standard deviation(SD) and competence of each trustee for different rounds and we detailed them in Tables 1 and 3. In Tables 1 and 3, the highest values are in bold and the lowest values are in italics. We verified that in Table 1 the benevolence of trustees are increased as the number of interaction increases. For instance, with only 20 rounds, when the number of interactions between any two partners is not large the benevolence is small. By increasing the number of rounds, the benevolence increases significantly. Indeed, this confirms that the number of interactions is, in fact, impact the benevolence existing between any pair of trustor-trustee (We have proved the main hypothesis of this work 1). In the case of competence (see Table 3), we also observed the same behavior from the simulation. The competence of agent is influence directly by the number of interactions. As we mentioned before, the simulation has been repeated for 50 and 100 rounds. The benevolence value reaches the maximum value of one by increasing the number of interactions between partners and the partners that

Table 2. Agent x asks different agents' opinion about agent z in the four situations

Situation →	s_1	s_2	s_3	s_4
Y	FDD,FD	FD,FD	FDD,FD	FDD,FDD
M	FDD,FD	FD,FD	FDD,FD	FDD,FDD
W	FDD,FD	FD,FD	FDD,FD	FDD,FDD
D	FDD,FD	FD,FD	FDD,FD	FDD,FDD

Table 3. Competence evaluation for agents a, z and y and the number of rounds

No. of rounds $\rightarrow$	20	50	100
$Com_{(x,a)}$	0.21	0.40	**0.65**
$Com_{(x,z)}$	0.28	0.43	**0.88**
$Com_{(x,y)}$	0.18	0.33	**0.54**
SD_a	0.059	0.051	**0.048**
SD_z	0.068	0.058	**0.042**
SD_y	0.081	0.066	**0.041**
M_a	0.927	0.938	**0.941**
M_z	0.910	0.927	**0.947**
M_y	0.917	0.936	**0.962**

are considered to be in a close relationship (Proposition 1). Indeed, each trustor can conclude the trustworthiness of trustee in each round and make a decision. Overall, we are able to confirm the truthfulness of Hypothesis 1.

5   Related Work

Many computational trust models have been presented by different scholars, nevertheless, only a few models are actually social computational models. Adalie *et al.* [15] presented a conceptual model of social trust based on Kelton *et al.*'s model [16]. Kelton *et al.*'s consider ability, positive intentions, ethics, and predictability as the trustworthiness components. Adalie *et al.* used a probabilistic approach to implement the model, but by recognizing the limits of such approach in the treatment of the social concepts, their model was not implemented.

Among all the presented computational trust models [17], the only computational approach that includes a comprehensive set of features grounded on the theory of trust is the socio-cognitive model of trust by Castelfranchi and Falcone [18]. This model considers that the trustor has a goal that can be achieved by the action of the trustee. In their view, trust is formed by considering the different beliefs that the trustor has about the trustee, either internal (beliefs on competence, disposition, and harmfulness) or external (opportunities and dangers). The values of these beliefs are further modulated by meta-beliefs about the relative strength of each belief. The richness of this model makes it hard to implement in practice. In fact, the current implementation of the model (e.g., [18]) requires extensive manual configuration by domain experts for each trustee and task under assessment and oversimplifies the theoretical model. Moreover, it requires explicit information about the competence and disposition (or similar beliefs) of the agent under evaluation, which may be hard to get in dynamic agent-based environments.

Another social trust model was presented by Urbano *et al.* [3] called situation-aware and social computational trust Model (SOLUM). Their computational model consists of two parts: the first part is a general framework of computational trust, which is based on two fundamental characteristics of trust, the trustor's disposition and emotional state. They adapted also Mayer's trustworthiness dimension that includes the ability, integrity, and benevolence to determine trust. For the second part, they proposed a set of distinct techniques to extract information about the individual dimensions of the agent's trustworthiness from the set of structured evidence available to the agent. The main difference between our model and Urbano's model is that we consider different stages of relationships for the competence function. We slightly adapted and modified the Marsh [2] competence formalization by considering three different situations for trustor to make a decision about the (future) collaboration with the trustee.

Finally, Herzig *et al.* [19] formalized the model of Castefranchi and Falcone, in multi-modal logic, adding the notions of occurring trust and dispositional trust (i.e., trust in a general disposition of the trustee to perform a similar task some point in the future). Skopik *et al.* [20] purposed a semi-distributed information sharing platform where different organizations can share the incidents information with their trusted peers. Skopik *et al.*, proposed a fuzzy method to evaluate trust among members. The major aim of social trust in their model is to personalize online interactions and prioritize collaboration with trustworthy individuals. The author claimed that trusted relations can be defined manually by users, e.g., by declaring "friend-relations" or can be determined automatically through mining of interactions. However, their social model is based on personal experience of each member and suffers from the scalability issue.

6   Conclusion and Discussion

Computational trust is crucial for decision making regarding possible agents' future joint activities such as the alliances. It heavily relies on the estimation of trustworthiness to assess the trust on particular trustees. To better estimate this trustworthiness, it is important to estimate, besides other relevant features, their competence and benevolence separately, and to combine them taking into consideration the particular situation and relationship. In this paper, we described a part of our trust computational model. We evaluated our approach in a simulated experimental environment. We have proved that the trustworthiness estimation grew with the increasing number of interactions between any trustor-trustee pair. Besides, we went beyond the traditional evaluation of computational trust models (such as Fuzzy logic evaluation) and used a model of agents' behavior where both trustors and trustees evolve their behaviors based on different stages of existing relationships (i.e. presented in the competence formula) between the agents. Concerning future work, we intend to further identify the particular circumstances in which the use of this sophisticated trust model is more relevant. Also, we intend to explore integrity as another dimension of trustworthiness, as well as exploring other ways of combining the trustworthiness dimensions, and to use other antecedents of trust, such as the trustors' own propensity to trust.

A lot of future work remains to be done to ensure that the framework is functional in practice. We plan to conduct experiments to evaluate the robustness of the proposed trust mechanism against the badmouthing attacks and noncompliant members. Furthermore, evidential reasoning in the case of conflicting on evidence and evaluate trust based on this method will need to be elaborated and evaluated. Another interesting direction for future work is to develop guidelines in consultation with policy makers to define sounds policy and standard for determining the contract importance based on the risk associated with the proposed methods and the members' preferences. Many different adaptations, tests, and experiments for our model have been left for the future due to lack of time. Future work concerns the a deeper analysis of our proposed model and validates the model with different computational models that proposed by other scholars such as Urbano et al.

Acknowledgment. This work is funded by the Dutch Science Foundation project SARNET (grant no: CYBSEC.14.003/618.001.016) and the Dutch project COMMIT (WP20.11). Special thanks go to our research partner KLM. The authors would also like to thank anonymous reviewers for their comments.

References

1. Sabater, J., Sierra, C.: Review on computational trust and reputation models. Artif. Intell. Rev. **24**(1), 33–60 (2005)
2. Marsh, S.P.: Formalising trust as a computational concept (1994)
3. Urbano, J., Rocha, A.P., Oliveira, E.: The impact of benevolence in computational trust. In: Chesñevar, C.I., Onaindia, E., Ossowski, S., Vouros, G. (eds.) AT 2013. LNCS (LNAI), vol. 8068, pp. 210–224. Springer, Heidelberg (2013). https://doi.org/10.1007/978-3-642-39860-5_16
4. Mayer, R.C., Davis, J.H., Schoorman, F.D.: An integrative model of organizational trust. Acad. Manag. Rev. **20**(3), 709–734 (1995)
5. Barney, J.B., Hansen, M.H.: Trustworthiness as a source of competitive advantage. Strateg. Manag. J. **15**(S1), 175–190 (1994)
6. Krishnan, R., Martin, X., Noorderhaven, N.G.: When does trust matter to alliance performance? Acad. Manag. J. **49**(5), 894–917 (2006)
7. Guo, G., Zhang, J., Thalmann, D., Yorke-Smith, N.: ETAF: an extended trust antecedents framework for trust prediction. In: 2014 IEEE/ACM International Conference on Advances in Social Networks Analysis and Mining (ASONAM), pp. 540–547. IEEE (2014)
8. Sabater, J., Sierra, C.: Regret: reputation in gregarious societies. In: Proceedings of the Fifth International Conference on Autonomous Agents, pp. 194–195. ACM (2001)
9. Abdul-Rahman, A., Hailes, S.: Supporting trust in virtual communities. In: Proceedings of the 33rd Annual Hawaii International Conference on System Sciences, 9-p. IEEE (2000)
10. Mui, L., Mohtashemi, M., Halberstadt, A.: A computational model of trust and reputation. In: HICSS, Proceedings of the 35th Annual Hawaii International Conference on System Sciences, pp. 2431–2439. IEEE (2002)

11. Abowd, G.D., et al.: Towards a better understanding of context and context-awareness. In: Gellersen, H.-W. (ed.) HUC 1999. LNCS, vol. 1707, pp. 304–307. Springer, Heidelberg (1999). https://doi.org/10.1007/3-540-48157-5_29
12. Levin, D.Z., Cross, R., Abrams, L.C., Lesser, E.L.: Trust and knowledge sharing: a critical combination. IBM Inst. Knowl.-Based Org. **19** (2002)
13. Koscik, T.R., Tranel, D.: The human amygdala is necessary for developing and expressing normal interpersonal trust. Neuropsychologia **49**(4), 602–611 (2011)
14. Braubach, L., Lamersdorf, W., Pokahr, A.: Jadex: implementing a BDI-infrastructure for JADE agents (2003)
15. Adali, S., Wallace, W., Qian, Y., Vijayakumar, P., Singh, M.: A unified framework for trust in composite networks. In: Proceedings of 14th AAMAS W. pp. 1–12. Trust in Agent Societies, Taipei (2011)
16. Kelton, K., Fleischmann, K.R., Wallace, W.A.: Trust in digital information. J. Am. Soc. Inform. Sci. Technol. **59**(3), 363–374 (2008)
17. Pinyol, I., Sabater-Mir, J.: Computational trust and reputation models for open multi-agent systems: a review. Artif. Intell. Rev. **40**(1), 1–25 (2013)
18. Castelfranchi, C., Falcone, R.: Trust Theory: A Socio-Cognitive and Computational Model, vol. 18. Wiley, New York (2010)
19. Herzig, A., Lorini, E., Hübner, J.F., Vercouter, L.: A logic of trust and reputation. Log. J. IGPL **18**(1), 214–244 (2009)
20. Skopik, F., Schall, D., Dustdar, S.: Modeling and mining of dynamic trust in complex service-oriented systems. In: Dustdar, S., Schall, D., Skopik, F., Juszczyk, L., Psaier, H. (eds.) Socially Enhanced Services Computing, pp. 29–75. Springer, Vienna (2011). https://doi.org/10.1007/978-3-7091-0813-0_3

CodeTrust
Trusting Software Systems

Christian Damsgaard Jensen$^{(\boxtimes)}$ and Michael Bøndergaard Nielsen

Department of Applied Mathematics and Computer Science,
Technical University of Denmark, Copenhagen, Denmark
cdje@dtu.dk

Abstract. The information society is building on data and the software required to collect and analyse these data, which means that the trustworthiness of these data and software systems is crucially important for the development of society as a whole. Efforts to establish the trustworthiness of software typically include parameters, such as security, reliability, maintainability, correctness and robustness.

In this paper we explore ways to determine the trustworthiness of software, in particular code where some of the constituent components are externally sourced, e.g. through crowd sourcing and open software systems. We examine different quality parameters that we believe define key quality indicators for trustworthy software and define CodeTrust, which is a content based trust metric for software.

We present the design and evaluation of a research prototype that implements the proposed metric, and show the results of preliminary evaluations of CodeTrust using well known open source software projects.

1 Introduction

We are increasingly dependent on software in all the systems and infrastructures that weave the fabric of our everyday life. From the systems that we rely on to do our work, the social media that occupy much of our spare time and the Internet of Things that provides the data and control necessary to support the intelligence and convenience that we expect from our modern way of life. As software becomes ubiquituous and we all need more software systems to function normally, there is an increasing pressure to reduce costs, e.g. through the integration of free (as in gratis) open source software in commodity products. The urgency of this problem is probably best illustrated by the HeartBleed [1] vulnerability discovered in the Open SSL library (e.g. used in the popular Apache web server) or the GNU Bash remote code execution vulnerability Shellshock [6], both discovered in 2014. In both cases, software failures had a crippling effect on popular software systems. The HeartBleed vulnerability in Open SSL was present in several versions of the security protocol library, which meant that many manufacturers, who had relied on Open SSL in their software systems, were unable to determine which of their products were actually vulnerable. Analysis of the Gnu Bash source code, showed

© IFIP International Federation for Information Processing 2018
Published by Springer International Publishing AG 2018. All Rights Reserved
N. Gal-Oz and P. R. Lewis (Eds.): IFIPTM 2018, IFIP AICT 528, pp. 58–74, 2018.
https://doi.org/10.1007/978-3-319-95276-5_5

that the Shellshock vulnerability in the popular Bash command interpreter had existed since September 1989. These examples show that software vulnerabilities may exist in code for a long time before they are discovered, even in otherwise well respected software like OpenSSL and GNU Bash.

Software systems are often based on components and services that integrate externally developed software libraries and execution engines. Establishing the trustworthiness of the components and services that are integrated into a software system is therefore of vital importance to software developers. This requires a consideration of both directly observable software quality attributes, such as size and complexity, and reputation factors, such as the history of vulnerabilities found in the software components and services and the track record of the software developers. In this paper we propose the CodeTrust software trust metric to evaluate the trustworthiness of a given software system. CodeTrust considers the vulnerability history of the specific software (both number and severity of vulnerabilities), the track record of the software's developers and several directly observable software quality attributes.

We have developed a prototype that implements CodeTrust and used this prototype to evaluate a number of well known Open Source Software (OSS) systems. The evaluation shows a significant variation in the CodeTrust metric for different OSS projects, but that missing data leads to some uncertainty, which suggests that it would be interesting to include a confidence score in the CodeTrust metric.

The rest of this paper is organized as follows. Section 2 presents the Heartbleed vulnerability to illustrate several of the concepts that we consider and provide an overall motivation for our work. Related work on software trust metrics and trust systems used in software development is examined in Sect. 3. We propose the CodeTrust metric in Sect. 4, where we also discuss different software quality attributes. We implemented a simple prototype to allow a preliminary evaluation of CodeTrust; this evaluation is presented in Sect. 5. Finally, we present conclusions and directions for future work are presented in Sect. 6.

2   Motivation

The HeartBleed vulnerability, mentioned in the Introduction, is one of the best known software vulnerabilities in recent years. HeartBleed was caused by a flawed implementation of the Heartbeat Extension [19] in OpenSSL,[1] which supports keep-alive functionality without performing a renegotiation. The vulnerable code allocates a memory buffer for the message to be returned by the heartbeat based on the length field in the requesting message with no length check for this particular memory allocation. The vulnerable implementation allocates this memory,

---

[1] OpenSSL is a widely used implementation of the Transport Layer Security (TLS) protocol [9], which allows two computers on the Internet to establish secure communication. It is often used by embedded systems and open source software, such as the Apache and nginx webservers which, at the time, powered around two thirds of the websites on the Internet.

without regard to the actual size of that message's payload, so the returned message returned consists of the payload, possibly followed by whatever else happened to be in the allocated memory buffer on the server. Heartbleed is exploited by sending a malformed heartbeat request with a small payload and large length field to the vulnerable party in order to elicit the victim's response. This allows an attacker to read up to 64 KB of the victim's memory that was likely to have been used previously by OpenSSL, e.g. this memory could include passwords of other users who had recently logged onto the webserver. HeartBleed was first disclosed in April 2014, but the bug was introduced in 2012, when the TLS Heartbeat Extension was first standardised. The flaw was introduced by a single programmer, who implemented the extension, and reviewed by one of OpenSSL's four core developers before being integrated into OpenSSL v. 1.0.1; the bug remained unnoticed in subsequent releases of OpenSSL, until OpenSSL v1.0.1g, which corrected the mistake. An article in the online media The Register indicates around 200,000 Internet sites still vulnerable to HeartBleed in January 2017 [17] and a quick search for the vulnerability in the search-engine Shodan indicates that more than 150,000 Internet sites are still vulnerable a year later.

The HeartBleed vulnerability is not only interesting because it affected an important and popular Internet security component, but mostly because it demonstrates how a small mistake in a software component can have major repercussions for global Internet security, i.e. we place a lot of trust in software, which is delivered for free and without warranty.

3   Related Work

Deciding whether code can be trusted has a long history, e.g. in his *Note on the Confinement Problem* from [13], Butler Lampson examines the problem of externally sourced software libraries leaking confidential data. Subsequent efforts to address this problem include a number of software evaluation criteria that were especially developed for military use [7,20], which inspired the development of common criteria for security evaluation of software [12]. Common to these evaluation criteria is that they introduce a well defined hierarchy of increasingly secure systems (encoded in a *Security Level*[2]) and that they do not apply to the software in itself, but to installed systems, e.g. the Common Criteria [12] introduces the notion of a Target of Evaluation (ToE) which defines the set of systems and services considered in the evaluation. Moreover, the official certification process according to these criteria requires significant efforts, resources and time, so they are not widely used outside high security environments, such as defence, aerospace or financial services.

Software quality has been studied from many different aspects over the years, such as reliability and fault tolerance [18] to the notion of dependability [3] and

---

[2] The Common Critera captures the *Protection Profile (PP)* and the *Security Target (ST)* and measures the *Evaluation Assurance Level (EAL)*, which depends on the depth and rigour of the security evaluation.

the necessary consideration of the full tool-chain [23]. In the following, we limit our presentation to a few efforts that have influenced our work the most.

The Trusted Software Methodology (TSM) [2] found 44 Trust Principles that determine the quality of software. These principles combine aspects of both security and software engineering as illustrated in Fig. 1 below.

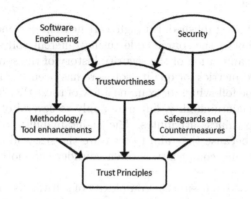

Fig. 1. Trust principles that reflect trustworthiness, quality and security of software.

The TSM recognises the role of both security techniques and software engineering practices in the development of trustworthy of software systems, i.e. secure software development can be considered a socio-technical system (STS), which has been examined by Mohammadi et al. [14]. They identified a number of attributes in STS that affect the trustworthiness of the developed software, these attributes are shown in Fig. 2.

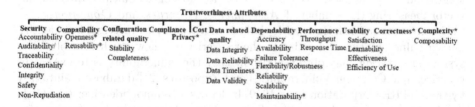

Fig. 2. Trustworthiness attributes identified by Mohammadi et al. [14].

These attributes capture different aspects of trustworthiness, but in this paper we focus on the attributes that are most directly linked with the security of the software product, i.e. Security and Dependability. The difficult part of using these attributes directly, is that it requires a general evaluation of the attributes in all types of software. The metrics created will have to apply to both small and large projects (and everything in between) without being biased toward one or the other.

The work on TSM and STS demonstrate that trustworthy software is defined by directly observable software artefacts of the developed systems, as well as indirectly perceivable characteristics of the software development process. This corresponds to the notions of direct and indirect trust in the trustee.

3.1   Direct Trust

Direct trust can be established through certification (as mentioned above,) through examination of the source code (using different software quality metrics,) or through examination of the security history of the software.

Software related metrics for quality software has been studied extensively in the literature. In the following, we examine a few of these that have been studied in the context of maintainability, but may apply to several of the Dependability related trustworthiness attributes. The maintainability attributes are particularly relevant, because they aim to measure the size and complexity of the developed software and complexity is often consider the mother of all security vulnerabilities.

The simplest way to measure the complexity of software is to measure the size of the program. This is most commonly done by counting the *lines of code* in the software, because smaller programs are often easier to comprehend, but several extensions to this metric are possible. In *effective lines of code*, lines consisting only of comments, blank lines, and lines with standalone brackets are ignored. The *logical lines of codes* counts the number of statements in the programming language, e.g. lines ending with a semicolon in "Java" or "C". The *comment to code ratio* is another simple metric is to measure the amount of actual code to the amount of information included to assist software developers. Other metrics have been proposed, e.g. Halstead complexity [11] tries to eliminate the impact of the programming language by considering the software vocabulary and the program length and the ABC metric [10] is measured as the length of a three-dimensional vector measuring the number of *A*ssignments, *B*ranches, and *C*onditions.

In order to establish the security history of software, it is necessary to identify known vulnerabilities and estimate their severity, i.e. how much control of the system an attacker may obtain and how easy the vulnerability is to exploit in practice. The Common Vulnerabilities and Exposures [21] database maintained by the MITRE Corporation since 1999. It defines a common identifier (the CVE number) and a short description of the vulnerability, which provides security professionals an unambiguous way to discuss vulnerabilities. In adition to naming and describing known vulnerabilities, the Common Vulnerability Scoring System (CVSS) [8] defines a way to capture the principal characteristics of a vulnerability and calculate a numerical score reflecting its severity. The CVSS scoring system is maintained by a special interest group (SIG) of the Forum of Incident Response and Security Teams (FIRST) and CVSS scores for most vulnerabilities listed in the CVE database can be found on the National Vulnerability Database [16]. The CVSS scores vulnerabilities from 0 to 10, where 10 is the most critical. Numerical scores are, however, difficult to communicate to a large audience, so

FIRSThas decided to define severity levels that map the CVSS scores to text. This mapping is shown in Table 1.

Table 1. Mapping CVSS scores to severity levels

Severity level	CVSS score
None	0.0
Low	0.1–3.9
Medium	4.0–6.9
High	7.0–8.9
Critical	9.0–10.0

3.2 Indirect Trust

Some software requires frequent patches and security updates, which reflects the competence, development methods and priorities of the development team, i.e. some development teams seem to favour feature rich software delivered at a high rate, while others favour more judicious methods focusing on formal specification, evaluation and testing. Indirect trust may therefore be established through the track record of the software developers. It is hard to know the development methodology of a software product that has not undergone certification, e.g. according to the Common Criteria mentioned above, so we need to rely on inference based on externally observable indicators, such as the number of CVEs and the CVSS scores mentioned above.

Wang et al. [24] proposes a security score based on the CVE and CVSS scores, which are used together with the Common Weakness Enumeration (CWE) [22] to define a security metric. The focus of the security metric is on the common types of vulnerabilities, and how the specific type are handled by the software developers. The calculations use the CVSS score and the duration of the vulnerability type to calculate a severity score of the project.

4 CodeTrust

As mentioned above, the trustworthiness of software depends on both software artefacts, that can be observed directly in the source code, and the methodology, processes and people involved in the software development. In this paper, we develop a metric for the trustworthiness of software called *CodeTrust*. This metric focus on the security aspects of trustworthiness and, in particular, aspects relating to the development process (the software development team) and the security history of a particular software project or product.

4.1 Overview

An overview of the CodeTrust metric is shown in Fig. 3, which should be read top down.

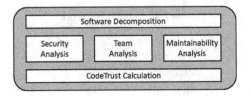

Fig. 3. Overview of the CodeTrust metric.

Most larger software systems, and many smaller systems, include externally sourced software modules or libraries. The first step is therefore to decompose the software into clearly identifiable components. Aggregation of software components is normally achieved through copying source code or through external calls to libraries or services - these are normally known as dependencies. We do not presume to be able to distinguish between internally and externally developed software from the source code alone, so in this paper we propose a decomposition based on the stated dependencies of a given software system or component.

Information about the development team and software source code are not normally available for external review, so the Team Analysis and Maintainability Analysis are only included for internal software projects or Open Source Software (OSS) projects. We believe that evaluating different OSS components to include in current development projects will be one of the principal uses for CodeTrust, which is why we include it in the general metric.

4.2 Security Analysis

The number of CVEs reported for a particular software reflects the number of vulnerabilities found in that software, so a low number of vulnerabilities is always preferred. The criticality of a vulnerability is rated by the CVSS on a 0–10 scale, where 10 is a vulnerability with critical severity and 0 has a low severity level. A large number of vulnerabilities with low severity is preferred to a few critical vulnerabilities, as the non-critical vulnerabilities may not provide much access to information, whereas a critical vulnerability may compromise the entire system.

Security Score. We calculate a *Security Score (SS)*, where the vulnerabilities and severity and are weighted as seen in Eq. 1. The Security Score correspond roughly to a classic definition of risk as the likelihood of an unwanted event multiplied by the consequences of that event happening.

$$security\_score = 0.2 \cdot vulnerability\_score + 0.8 \cdot severity\_score \qquad (1)$$

Vulnerability Score. The *vulnerability_score* indicates the general amount of CVEs registered for the software and thus the developer's ability to create secure software. The *vulnerability_score* calculation is found in Eq. 2. The severity score is an indication of how the software matures, by tracking the severity levels of reported vulnerabilities; the calculations are found in Eq. 6. The weight between the vulnerability score and severity score favours severity, because the criticality of a vulnerability is more important than the amount of vulnerabilities overall.

$$vulnerability\_score = grade\_ncve \cdot grade\_tcve \tag{2}$$

The vulnerability score is made up by the average annual number of recorded vulnerabilities for the software and is represented by the factor *grade_ncve*; the calculations can be found in Eq. 3.

$$grade\_ncve = \begin{cases} User\,evaluation & \text{if } ncve <= 5 \\ 0.7 & \text{if } 5 < ncve <= 20 \\ 0.9 & \text{if } 20 < ncve <= 70 \\ 1.0 & \text{if } 70 < ncve \end{cases} \tag{3}$$

The ncve is the average annual number of recorded CVEs, which has a tendency to discriminate against larger projects, because a project with 20 million lines of code is more likely to produce a large number of vulnerabilities compared to a project in the tens of thousands lines of code. This is an issue when CodeTrust evaluation is used as an absolute estimate of software trustworthiness, but it allows comparison of similar software, such as the most popular web browsers Edge, Chrome and Firefox. Possible solutions to the size bias include weighting the *grade_ncve* by the size of the project or separating software projects into size intervals for comparison with other projects of similar size. The *User evaluation* relies on the registered number of users for a particular software project. Such data can be obtained as sales numbers for commercial software or taken from OpenHub [4], which have extensive data on a large set of OSS Projects, including numbers of users and contributors.

$$User\,evaluation = \begin{cases} 0 & \text{if } project\,not\,found \\ 0 & \text{if } 500 < users \\ 0 & \text{if } users < 500 \text{ and } 15 < contributors \\ 10 & \text{if } users < 500 \text{ and } contributors < 15 \end{cases} \tag{4}$$

The second part of the vulnerability score is the CVE trend, which is a simple linear regression of the CVEs for every year. The evaluation does not focus on the amount of CVEs but the trends, which is indicated by the slope in a linear regression.

$$grade\_tcve = \begin{cases} 4 & \text{if } a < -0.2 \\ 7 & \text{if } -0.2 < a < 0.2 \\ 10 & \text{if } 0.2 < a \end{cases} \tag{5}$$

For simplicity, we only operate with a positive trend, i.e. there are fewer vulnerabilities so the slope (a in Eq. 5) is negative, a neutral trend (the slope is roughly flat) and a negative trend (the slope is positive). The possible values returned by the calculation have been distributed evenly in the domain 0–10, as indicated in the equation above.

Severity Score. The *severity score* is based directly on the CVSS reports from the National Vulnerability Database [16].

The severity score, shown in Eq. 6, measures whether the average of vulnerabilities with severity *Critical* or *High* is greater than 25% (*average_critical* and *average_high* are binary variables that are true if this is the case.) It also includes the trends, for each of the CVSS severity levels, calculated using Eq. 5, in the same way as the CVE trend. The coefficients for the trend variables reflect the relative importance of the severity levels for the final security of the software. They have been established through minor tests with known open source software projects; more fundamental experimentation will be carried out as part of our future work.

$$
\begin{aligned}
severity\_score =(&0.6 \cdot average\_critical+ \\
&0.4 \cdot average\_high) + 0.45 \cdot trend\_critical+ \\
&0.3 \cdot trend\_high + 0.1 \cdot trend\_medium + 0.05 \cdot trend\_low
\end{aligned}
\tag{6}
$$

The security score is in the same range (0–10) as the CVSS score, with severity 10 meaning the least secure system. We believe this is counter intuitive, so we define the *security_history_score*, in Eq. 7, where 10 reflects a system with the best security history.

$$
security\_history\_score = 10 - security\_score \tag{7}
$$

In the following, we examine the two remaining constituent elements of the CodeTrust metric, namely the team analysis and the maintainability analysis. As mentioned earlier, we focus these efforts on OSS, because numbers to support our analysis are more easily obtained. It should be possible for most software development companies to obtain similar numbers from their own products.

4.3   Team Analysis

The quality of software developed by a development team depends on the project management methodologies, processes and tools employed by the team, but to a higher degree on the security consciousness and experience of the individual team members. The experience of a developer in OSS projects can be roughly estimated by looking at the security history of previous projects. This *contributor score* can be determined as a sum of the *security_history_score* of all of all other projects that the contributor has contributed to, weighted by the relative size of the contributions as shown in Eq. 8. This estimation is obviously rough, because the contributor may not have committed any of the vulnerable code to software with a poor security history, but we believe that security conscious programmers will migrate away from projects where security has low priority (in open source projects, the satisfaction of contributing to a meaningful is the primary reward for programmers.)

$$contributor\_score = \sum_{projects} \frac{commits_{contributor\ in\ project} \cdot security\_history\_score_{project}}{total\_commits_{contributor}}$$

(8)

Having estimated the experience of the individual contributors to a software project, we can now calculate a team score as the sum of the contributor scores for the individual developers weighted by the relative size of their contributions to the overall software project, as shown in 9 below.

$$team\_score = \sum_{contributors} \frac{contributor\_commits_{project} \cdot contributor\_score}{total\_commits_{project}}$$

(9)

The information about contributors to OSS projects and the number of commits that they have contributed to different project can be found on Open-Hub [4].

4.4   Maintainability Analysis

As discussed in Sect. 3, there are many metrics for measuring the maintainability og software. In the current definition of CodeTrust, we favour a simple definition based on the comments to code ration defined in Eq. 10, but we clearly identify this as an interesting area for future work.

$$comments\_code\_ratio = \frac{lines_{comments}}{lines_{code} + lines_{comments}}$$

(10)

The necessary information for these calculations can be found on OpenHub for many OSS projects. This allows us to benchmark individual projects against the other projects, i.e. normalize the comment to code ration for a particular project to the average project. Table 2 presents data for a number of well known projects; these were collected in December 2016.

The table shows that the majority of OSS projects has a comment to code ration between 10% and 25%, so we define the Maintainability score as the normalized comment to code ratio as defined in Eq. 11.

$$Maintainability\_score = \frac{comment\_code\_ratio - 0.1}{0.25 - 0.1} \cdot 10$$

(11)

4.5   CodeTrust Metric

Having calculated the *security history score*, the *team score* and the *maintainability score* for the projects above, we are now able to define the CodeTrust metric as shown in Eq. 12.

$$\begin{aligned} codetrust = \ &0.65 \cdot security\_history\_score \\ &+ 0.25 \cdot team\_score + 0.1 \cdot maintainability\_score \end{aligned}$$

(12)

Table 2. OpenHub data for popular open source projects.

Project	Lines of code	Lines of comments	Comments/code ratio
Apache subversion	660, 711	208, 243	24.0%
MySQL	2, 862, 087	692, 663	19.5%
Ubuntu	911, 004	187, 691	17.1%
Linux kernel	18, 963, 973	3, 872, 008	17.0%
Mozilla firefox	14, 045, 424	2, 825, 225	16.8%
Chromium	14, 945, 618	2, 752, 467	15.6%
Python	1, 030, 242	184890	15.2%
PHP	3, 617, 916	587, 629	14.0%
Git	774, 674	96, 554	11.1%
Apache HTTP server	1, 832, 007	210, 141	10.3%
neat project	23708	1695	6.67%

The weighting of the different scores reflect our estimate of the relative importance of these scores to the overall trustworthiness of the developed software. As each of these scores are subject to further research, it is possible that these weights will change, but we feel confident that the relative importance of the different aspects are captured by the weights above.

5   Evaluation

We have developed a simple prototype that implements the CodeTrust metric, which allows us to present a preliminary evaluation. The prototype is written in Java, with the incorporation of a few external components and libraries, such as the Debian Linux package manager program `apt-rdepends` for resolving dependencies and the RoboBrowser [5] for scraping web pages. For a more detailed description of the prototype and the evaluation presented in this paper, please refer to the M.Sc. thesis of Nielsen [15].

We evaluate each of the three components before we present the evaluation of the full CodeTrust prototype.

5.1   Security History Score

We have selected a number of popular OSS projects, where information is available on OpenHub; this is simply to make our evaluation task easier. The results of this evaluation are presented in Table 3.

The dashes indicates that there were no CVEs registered for the project at the time of evaluation. This may be explained by projects being new (no vulnerabilities have been found yet), small (few users to find vulnerabilities and little interest from criminals) or well engineered and competently programmed.

Table 3. Security history score for selected OSS projects.

Project	ncve	tcve	vs	lt	mt	ht	ct	ah	ac	sev	ss
Apache server	0.9	10	9	7	10	10	10	0	0	8.85	8.88
Atom editor	-	-	-	-	-	-	-	-	-	-	0
Docker	-	-	-	-	-	-	-	-	-	-	0
Mozilla Filezilla	-	-	-	-	-	-	-	-	-	-	0
Firefox	1	10	10	7	10	10	7	0	1	8.1	8.48
Keepass2	-	-	-	-	-	-	-	-	-	-	10
MongoDB	-	-	-	-	-	-	-	-	-	-	0
MySQL	0.9	10	9	10	10	4	7	0	0	5.85	6.48
neat-project	-	-	-	-	-	-	-	-	-	-	0
OpenSSL	0.7	10	7	7	10	10	10	0	0	8.85	8.48
PHP	1	10	10	4	4	4	4	1	0	4	5.2
Python	0.7	10	7	7	7	4	7	0	0	5.4	5.72
Ruby	0.7	10	7	7	10	7	7	0	0	6.6	6.68
Ruby on Rails	0.7	10	7	7	10	7	7	0	0	6.6	6.68
tar	0.7	10	7	7	7	7	7	0	0	6.3	6.44
Wordpress	1	10	10	10	10	10	7	0	0	7.65	8.12

We note that most of the projects that have no CVE data receives the lowest possible security score, apart from the password manager Keypass which receives the highest score. This demonstrates that it is possible for a project to receive a high score based on user evaluations and that projects developed for security purposes are likely to be more security concious, which should result in a higher security score. The relative high score of OpenSSl confirms this belief, despite the bad publicity attracted because of the HeartBleed vulnerability.

5.2   Team Score

The team score is used to describe how the current contributors experience and performance have been with their previous projects. The perfect situation would be to test each contributors performance in their commits, but this is unfortunately not possible. The contributors found are only the contributors currently contributing, which means the contributors with commits during the last 12 months. The contributors are thus evaluated on the projects which they have been part of and committed to. The data from each project is found in Table 4.

We note that two projects (Filezilla and Keepas2) have very few contributors, so if these contributors have not recently contributed to other projects, the team score is essentially determined by the user evaluation of the security history score calculation (this explains the extreme values 0 and 10).

Table 4. Team score for selected OSS projects.

Project	Contributors	Team score
Apache server	27	5.71
Atom editor	822	9.89
Docker	532	9.91
Filezilla	1	10
Firefox	1087	5.14
Keepass2	2	0
MongoDB	106	9.96
MySQL	126	4.62
neat-project	23	9.87
OpenSSL	126	3.02
PHP	170	5.49
Python	47	9.08
Ruby	42	7.29
Ruby on Rails	554	6.29
tar	4	5.63
Wordpress	34	3.49

5.3 Maintainability Score

The maintainability score simply reflects the code to comment ratio as discussed earlier. The score is shown in Table 5.

We observe that two projects (Atom editor and neat-project) receives the lowest score and one project (Wordpress) scores the highest. We explain this by the effects of normalizing the ratio to the range 10%–25%, i.e. the two lowest scoring projects both have a comment to code ratio below 10% and the highest scoring project has a ratio above the 25%.

5.4 CodeTrust

The results of our evaluation of selected OSS projects are shown in Table 6, which shows the project, the security history score (SH score), the team score, the maintainability score and the CodeTrust score for the project.

We first note that several projects received a very low score because of a "0" in the Security History Score. This is how the CodeTrust metric is designed, but it highlights the problem of incomplete information. In most cases, the low security score reflects the fact that no CVEs have been registered for the project.

We also note that the OpenSSl, which contained the bug that caused the HeartBleed vulnerability described in Sect. 2, receives a respectable score of 6.81, which means that OpenSSL belongs to the upper quartile of the evaluated projects.

Table 5. Maintainability score for selected OSS projects.

Project	Code/comment ratio	Maintainability score
Apache server	10.29	0.19
Atom editor	8.26	0
Docker	10.93	0.62
Mozilla Filezilla	12.98	2.00
Firefox	16.75	4.5
Keepass2	16.74	4.49
MongoDB	21.29	7.53
MySQL	19.49	6.32
neat-project	6.67	0
OpenSSL	18.20	5.47
PHP	13.97	2.65
Python	15.22	3.48
Ruby	12.18	1.46
Ruby on Rails	16.07	4.04
tar	11.99	1.32
Wordpress	27.49	10

Table 6. CodeTrust metric for selected OSS projects.

Project	SH score	Team score	Maintainability score	CodeTrust score
Apache server	8.88	5.71	0.19	7.22
Atom editor	0	9.89	0	2.47
Docker	0	9.91	0.62	2.5
Filezilla	0	10	2	2.7
Firefox	8.48	5.14	4.5	7.2
Keepass2	10	0	4.49	6.95
MongoDB	0	9.96	7.53	3.24
MySQL	6.48	4.62	6.32	6
neat-project	0	9.87	0	2.47
OpenSSL	8.48	3.02	5.47	6.81
PHP	5.2	5.49	2.65	5.02
Python	5.72	9.08	3.48	6.34
Ruby	6.68	7.29	1.46	6.31
Ruby on Rails	6.68	6.29	4.04	6.32
tar	6.44	5.63	1.32	5.73
Wordpress	8.12	3.49	10	7.15

Finally, we note that the CodeTrust makes it possible to compare competing frameworks, such as the combination of `Python` and `PHP` against `Ruby` and `Ruby on Rails`. Both frameworks are relatively mature frameworks for dynamic web content and generally score well, but `PHP` scores a little lower than the others, which suggests that the `Ruby` based combination is a little more secure.

6   Conclusions

In this paper, we examined the problem of trustworthiness of software, in particular software developed in Open Source Software projects. Trustworthiness concerns both functional and non-functional requirements for the developed software, but in this paper we focused on the non-functional requirement *security*.

We have defined the CodeTrust metric to measure the trustworthiness of software, through an evaluation og the security history of the software itself and the development team responsible for the software. We also included a rough estimate of the maintainability of the software in our metric, because complexity of code is one of the main causes for insecure software.

We have employed the CodeTrust metric to evaluate a number of OSS projects, including `OpenSSL`, which contained the bug that caused the highly publicized HeartBleed vulnerability. The CodeTrust evaluation gave a high score to `OpenSSL`, which indicates that the CodeTrust metric is robust against short term effects og widely publicized vulnerabilities.

No metric is more reliable than the input it receives, which is also a problem identified in the evaluation of CodeTrust. New software has no security history, so it is possible that CodeTrust should emphasize the team analysis more in this case. This would, however, only solve the problem when the team consists of experienced software developers with a public track record, so software by many student start-ups would not be trusted (it is an open question whether it should).

The problem of missing data is an important issue that we intend to address in future work. There are two main direction that we plan to pursue: acquisition of more data, through more comprehensive web-scraping techniques, and including a confidence score in the metric, which indicates the quality of the data that the evaluation is based on.

The overall result of our evaluation shows that the CodeTrust metric works well for larger and more mature OSS projects, but that there are some problems evaluation new or small projects. The evaluation shows that most of the projects that rated poorly, did so because of missing data, which means that the current prototype cannot be used to make automated decisions about whether to rely on particular software or not. Our evaluation of the two dynamic web-page frameworks `Ruby on Rails` and `PHP` shows that there is a difference in trustworthiness, but also that both frameworks are mature and have a reasonable security track record. The difference may persuade an organisation to choose one framework over the other, which is another reason for evaluating the trustworthiness of software.

Finally, we wish to further examine the relationship between the Security History Score and the Team Score, in particular for software developers that primarily work on a single project. In this case, the CodeTrust evaluation is based almost exclusively on the security history data.

References

1. The heartbleed bug. http://heartbleed.com/
2. Amoroso, E., Taylor, C., Watson, J., Weiss, J.: A process-oriented methodology for assessing and improving software trustworthiness. In: Proceedings of the 2nd ACM Conference on Computer and Communications Security, pp. 39–50 (1994)
3. Avizienis, A., Laprie, J.C., Randell, B.: Fundamental concepts of dependability. In: Proceedings of the 3rd IEEE Information Survivability Workshop (2000)
4. Black Duck: Open Hub. https://www.openhub.net/
5. Carp, J.: robobrowser. https://github.com/jmcarp/robobrowser
6. Cerrudo, C.: Why the Shellshock Bug is Worse than Heartbleed. MIT Technology Review, Cambridge (2014)
7. Commission of the European Communities: Information Technology Security Evaluation Criteria (ITSEC): Preliminary Harmonised Criteria
8. Common Vulnerability Scoring System SIG: The Common Vulnerability Scoring System (CVSS). https://www.first.org/cvss/
9. Dierks, T., Rescorla, E.: The Transport Layer Security (TLS) Protocol Version 1.2. RFC 5246, The Internet Engineering Task Force (2008)
10. Fitzpatrick, J.: Applying the ABC metric to C, C++, and Java. In: More c++ Gems, pp. 245–264. Cambridge University Press, New York (2000). Originally published in C++ Report, June 1997
11. Halstead, M.H.: Elements of Software Science (Operating and Programming Systems Series). Elsevier Science Inc., New York (1977)
12. ISO/IEC 15408: Common Criteria for Information Technology Security Evaluation
13. Lampson, B.W.: A note on the confinement problem. Commun. ACM **16**(10), 613–615 (1973)
14. Mohammadi, N.G., Sachar Paulus, M.B., Metzger, A., Koennecke, H., Hartenstein, S., Pohl, K.: An analysis of software quality attributes and their contribution to trustworthiness. In: Proceedings of the 3rd International Conference on Cloud Computing and Services Science, Closer 2013, vol. 3, no. 3, pp. 542–552 (2013)
15. Nielsen, M.B.: Quality and IT security assessment of open source software projects. M.Sc. thesis, DTU Compute, Technical University of Denmark (2017)
16. NIST: National vulnerability database. https://nvd.nist.gov/
17. Pauli, D.: It's 2017 and 200,000 services still have unpatched heartbleeds. https://www.theregister.co.uk/2017/01/23/heartbleed_2017/
18. Randell, B.: System structure for software fault tolerance. SIGPLAN Not. **10**(6), 437–449 (1975)
19. Seggelmann, R., Tuexen, M., Williams, M.: Transport Layer Security (TLS) and Datagram Transport Layer Security (DTLS) Heartbeat Extension. RFC 6520, The Internet Engineering Task Force (2012)
20. The Department of Defense (DoD): Trusted Computer System Evaluation Criteria (TCSEC), TCSEC Rainbow Series Library, Orange Book
21. The MITRE Corporation: Common vulnerabilities and exposures. https://cve.mitre.org/

22. The MITRE Corporation: Common Weakness Enumeration (CWE). http://cwe.mitre.org/about/index.html
23. Thompson, K.: Reflections on trusting trust. Commun. ACM **27**(8), 761–763 (1984)
24. Wang, J.A., Wang, H., Guo, M., Xia, M.: Security metrics for software systems. In: Proceedings of the 47th Annual Southeast Regional Conference, no. 47, pp. 1–6 (2009)

Visualisation of Trust and Quality Information for Geospatial Dataset Selection and Use: Drawing Trust Presentation Comparisons with B2C e-Commerce

Victoria Lush$^{(\boxtimes)}$, Jo Lumsden, and Lucy Bastin

Aston University, Birmingham B4 7ET, UK
{lushvl,j.lumsden,l.bastin}@aston.ac.uk

Abstract. The evaluation of geospatial data quality and trustworthiness presents a major challenge to geospatial data users when making a dataset selection decision. Part of the problem arises from the inconsistent and patchy nature of data quality information, which makes intercomparison very difficult. Over recent years, the production and availability of geospatial data has significantly increased, facilitated by the recent explosion of Web-based catalogues, portals, standards and services, and by initiatives such as INSPIRE and GEOSS. Despite this significant growth in availability of geospatial data and the fact that geospatial datasets can, in many respects, be considered commercial products that are available for purchase online, consumer trust has to date received relatively little attention in the GIS domain.

In this paper, we discuss how concepts of trust, trust models, and trust indicators (largely derived from B2C e-Commerce) apply to the GIS domain and to geospatial data selection and use. Our research aim is to support data users in more efficient and effective geospatial dataset selection on the basis of quality, trustworthiness and fitness for purpose. To achieve this, we propose a GEO label – a decision support mechanism that visually summarises availability of key geospatial data informational aspects. We also present a Web service that was developed to support generation of dynamic GEO label representations for datasets by combining producer metadata (from standard catalogues or other published locations) with structured user feedback.

Keywords: Geospatial data quality and trustworthiness · Trust visualisation Trust indicators

1 Introduction

To address issues of geospatial data quality, international organisations, initiatives, and working groups such as the International Organisation for Standardization (ISO) [1], the Open GIS Consortium (OGC) [2], INSPIRE [3], and many more, are actively working to establish, improve and extend geospatial data and metadata standards. Despite the detailed recommendations of standardisation bodies, and despite the existence of formal metadata standards such as ISO 19115:2003, data quality information is, however, often not communicated to users in a consistent and standardised

© IFIP International Federation for Information Processing 2018
Published by Springer International Publishing AG 2018. All Rights Reserved
N. Gal-Oz and P. R. Lewis (Eds.): IFIPTM 2018, IFIP AICT 528, pp. 75–90, 2018.
https://doi.org/10.1007/978-3-319-95276-5_6

way [4]. While standardisation efforts have significantly improved metadata interoperability, an increasing choice of metadata standards poses a number of unresolved questions: Which standards are best to follow? How much metadata to provide? How to make metadata 'useful' and not just 'usable'? [5]. Since metadata standards are mostly focused on data production rather than potential data use and application, a typical metadata document is not sufficient to effectively communicate dataset fitness for purpose to users from a variety of domains and expertise levels [4, 6].

Geospatial data users are presented with an increasing choice of data available from various data portals, repositories, and clearinghouses [4]. This means that the inter-comparison of dataset quality and the evaluation of a dataset's fitness for purpose can present a major challenge for geospatial data users. Over the past decade, many researchers and scholars have attempted to address the challenge of communicating geospatial data fitness for purpose information, proposing a more 'user-centric approach' to geospatial metadata [7]. Researchers argued the case for enriching metadata records with: references to relevant literature (citations information); less formal opinions from the data producers; expert opinions of data quality; and user feedback regarding previous data use [8]. Recent reviews, however, suggest that these recommendations have not yet been put into practice, with no practical means for collating and searching user-focused metadata, added to which many metadata records that are available are incomplete [4, 7, 9, 10].

Trust significantly influences our decision making. In the field of Business to Consumer (B2C) e-Commerce, trust is considered to be a crucial enabler for online transaction decisions [11]. The impersonality of geospatial dataset selection decisions closely mirrors that of the e-Commerce transaction experience. Transactional risk is a vital precondition of e-Commerce trust [12]: similarly, the risks involved in dataset selection and use (i.e., the importance of selecting the right dataset for a given purpose) establish a need for dataset users to trust in dataset providers to deliver a reliable, quality dataset to meet their needs. In B2C e-Commerce, trust indicators are used to engender consumer trust in e-Vendors; it can, therefore, be argued that it should be possible to establish and deploy similar trust indicators in the GIS domain to convey information about the trustworthiness of geospatial datasets and dataset providers. In essence, drawing on the parallels with B2C e-Commerce, it can be argued that representation and visualisation of key trust indicators associated with geospatial datasets and their producers has the potential to support more effective, informed, and trust-based selection of quality datasets. Surprisingly, research into mechanisms of representing trust in the GIS domain has not yet received the same level of attention as it has in the e-Commerce domain [13, 14].

To tackle the challenge of data quality and trustworthiness assessment and dataset selection decision making, we present a GEO label – a voluntary label designed to improve user assessment of the quality of geospatial datasets and promote trust in datasets that carry the label. This paper presents research conducted to define a GEO label that has the capacity to act as a trust indicator for geospatial data. We also introduce a Web service developed to support GEO label generation for datasets by combining producer metadata (from standard catalogues or other published locations) with structured user feedback.

The following section of this paper outlines a review of related work (much of it from the field of B2C e-Commerce which considers consumer trust in service provision, aligning well with the concept of consumer trust in GIS dataset provision) which illustrates some of the important concepts underpinning this research arena. Subsequent to this, we present the research we have conducted to define and develop a GEO label and to establish a Web-service for the generation of GEO labels. We conclude with a discussion and reflection on trust in the GIS domain based on our research experience.

2 Related Work

Prior to its recent introduction to the GIS domain, trust has been extensively researched and successfully adopted in B2C e-Commerce to enable online marketplace transactions [14]. In this section, we review related work on trust to draw important parallels with the GIS domain and demonstrate the significance of trust in geospatial dataset selection and use.

2.1 Concept and Models of Trust

Trust is a fundamental part of our everyday life [15]. Without the presence of trust, society would experience a loss of effectiveness, task performance and dynamism leading to its inevitable destruction [16]. There exist many types of trust – with trust being viewed as a multi-dimensional concept – and there are many disciplines and research fields (e.g., economics, social psychology, sociology, management, marketing, information systems, commerce, and e-Commerce) that study this phenomenon. The definition of trust largely depends on the nature of the relationships and contexts to which it applies [15]. In sociology, trust is described as a mechanism for coping with the freedom of others [17]. In psychology, trust is viewed as a personality characteristic (interpersonal trust) [18] or a *"psychological state"* [19, p. 398]. In e-Commerce, many researchers adopt a common definition of trust as being a belief or positive expectation that a vendor will fulfil promised obligations and that the vendor will not take any actions that will negatively affect the trustee [20].

A series of models of trust have been proposed [e.g., 21–25]. Ganesan and Hess [21] present two dimensions of trust – *credibility* and *benevolence*. Business studies of trust have identified *credibility* (the belief that the vendor has the necessary capacity to complete a task effectively and reliably) and *benevolence* (the belief that the vendor has good intentions and will behave in a favourable manner even in the absence of existing commitment) as critical factors of trust [26].

Institutional trust comes from sociology and refers to trust in institutions, such as laws and regulation in society [27] and the presence of essential structural conditions [22]. In e-Commerce, *institutional trust* denotes trust in the Internet as a whole and particularly trust in the technology that it offers [27]. *Interpersonal trust* is an individual's trust in another specific party [24]; in e-Commerce, this type of trust can represent a customer's trust in an e-vendor, trust in third-party assurances of e-vendor trustworthiness and integrity, or a friend's recommendation of an online vendor [27]. *Dispositional trust* was defined in the area of psychology, and refers to an individual's ability and willingness to trust in general. *Dispositional trust* is particularly important in the initial stages of a relationship and in novel situations where familiarity is absent [27].

Further trust classifications include *initial* and *experiential* trust [28], *vertical* and *horizontal trust* [25], and *technological* and *relational trust* [23]. *Initial* or 'grabbing' trust refers to a first trusting judgement at the commencement of a novel situation or relationship and is highly influenced by an individual's disposition to trust. *Experiential trust* comes with experience and familiarity and is considered to be much more complex than initial trust. Lee and Yu [25] describe the notion of *vertical* and *horizontal* types of trust: "*vertical trust captures the trust relationships that exist between individuals and institutions, while horizontal trust represents the trust that can be inferred from the observations and opinions of others*" [25, p. 9]. McCord and Ratnasingam [23] discuss *technological* and *relational* types of trust. They define technological trust as "*the subjective probability by which an individual believes that the underlying technology infrastructure and control mechanisms are capable of facilitating inter-organizational transactions according to its confident expectations*" [23, p. 921]; they refer to *relational trust* as "*a consumer's willingness to accept vulnerability in an online transaction based upon positive expectations of future e-retailer behaviours*" [23, p. 921]. In Sect. 7, we reflect on the parallels between established models of trust as outlined here and trust processes/mechanisms in the domain of GIS dataset provision and use based on our research outcomes.

2.2 e-Commerce Trust Indicators

Extensive research has been conducted in the e-Commerce domain to identify trust indicators that can be embedded within e-Commerce websites to engender user willingness to engage in online transactions [29]. Many researchers [e.g., 29–31] either directly or indirectly illustrate that these trust indicators (known as trust triggers) can be effective in engendering consumer trust in e-Commerce and, hence, in promoting online transactions. In essence, an online trust trigger is an element of a website that acts as an indicator of the trustworthiness of the website [30]. Lumsden and MacKay [30] identify nine of the most generally agreed-upon trust triggers that are commonly used in e-Commerce, namely: customer testimonials and feedback; professional website design; branding; third party security seals; up-to-date technology and security measures; alternative channels of communication between consumers and the vendor; clearly stated policies and vendor information; consistent (professional) graphic design; and ease of navigation. The parallels between trust triggers in e-Commerce and the facets of GIS datasets on which dataset users base selection decisions (according to the outcomes of our research) are discussed in Sect. 7.

2.3 Trust in the GIS Domain

There are a number of parallels between consumers' decisions to transact with a given e-Commerce vendor and dataset users' decisions to adopt one from *n* datasets for their given needs. While trust has to date received relatively little attention in the GIS domain, some GIS researchers and scholars have made attempts to highlight the importance and relevance of trust to geospatial data and systems. Harvey [32] evaluated effects of trust on development of the National Spatial Data Infrastructures (NSDI) in the United States. The results of telephone and face-to-face interviews, surveys and workshops with local government agencies' staff indicated that trust directly impacts willingness to share data. Bertino *et al.* [33] discuss the role of trust in terms of managing, accessing and sharing of geospatial data that is used for safety-critical applications. They propose that, to engender user trust in geospatial data, geospatial data repositories should: maintain complete logs of data provenance including data source and the submission date; utilise mechanisms for dynamic verification of the data source; and introduce privacy policies for protecting sensitive information from privacy violations.

With recent growth in production and availability of volunteered geographic information (VGI) which is commonly generated by non-experts, trustworthiness of VGI is increasingly attracting the attention of the GIS community. With a focus on filtering more reliable socially-generated geospatial content, Bishr and Janowicz [34] propose using trust as a proxy measure of VGI quality. They argue that quality is a subjective measure, but if trust-rated geospatial information is useful and relevant to many users then it is of satisfactory quality. Keßler and de Groot [35] also support the idea of using trust as a proxy measure of VGI quality and identify five provenance-based trust parameters of VGI observations, namely: versions; users; confirmations; tag corrections; and rollbacks. Moreri *et al.* [14] present a novel trust and reputation modelling methodology to establish the quality and credibility of VGI such that it can be considered in land administration systems on a fit for purpose basis. Their research is motivated by lack of official geospatial data in developing countries.

Despite recent research efforts to highlight the importance of trust in the GIS domain, thus far no practical work has been done to establish a standard visualisation of trust that users can utilise to compare the trustworthiness of datasets. There is also a lack of transition of trust knowledge from other domains such as psychology, sociology and e-Commerce where notions of trust and trust cues have been established and empirically confirmed.

3 GEO Label Initiative

The Global Earth Observation System of Systems (GEOSS) [36] is a distributed 'system of systems' which is being constructed by the Group on Earth Observation (GEO) [37] to provide decision-support tools to a wide variety of users. Given that the GEOSS is estimated to contain more than 28 million dataset records and is constantly growing [38], choices faced when selecting a dataset can (depending on usage domain) be quite daunting. With such a huge choice of datasets comes the problem of data quality assessment and dataset selection decision making. To tackle this challenge, the GEO Science and Technology Committee (STC) [39] proposed to establish a GEO label – a label *"related to the scientific relevance, quality, acceptance and societal needs for activities in support of GEOSS as an attractive incentive for involvement of the S&T communities"* [40, p. 2]. The STC suggested that the development of such a label could significantly improve user recognition of the quality of geospatial datasets and that its use could help promote trust in datasets that carry the established GEO label [40]. Research presented in this paper was conducted to define and develop the proposed GEO label to act as a quality and trustworthiness indicator and support fitness for purpose dataset evaluation.

4   Method

The main focus of our research was to design the concept of a GEO label founded on knowledge elicited about how geospatial data users select datasets to use, the reasoning behind their selection decisions, and what mechanisms could improve their experience. Our research adopted an iterative user-centered design (UCD) approach in order to generate solutions that are tailored to geospatial data users' needs and that are likely to garner user acceptance once deployed.

Utilising various tried-and-tested UCD methods, our research comprised a series of phases of research (exploration, development, evaluation and validation), with each phase building upon the knowledge gathered in the previous phase(s) [9].

A preparatory phase [9, 10] was conducted using a series of semi-structured, face-to-face and telephone interviews with geospatial data expert users and producers. The intention was to uncover initial information about dataset selection, including their use and production within representative application areas, in order to inform later research phases. A total of 18 interviewees were recruited, representing a variety of expert groups including end data users, researchers, data archivists, academics, and data producers.

Phase I [9] was conducted via a comprehensive online questionnaire-based survey that comprised over 60 questions to solicit initial geospatial data producers' and users' views on the concept of a GEO label and the role it should serve. A total of 87 valid questionnaire responses were received: 57 from self-identified dataset users and 30 from self-identified dataset producers.

Phase II [9] focused on the iterative design of the graphical representation of the GEO label. A comprehensive questionnaire-based study that also comprised over 60 questions was conducted to solicit geospatial data producers' and users' views on the proposed GEO label visualisations. A total of 26 valid questionnaire responses were received, 10 from 'primarily dataset users', 3 from 'primarily dataset producers', and 13 from 'equally data users and data producers'. Following this, GEO label designs were adapted and improved in line with geospatial experts' feedback and recommendations.

5   Findings and Outcomes

In this section, we highlight the key findings from the studies conducted to define and develop a GEO label.

5.1   Initial Investigation

Verbatim transcripts of the interview recordings were generated to support detailed data analysis. The transcripts were thematically analysed to identify the informational facets of importance to users when assessing dataset fitness for purpose and to derive detailed user requirements that relate specifically to quality and trustworthiness assessment of datasets for the purpose of making dataset selection decisions.

The analysis of the interview transcripts identified that geospatial data users highly value good *quality metadata records*. The study participants stated that complete and well-documented metadata records are essential in the assessment of geospatial data quality and trustworthiness. Core metadata defined in ISO standards must be provided with geospatial datasets to enable comparative evaluation of dataset quality and trustworthiness. The study revealed the importance of *dataset provenance* and *licensing* information when assessing whether to trust that a dataset was fit for purpose. Data users confirmed that provenance information is usually incomplete and licensing information is normally missing from the metadata records of datasets. Dataset users are also interested in soft knowledge about data quality – i.e., *data providers' comments* on (a) the overall quality of a dataset, (b) known data errors, (c) potential data use, and (d) any other information that can help in the assessment of fitness for use of datasets. Also important when selecting a quality dataset are *peer recommendations* and *reviews*: dataset users are keen to be able to obtain feedback from their peers and are willing to accept peer recommendations when trying to select the most appropriate dataset for their given needs. The study results revealed the importance of *citation information* when assessing whether a dataset is fit for purpose, yet there was general consensus that *citation information* is, unfortunately, hard to acquire. It was discovered that, when selecting a dataset, users typically seek information about *dataset providers* and, in particular, value the availability of valid contact details for providers. Finally, study findings indicated that having side-by-side dataset and metadata comparison functionality would make the dataset selection process much easier for users.

The results suggested that a GEO label would best serve a drill-down function whereby, at the top level, it visually represents the availability of specific informational elements for its associated dataset and, thereafter, permits users to click the label to drill down into the detail for each informational element. Based on the interviewees' responses, GEO label-appropriate facets were identified as potential candidates for inclusion in the GEO label, namely: the reputation of the dataset producer; producer comments on the dataset quality; the dataset's compliance with international standards; community advice; dataset ratings; expert value judgments; links to dataset citations; quantitative quality information; and side-by-side metadata comparison. It was decided that provenance information could be effectively conveyed via the producer profile, producer comments and citations information facets. Licensing information was not included due to perceived lower importance and the fact that it is nearly always missing from dataset descriptions.

5.2   Phase I and Phase II Studies

To investigate geospatial data producers' and users' views on the concept of a GEO label and the role it should serve, an online questionnaire-based survey was conducted. The questionnaire presented various examples of e-Commerce review/rating systems (some incorporated click-to-verify/drill-down functionality to access additional information) and certification programmes and seals in order to explore respondents' preferences for the role of a GEO label.

Overall, the results of this study showed that users and producers of geospatial datasets appeared to have generally very positive attitudes towards the development and introduction of a GEO label. The study illustrated that geospatial dataset users rely heavily on metadata records when assessing dataset fitness for use, and reiterated the problems associated with the lack of uniform availability of quality-associated information despite ongoing standardisation efforts. For these reasons, many respondents agreed that a GEO label could potentially fulfil a certification or assurance seal function and be used to impose higher standards on provision of metadata records. Respondents demonstrated positive attitudes towards the concept of a GEO label that provides some sort of rating and review facilities, seeing this as appropriate support for more subjective metadata recording and assessment for datasets. The majority of users and producers strongly supported the notion of a GEO label providing an all-in-one drill-down interrogation facility that would combine expert value judgements, community advice, links to citation information, side-by-side visualisation of metadata records, etc.

Based on the study findings, prototypic GEO label graphic representations (i.e., static images) were developed which could potentially be used to convey availability of spatial dataset quality information (see Fig. 1). These GEO label visualisations combined the 8 identified and confirmed informational aspects, namely: dataset producer information; producer comments on the dataset quality; the dataset's compliance with international standards; user feedback (community advice); user ratings of the dataset; expert reviews (expert value judgments); dataset citations; and quantitative dataset quality information. Side-by-side metadata visualisation would require at least two datasets and does not represent an informational facet of a single dataset alone, consequently it was decided not to include this function in the GEO label visualisation itself.

Each informational facet was designed to show whether the information it represents is 'available', 'not available' or 'only available at a higher level' (i.e., information is available for a parent dataset) for the dataset with which the GEO label is associated.

A questionnaire-based study was designed to evaluate the effectiveness of, or potential issues with, the proposed GEO label designs and to arrive at a final, community-supported GEO label representation. Overall, the study results indicated that, unfortunately, none of the proposed GEO label visualisations were as yet sufficiently effective (in the eyes of the intended community of use at least) to stand as the

Fig. 1. Prototypic graphic representations of the GEO label.

final GEO label design. Nevertheless, respondents' feedback provided rich information on which basis to identify essential GEO label design modifications and improvements and derive user-defined GEO label requirements. The GEO label facet icons and the overall label design underwent some modifications and improvements. Despite the attempt to convey provenance information via the producer profile, producer comments and citations information facets, data producers argued that producer-related quality information was underrepresented in the label and requested that an additional facet was established to solely represent lineage information: as such, a data provenance information facet was added to the final GEO label design. Conversely, feedback and ratings facets were combined into a single user feedback facet because the study results indicated relatively low attributed importance and perceived redundancy of the user ratings facet. The final GEO label therefore comprised the following facets (see Table 1): producer information; producer comments; the dataset's lineage/provenance information; the dataset's compliance with international standards; user feedback (community advice); expert reviews (expert value judgments); dataset citations; and quantitative dataset quality information. These were combined into a label as shown in Fig. 2.

Table 1. Graphical representations and descriptions of the GEO label informational aspects.

Facet Icon	Facet Description
	Producer profile conveys availability of information about the producer of the dataset, e.g., organisation or individual who produced the dataset.
	Producer comments conveys availability of any informal comments about the dataset quality as provided by the dataset producer, e.g., any identified problems.
	Lineage information conveys availability of lineage/provenance information, e.g., processing applied to data and number of process steps.
	Standards Compliance conveys availability of information about dataset's compliance with international standards, e.g., compliance with ISO 19115.
	Quality information conveys availability of formal quality measures of the dataset, e.g., uncertainty measures, errors, accuracy information, etc.
	User feedback conveys availability of feedback, comments and ratings provided by the users of the dataset, e.g., identified problems, etc.
	Expert reviews conveys availability of domain experts' comments on dataset quality, e.g., results of formal quality checks, expert suggestions, etc.
	Citations information conveys availability of citations where the dataset was used and cited, e.g., formal reports on dataset quality checks, journal articles, etc.

To convey the availability of quality information, each informational facet can represent one of three data availability states: 'available'; 'not available'; and 'available only at a higher level' (to indicate that information is not immediately available for the dataset, but is available for a parent dataset). These three information availability states

Fig. 2. Final GEO label design: left: information is available; middle: information is available at a higher level; right: information is not available.

Table 2. Graphical representations and descriptions of the GEO label availability states.

Facet Appearance	Availability State Description
	Fully filled-in background + white icon with black outline – *information is available* for this dataset.
	White background + white icon with black outline – *information is not available* for this dataset (at any level).
	Partially filled-in background + white icon with black outline – *information is available only at a higher level* for this dataset.

are expressed by varying the appearance of the facet icons as shown in Table 2. The final GEO label design was formally evaluated as part of a study of a decision-support system which was developed to utilise the label in selection of datasets: discussion on this is outside the scope of this paper but interested readers can read more here [9].

6   GEO Label Service Implementation

To support use of the graphical GEO label, we developed a GEO label service as a stand-alone Web-based server-side application, exposed via a publicly available RESTful API. Representational State Transfer (REST) is an abstract architectural style that constrains the implementing application to adopt a stateless client-server model with a uniform interface, meaning that "resources" made available by an application are represented by a Uniform Resource Identifier (URI) with a communication protocol that defines methods for accessing and modifying the state of these resources. A prime example of a system implementing this architecture with the Hypetext Transfer Protocol (HTTP) used for communication is the World Wide Web, where clients use HTTP method verbs to inform a server how to process their requests for a resource's URI – e.g., GET for the retrieval of information and POST for accepting data (commonly used when creating new resources).

The GEO label service is designed to dynamically process producer metadata and feedback XML documents for a given dataset and, based on evaluated information availability, build a clickable SVG (Scalable Vector Graphic) GEO label representation for that dataset. The service accepts encoded URLs of publicly available metadata documents or metadata XML files as part of an HTTP GET request, or locally-available files uploaded through a POST request, and applies XPath and XSLT mappings to transform the supplied XML documents into SVG representations. The service is underpinned by two metadata XML-based quality models that were developed by the GeoViQua project [41]. The first is the Producer Quality Model (PQM) [42] that extends ISO 19115:2003 [43], ISO 19115-2:2009 [44] and ISO 19157:2013 [45], adding means to report publications, discovered issues, reference datasets used for quality evaluation, traceability, and statistical summaries of quantified uncertainty. This model introduces elements to record qualitative and quantitative quality information, and to identify resources (i.e., geospatial datasets) in order to relate metadata in hierarchical or other ways. The second is the User Quality Model (UQM) [42, 46], developed to enable application of 'customer' reviews to datasets which span a variety of user expertise levels, thematic, temporal and spatial domains. This model re-uses a few ISO quality and metadata elements, and elements of the PQM, but is far less strictly bound to existing ISO schemas. These two models aim to fill significant perceived gaps identified by users and producers of geospatial data, such as the formalisation of soft knowledge quality parameters (e.g., discovered issues, publications, lineage), the standardisation of statistical quality metrics, and the ability to collect feedback from users to support the more 'user-centric' metadata. Although the services primarily rely on the GeoViQua quality models, an external XPath configuration file which is used for determining whether information is available can be adapted to support any XML-based metadata models.

Generated SVG GEO labels offer dynamic hover-over functionality for obtaining quick summary information. Hovering over an individual facet in the GEO label displays a summary of the information related to the facet for the associated dataset – e.g., producer name, producer comments, the name of the standard to which the dataset complies, etc. (see Fig. 3).

Fig. 3. Examples of producer profile and producer comments hover-over functionalities.

A drilldown GEO label function is designed to provide detailed structured information extracted from the associated dataset's metadata record when a facet is clicked. The GEO label service API is used to transform producer metadata and feedback XML documents into styled, structured HTML pages. Figure 4 provides an example of a citations information summary page that was generated using the GEO label drilldown function.

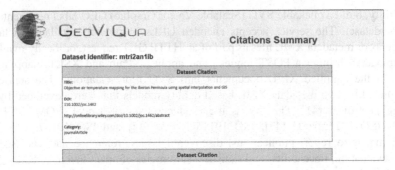

Fig. 4. Example of citations information drilldown page.

The practical implementation of the GEO label demonstrated that producer meta-data documents can, in practice, be effectively combined with user feedback to generate an integrated visualisation of a user-focused summary of geospatial dataset quality and trustworthiness. It has, additionally, confirmed the feasibility of not only the drilldown GEO label function for obtaining detailed dataset information, but also the hover-over function for viewing a quick quality summary. The SVG format of the GEO label representation allows for integration of the essential dataset quality and trustworthiness information and ensures label interactivity. Regarding the technological side of the GEO label implementation, the key advantage of the service is in its interoperability – it allows for the GEO label to be integrated within any GIS application that supports HTTP requests.

7 Discussion and Reflection on Trust in the GIS Domain

The findings from the studies presented here lend empirical evidence supporting observations of direct parallels between geospatial data quality and trust themes and well-defined trust models and trust triggers that are already used extensively in B2C e-Commerce to engender consumer trust and increase user willingness to engage in online transactions. Compliance of geospatial data and metadata with international standards directly relates to *vertical* and *institutional trust* and is comparable to use of B2C e-Commerce trust seals. Peer reviews and recommendations on quality of geospatial datasets together with ratings of datasets relate to *horizontal trust* and reflect consumer testimonials that are widely used by online vendors to engender consumer trust in the products and/or services that a vendor provides. Expert reviews also relate to *horizontal trust* but are different from consumer testimonials; hence this informational aspect does not have an exact counterpart in terms of an e-Commerce trust trigger. Producer reputation relates to *credibility* and *benevolence* dimensions of trust and reflects the e-Commerce branding trust trigger. The B2C e-Commerce trust trigger relating to alternative channels of communication is also relevant here since geospatial data users are highly interested in the availability of dataset producers' contact infor-mation. Informal producer comments (soft knowledge) also relate to producer *credibility* and *benevolence*, although this informational aspect does not have a corresponding e-Commerce trust trigger. Availability of citations information relates to both *horizontal* and *vertical* dimensions of trust – *horizontal* trust is supported by descriptions of the dataset quality and recommendations on the dataset's use supplied in scientific papers, while *vertical* trust is trust in a journal or a conference where the document was published. Availability of quantitative quality information and licensing information links to *institutional* trust since it indicates that the dataset adheres to some international standard and is supplied in a structured manner. Geospatial dataset provenance and the method(s) adopted for data collection and processing relate to *vertical* and *technological* dimensions of trust, respectively – i.e., trust in the organisation that produced the dataset and technologies that were used to collect and process the data to produce the dataset. Citations information, quantitative quality information, data provenance and licensing do not have corresponding B2C e-Commerce trust triggers.

Trust clearly has the potential to have a major impact on users' geospatial dataset selection and quality evaluation processes. When searching for a suitable geospatial dataset, users may come across new data repositories or unknown data providers, in which case they have to decide whether to engage in a trusting relationship (*initial trust*) with that provider. Users may reflect on their previous experiences with geospatial data producers and providers to decide whether or not to return to a dataset provider to acquire future data sets (*experiential trust*). Furthermore, in any decision to trust a dataset provider, a user is essentially making an assessment of the provider's credibility, the technological trustworthiness of the provider or producer, and the observance of standards set by higher orders (*vertical trust*). Users may also contact their peers, work colleagues or friends to get advice and recommendations on what data could be suitable for given tasks (*horizontal* and *interpersonal trust*), they may seek information on projects or companies who have previously used a given dataset (*horizontal trust*), or they may look to journal papers, expert reviews and technical reports where dataset quality checks have been reported when making a selection decision (*horizontal trust*). When selecting from several dataset options, some users may be more keen on datasets that adhere to international standards and are supported with standardised metadata documentation (*institutional* and *vertical trust*). In contrast, in situations where consequences of data misuse are very severe, users may choose not to select datasets themselves but to use a third-party organisation to select datasets for them (*institutional trust* and *third-party credibility*).

The mapping between trust concepts and GIS dataset selection and use suggests that trust plays a vital role in geospatial data selection and use. Every time geospatial data users select a dataset to use, they are likely to have to make a trusting decision, often without even realising they are doing so. We believe that the GEO label effectively combines various notions of trust discussed above and can act as an all-in-one geospatial data trust indicator. It represents a novel decision support mechanism that enables a more efficient and informed evaluation of geospatial dataset quality and trustworthiness, and facilitates more effective dataset intercomparison and selection.

8 Conclusion

This paper described, in brief, user-centred design research conducted to establish the concept of a GEO label and identify the role it should serve in the visualisation of geospatial data quality and trustworthiness. The paper presented three phases of research conducted to: (a) identify the informational aspects upon which users rely when assessing geospatial dataset quality and trustworthiness; (b) elicit initial user views on the role of a GEO label in supporting dataset comparison and selection; and (c) evaluate prototype label visualisations to arrive at a final GEO label representation. The findings indicated that, to engender user trust, geospatial data producers need to supply complete metadata records, supporting documentation, and contact information with the datasets that they produce. It was also discovered that peer recommendations are of great value to geospatial data users and that users would want to see e-Commerce review functionality available in geospatial data portals, catalogues and clearinghouses.

Practical implementation of the GEO label demonstrated that it is possible to develop an effective voluntary quality label without having to establish a new standard, standardisation body or a certification programme. The developed solution not only fulfills the needs of the geospatial community, but also addresses the STC's initial vision of a GEO label that would comprise objective labelling (producer metadata) and subjective labelling (user-focused metadata).

The GEO label integration into geospatial data portals should raise community awareness of metadata incompleteness. It is much easier to conceal metadata incompleteness in complex XML files; even tabular views can give a false impression of information availability since some records provide long lists of keywords, responsible parties, and points of contact. For geospatial data producers, the GEO label can act as a graphical template of quality and trust information that should be provided with every geospatial dataset and should encourage producers to supply rich metadata.

Via literature review, discussion and reflection on our findings, this paper also demonstrated how research on trust in other domains can be applied to geospatial data and GIS applications. It was revealed that geospatial data quality and trust indicators largely mirror B2C e-Commerce trust triggers. Drawing on the research and knowledge in the e-Commerce domain, it is suggested that the GIS domain should employ similar trust promoting mechanisms to engender user trust in geospatial data and GIS applications.

References

1. ISO/TC211. https://committee.iso.org/home/tc211
2. OGC. http://www.opengeospatial.org/
3. INSPIRE. https://inspire.ec.europa.eu/
4. Griraa, J., Bedard, Y., Roche, S., Devillersb, R.: Towards a collaborative knowledge discovery system for enriching semantic information about risks of geospatial data misuse. In: Shi, W., Wu, B., Stein, A. (eds.) Uncertainty Modelling and Quality Control for Spatial Data. CRC Press, Boca Raton (2015)

5. Brown, M., Sharples, S., Harding, J., Parker, C., Bearman, N., Maguire, M., Forrest, D., Haklay, M., Jackson, M.: Usability of geographic information: current challenges and future directions. Appl. Ergon. **44**, 855–865 (2013)

6. Boin, A.T., Hunter, G.J.: What communicates quality to the spatial data consumer? In: Stein, A., Bijker, W., Shi, W. (eds.) 5th International Symposium on Spatial Data Quality (ISSDQ 2007), Enschede (2007)

7. Pôças, I., Gonçalves, J., Marcos, B., Alonso, J., Castro, P., Honrado, J.P.: Evaluating the fitness for use of spatial data sets to promote quality in ecological assessment and monitoring. Int. J. Geogr. Inf. Sci. **28**, 2356–2371 (2014)

8. Comber, A.J., Fisher, P.F., Wadsworth, R.A.: Approaches for providing user relevant metadata and data quality assessments. In: Geographical Information Science Research UK Conference (GISRUK), Maynooth, pp. 79–82 (2007)

9. Lush, V.: Visualisation of quality information for geospatial and remote sensing data: providing the GIS community with the decision support tools for geospatial dataset quality evaluation. Thesis, Aston University (2015)

10. Lush, V., Bastin, L., Lumsden, J.: Developing a geo label: providing the GIS community with quality metadata visualisation tools. In: 21st GIS Research UK (GISRUK 3013), Liverpool, pp. 3–5 (2013)

11. Kim, C., Tao, W., Shin, N., Kim, K.-S.: An empirical study of customers' perceptions of security and trust in e-payment systems. Electron. Commer. Res. Appl. **9**, 84–95 (2010)

12. Chopra, K., Wallace, W.A.: Trust in electronic environments. In: 36th Annual Hawaii International Conference on System Sciences, Hilton Waikoloa Village, pp. 1–10 (2003)

13. Skarlatidou, A., Cheng, T., Haklay, M.: Guidelines for trust interface design for public engagement Web GIS. Int. J. Geogr. Inf. Sci. **27**, 1668–1687 (2013)

14. Moreri, K.K., Fairbairn, D., James, P.: Volunteered geographic information quality assessment using trust and reputation modelling in land administration systems in developing countries. Int. J. Geogr. Inf. Sci. **32**, 1–29 (2018)

15. Hosmer, L.T.: Trust: the connecting link between organizational theory and philosophical ethics. Acad. Manag. Rev. **20**, 379–403 (1995)

16. Marsh, S.P.: Formalising trust as a computational concept. Thesis, Stirling (1994)

17. Luhmann, N.: Trust and Power. Wiley, Chichester (1979)

18. Rotter, J.B.: Interpersonal trust, trustworthiness, and gullibility. Am. Psychol. **35**, 1–7 (1980)

19. Rousseau, D.M., Sitkin, S.B., Burt, R.S., Camerer, C.: Not so different after all: a cross-discipline view of trust. Acad. Manag. Rev. **23**, 393–404 (1998)

20. Geyskens, I., Steenkamp, J.-B.E.M., Scheer, L.K., Kumar, N.: The effects of trust and interdependence on relationship commitment: a trans-atlantic study. Int. J. Res. Mark. **13**, 303–317 (1996)

21. Ganesan, S., Hess, R.: Dimensions and levels of trust: implications for commitment to a relationship. Mark. Lett. **8**, 439–448 (1997)

22. McKnight, D., Choudhury, V., Kacmar, C.: Developing and validating trust measures for e-Commerce: an integrative typology. Inf. Syst. Res. **13**, 334–359 (2002)

23. McCord, M., Ratnasingam, P.: The impact of trust on the technology acceptance model in business to consumer e-Commerce. In: International Conference of the Information Resources Management Association: Innovations through Information Technology, New Orleans, pp. 921–925 (2004)

24. Tan, F.B., Sutherland, P.: Online consumer trust: a multi-dimensional model. J. Electron. Commer. Organ. **2**, 40–58 (2004)

25. Lee, A.J., Yu, T.: Towards a dynamic and composite model of trust. In: 14th ACM Symposium on Access Control Models and Technologies, Stresa (2009)

26. Doney, P.M., Cannon, J.P.: An examination of the nature of trust in buyer-seller relationships. J. Mark. **6**, 35–51 (1997)
27. Pennanen, K., Paakki, M.-K., Kaapu, T.: Consumers views on trust, risk, privacy and security in e-Commerce: a qualitative analysis. In: Kautonen, T., Karjaluoto, H. (eds.) Trust and New Technologies Marketing and Management on the Internet and Mobile Media, pp. 108–123. Edward Elgar Publishing, Cheltenham (2008)
28. Marsh, S., Meech, J.: Trust in design. In: CHI Conference on Human Factors in Computing Systems (CHI 2000), The Hague, p. 45. ACM Press (2000)
29. Jarvenpaa, S.L., Noam, T., Vitale, M.: Consumer trust in an internet store. Inf. Technol. Manag. **1**(2), 45–71 (2000)
30. Lumsden, J., MacKay, L.: How does personality affect trust in B2C e-Commerce? In: 8th International Conference on Electronic Commerce, New Brunswick (2006)
31. Liu, Y., Li, H., Hu, F.: Website attributes in urging online impulse purchase: an empirical investigation on consumer perceptions. Decis. Support Syst. **55**, 829–837 (2013)
32. Harvey, F.: Developing geographic information infrastructures for local government: the role of trust. Can. Geogr. **47**, 28–36 (2003)
33. Bertino, E., Thuraisingham, B., Gertz, M., Damiani, M.L.: Security and privacy for geospatial data: concepts and research directions. In: International Workshop on Security and Privacy in GIS and LBS, Irvine, pp. 6–19 (2008)
34. Bishr, M., Janowicz, K.: Can we trust information? - The case of volunteered geographic information. In: Future Internet Symposium, Berlin (2010)
35. Keßler, C., de Groot, R.T.A.: Trust as a proxy measure for the quality of volunteered geographic information in the case of OpenStreetMap. In: Vandenbroucke, D., Bucher, B., Crompvoets, J. (eds.) Geographic Information Science at the Heart of Europe, pp. 21–37. Springer, Cham (2013). https://doi.org/10.1007/978-3-319-00615-4_2
36. GEOSS. https://www.earthobservations.org/geoss.php
37. GEO. https://www.earthobservations.org/index2.php
38. Zabala, A., Riverola, A., Serral, I., Díaz, P., Lush, V., Masó, J., Pons, X., Habermann, T.: Rubric-Q: adding quality-related elements to the GEOSS clearinghouse datasets. IEEE J. Sel. Top. Appl. Earth Obs. Remote Sens. **6**, 1676–1687 (2013)
39. STC. http://www.earthobservations.org/com_stc_docs_6.shtml
40. ST-09-02: A GEO label: informing users about the quality, relevance and acceptance of services, data sets and products provided by GEOSS. Technical report (2010)
41. GeoViQua. http://www.geoviqua.org/Index.htm
42. Bastin, L., Thum, S., Masó, J.: Deliverable D6.1 data quality encoding as a best practice paper. Technical report (2012)
43. ISO/TC211. http://www.iso.org/iso/catalogue_detail.htm?csnumber=26020
44. ISO/TC211. http://www.iso.org/iso/catalogue_detail.htm?csnumber=39229
45. ISO/TC211.http://www.iso.org/iso/iso_catalogue/catalogue_tc/catalogue_detail.htm?csnumber=32575
46. Broek, M., Smeets, J., Thum, S., Masó, J.: Deliverable D3.2 user feedback elicitation tool. Technical report (2012)

Crowdsourcing Under Attack: Detecting Malicious Behaviors in Waze

Luis Sanchez[1], Erika Rosas[2(✉)], and Nicolas Hidalgo[3]

[1] Departamento de Ingeniería Informática, Universidad de Santiago de Chile,
Santiago, Chile
luis.sanchezgu@usach.cl
[2] Departamento de Informática, Universidad Técnica Federico Santa María,
Valparaíso, Chile
erosas@inf.utfsm.cl
[3] Escuela de Informática y Telecomunicaciones, Universidad Diego Portales,
Santiago, Chile
nicolas.hidalgoc@mail.udp.cl

Abstract. Social networks that use geolocalization enable receiving data from users in order to provide information based on their collective experience. Specifically, this article is interested in the social network Waze, a real-time navigation application for drivers. This application uses methods for identifying users that are open and free, where people are able to hide their identity by using a pseudonym. In this context, malicious behaviors can emerge, endangering the quality of the reports on which the application is based. We propose a method to detect malicious behavior on Waze, which crawls information from the application, aggregates it and models the data relationships in graphs. Using this model the data is analyzed according to the size of the graph: for large interaction graphs, we use a Sybil detection technique, while for small graphs we propose the use of a threshold-based mechanism to detect targeted behaviors. The results show that it is complex to use the large-scale Sybil attack detection techniques due to parameter tuning. However, good success rates can be achieved to tag users as honest and malicious if there are a small number of interactions between these groups of users. On the other hand, for small graphs, a straightforward analysis can be performed, since the graphs are sparse and the users have a limited number of connections between them, making clear the presence of outliers.

Keywords: Online Social Networks · Malicious Behaviors
Sybil attack · Sybil detection

1 Introduction

In recent years, Online Social Networks (OSN) usage has increased exponentially and some of them have become part of most people's everyday life. Facebook[1],

---

[1] www.facebook.com.

© IFIP International Federation for Information Processing 2018
Published by Springer International Publishing AG 2018. All Rights Reserved
N. Gal-Oz and P. R. Lewis (Eds.): IFIPTM 2018, IFIP AICT 528, pp. 91–106, 2018.
https://doi.org/10.1007/978-3-319-95276-5_7

Instagram[2], Twitter[3] and Waze[4] are only a few examples of OSNs accounting for millions of users that interact daily creating and sharing information. In large OSNs, threats are just around the corner, not only menacing users' private data, but also the whole network goals. Identity theft, malwares, fake profiles (or Sybils) are common examples of threats present in this type of networks [8]. In this work, we are particularly interested in Sybil-based attacks under the well-known OSN for drivers, Waze.

Waze is a crowdsourcing application to assist drivers by providing online information on traffic and road conditions. It was created in 2008 and to-date, it has approximately 50 million users [10]. Waze creates an online report of traffic conditions for a given route based on the information collected from and reported by users: current speed, position, origin and destination, police controls, traffic jams, accidents, etc. One of Waze's main features is user engagement to contribute to the common good, i.e., Waze is not just crowdsourcing, but personal participation [10]. Waze's success is directly related to the good-will of users; therefore, malicious behaviors such as Sybil attacks can seriously compromise the application's precision and success.

In the last years, some of these attacks have been reported in [1,13]. In the former, researchers were able to generate fake users and mobile devices using virtual machines in Android and they created fake traffic jams by setting low speed configurations to their fake devices. In the latter, people coordinated to emulate a traffic jam in a residential area, in order to reduce car passing in their neighborhood. Attacks like these can seriously compromise the behavior of the application and detecting this can be challenging in the presence of millions of users dynamically interacting online with the presence of anonymous users in the system. Sybil detection in similar environments such as Twitter have been studied; however, in the context of Waze, the application of state-of-the-art Sybil detection mechanisms requires modelling the malicious behaviors in terms of the data collected from the network.

In this work, we propose three models that attempt to characterize three different behaviors on which we focus our study: (1) Collusion for traffic jams: people collude in order to simulate a traffic jam by not moving [1]; (2) Driver speed attack: a coordinated group of Sybils simulate slow driving so that Waze declares a false traffic jam [13]; and (3) False event attacks: a coordinated group of Sybils vote for a false event, that obscures honest users.

The main contributions of this work are the models associated to the three malicious Sybil behaviors previously exposed. Our models were tested with real Waze traces and our results that show that malicious behaviors can be detected using a state-of-the-art Sybil attack detection mechanism and a threshold-based mechanism. In our experiments, we have exploited SybilDefender [14] and a threshold-based mechanism to detect abnormal behaviors. The former is applied over large interaction graphs and the latter, over small ones.

The remainder of this work is organized as follows: Sect. 2 briefly introduces the identity problems and their relationship with Sybil attacks. Also, we present some literature works that attempt to tackle this problem. Section 3 presents the main contribution of this work, the graphs that model the malicious behaviors we attempt to detect. In Sect. 4, we evaluate the proposed malicious behavior models using SybilDefender as the mechanism to detect Sybils and a threshold-based mechanism for those small interactions graphs. Finally, our conclusions and future work is stated in Sect. 5.

2 Background and Related Work

2.1 Identity Attacks in Social Networks

An identity in a social network is the set of characteristics of a particular person or group (entity) that distinguishes it from others in the network. Different to real-life identities, such as identification cards or a passport that are shown by a person and that can be confirmed comparing a picture and the biometric indexes, in the online world it is more difficult to establish the link between a physical entity and the online identity that represents it.

This problem has been widely discussed because it is easy to change one's identity in several OSNs, whereas in real life, this is a complex process. Friedman and Resnick have called this type of identity *cheap pseudonyms* [9], and allows a person interacting anonymously to constantly change identifiers or to maintaining a persistent identity.

In this context, one unique entity can build a set of pseudonyms in the system, which makes it appear as different entities. What we call a Sybil attack occurs when one physical entity creates and uses a set of identities in the system in order to perform malicious behaviors [6]. The malicious behaviors may vary according to the online environment and it may range from exploiting more resources than allowed to performing active attacks that hamper the veracity of the information exchanged in the network.

The problem of cheap pseudonyms is that they reduce the number of accountable actions in the system, and in the case of Waze, one user that has multiple identities in the system or multiple users may collude to spread false information for other drivers. This network shows relevant information to the users based on their localization and false information may show false traffic jams, which may produce longer routes for other drivers.

This kind of problem has been studied by [17] in the context of the social network Dianping. They have found that some user accounts make positive comments about places that are very far from each other in time intervals that are impossible to achieve. A few users control these accounts that give good rating to some places and bad rating to the competence, in exchange for money.

In the case of Waze, Sinai et al. [13] coordinated a Sybil attack by creating multiple identities using multiple virtual machines in Android that ran the Waze application. They simulated slow driving in all the identities on a specific street so the system detected a false traffic jam. They have proved that it is possible to control routes, which may produce important problems for other drivers. A collusion attack has also been documented by Carney [1] in LA, USA. In this case, the neighbors colluded and activated Waze outside their houses in order to simulate a false traffic jam, in order to force Waze to not recommend that neighborhood to drivers.

2.2   Managing Sybil Attacks and Collusions

In the context of large-scale systems, we can find two types of approaches to prevent the Sybil attack and collusion: detection and tolerance. The *detection* of malicious behaviors is focused on detecting identities that are acting with malice in the system, and evict them from the system. However, in presence of cheap pseudonyms, there is no problem for them to obtain a fresh new identity. For this reason, in large-scale networks, a more common approach is to *tolerate* malicious behaviors, for example, by avoiding using information generated by suspicious identities.

Community detection techniques have been used to detect suspicious entities in the presence of the Sybil attacks, assuming that the number of interactions of these types of identities with real users is limited, that there is at least one honest known user in the network, and the honest region is densely connected. Several Sybil detection algorithms have been proposed [4,14,16] that classify identities as Sybils or normal.

In this work, we used SybilDefender [14], but any other Sybil detection system can be used in its place. SybilDefender proposes four algorithms; the first one obtains statistics from the neighborhood of an honest node identifying J judges from its vicinity and performing R random walks of length L. The second one identifies a suspicious node as Sybil or non-Sybil using the results of the first algorithm. This is performed through R random walks of length L from the suspicious node, and comparing the values of recurrent nodes in the results of algorithm 1. The third and fourth algorithms enable detecting a Sybil region around a node classified as Sybil. A detailed description of the algorithms is presented in [14].

Recently, Sybil attacks have been studied in the context of Vehicular Ad-hoc Networks (VANETs) [7,11,12]. In [7], the authors built an event-based reputation system that feeds a trust management system that restricts the dissemination of false messages. In [11,12], the authors use driving patterns of vehicles and detect Sybils using classifiers, such as minimum distance classifier and support vector machines. In location-based social networks, [15] states that it is not normal the appearance of continuous gatherings, and use the detection of these events to identify Sybils. However, we argue that traffic jams may produce continuous gathering in urban zones. Other graph-based solution has been proposed for mobile online social networks in [3], where the authors use a connection analysis to differentiate honest versus fake nodes. Finally, in the context of mobile crowdsourcing, recent work proposes a passive and active checking scheme that verify traffic volume, signal strength and network topology [2], differentiating nodes using an adaptive threshold.

3   Modeling Sybil Behaviors

The goal of the model is to identify Sybil attacks in Waze. The key contribution is the way of modeling the data of Waze in order to detect Sybils or collusion. Figure 1 shows the proposed pipeline that is detailed in the following subsections. In general, data is captured from the LiveMap of Waze, reordered, and aggregated in order prevent redundant information. Then, we generate graphs that model the interactions between the users according to the malicious behavior we target. Then, an analysis of the graphs is performed using state-of-the-art Sybil detection mechanisms.

3.1   Crawling and Indexing

We crawled data from Waze using the endpoint that feeds the LiveMap[5] of Waze. This is public data that is delivered in JSON format of the current state of the requested area, defined by coordinates. The data captured was requested every 1 min, obtaining a snapshot of the map at that time. We categorize data in three types:

- **Alerts:** Alerts are events explicitly reported by Waze users, such as vehicle accidents, police locations, traffic jam reports, etc. These alerts are characterized by a point on a map and the number of votes received by other users that corroborate the information.
- **Jams:** Traffic jams are events that Waze reports using the location data of users. They are created when large traffic is detected on a street and are represented by geographic coordinates that build a line, and other data such as the severity of the traffic jam and current user speed, among others.
- **Users:** The data of users on the map shows their current location and is represented by an identifier, geographic coordinates, and current speed, among others.

We have indexed the data by user identifier and event identifier. The information about traffic jams is not used in this study, since it does not contain user information, which is the main focus of this study.

3.2   Data Aggregation

We mainly produce two structures that facilitate graph modeling:

- **Event fusion:** Generally, users create several Waze alerts that correspond to one real traffic event. In order to build the relationship between users that interact with a real event, we fuse the votes that are close in time and space. We have set the time and space parameters for 30 min and 200 m respectively.

---

[5] http://www.waze.com/livemap.

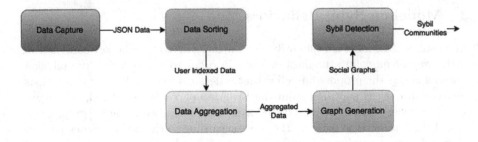

Fig. 1. Overview steps of the solution

- **Routes generation:** In order to relate users to a route trip they have followed, we have generated routes from the geographic coordinates of the users. The routes are built from the user geographic points that are relatively close in time. Since the data is captured every 1 min, it is not easy to generate a route from two geographically different points. We have used the process called map matching first, in order to deal with vagueness of the GPS location, so that the points are inside a street. Then, we have used Google Roads API, to correct the coordinates and infer the route that the user took.

3.3   Graph Modelling

As we attempt to exploit state-of-the-art Sybil detection mechanisms, we must model the data associated to the different malicious behaviors that we attempt to detect. In this work, we focus on three problems, some of them already reported in literature. The malicious behaviors we target are:

- **Collusion for traffic jam:** A group of users is detained on a street so that Waze declares a false traffic jam. This behavior is described in [1].
- **Driving speed attack:** A coordinated group of Sybils that simulate slow driving that Waze declares a false traffic jam. This behavior is described in [13].
- **False event attacks:** A coordinated group of Sybils that vote for a false event that obscure the honest users.

The generated interaction graphs are non-directed defined as $G = (V, A)$, where V is the set of vertexes that represent users, and A indicates the set of edges that represent interactions between two users. The weight of the edge is related with the amount of interactions the users had in time.

If the modeled graphs are fast mixing and the number of connections from the malicious to the honest area is limited, then, we can apply a Sybil Detection algorithm. With these properties, we guarantee that random walks can iterate all over the honest area, and it is difficult to walk outside this area.

Traffic Jam Graph. This graph is built with the users that do not move at the same time and within a close distance. Then, an interaction between two users a, b is defined as the number of times they were standing still at the same time in any of their trips v. Equation (1) shows how the weight of an edge between two users is computed: the sum of the number of times they may be colluded. ST is the set of trips where the users had the same origin and destination, meaning that they did not move from the beginning of the trip.

Equation (2) shows when a possible collusion is detected: when in a time window t the users were within a distance of less than d meters. We consider that the function $distance(v_1, v_2)$ gives the distance in meters from the position of the trip v_1 to the position of the trip v_2 and $time(v)$ gives the time when the travel v happened.

$$w_{g1}(a, b) = \sum^{v_{ua}, v_{ub} \in ST} col(v_{ua}, v_{ub}) \tag{1}$$

$$col(v_1, v_2) = \begin{cases} 1, \text{ if } distance(v_1, v_2) < d \text{ and} \\ \quad |time(v_1) - time(v_2)| < t \\ 0, \text{ in any other case} \end{cases} \tag{2}$$

If the users collude to stand still in the streets in order to produce a traffic jam, then they will appear more connected in the graph, and we would like to detect this malicious area.

Driving Speed Graph. The goal of this graph is to detect inconsistencies in the user behaviors that share part of their travel routes. We compare speed and temporality in order to check if their characteristics validate each other. The weight of an edge in this graph is high when two users share routes close in time and their driving speeds were similar. A lower weight of an edge indicates that their driving speeds were very different. Equation (3) shows the weight of the edge between users a and b: In the sum of all the times there is a similarity found between their trips T, normalized by the minimum number of trips of the users. We call v_{ua} a trip of the user a and v_{ub} a trip of the user b.

Equation (4) shows what we consider a similarity in this case. We take into account three properties of the trips, the time, the routes and the speed. Route similarity $s_{routes}(v_1, v_2)$ computes the number of segments shared in the trip v_1 and v_2, divided by the number of segments of the longest trip between v_1 and v_2. This route similarity is modified by factor α and β so to favor a homogeneous distribution, incrementing the similarity to 1 in cases there is a high similarity in speed and time, and generating a medium effect when there is a regular similarity in speed and time.

The temporal similarity $s_{time}(v_1, v_2)$ is equal to zero if v_1 and v_2 were separated in time more than a value min and equal to 100% if v_1 and v_2 occurred at the same time. Temporal distances in between are proportionally computed. The speed similarity $s_{speed}(v_1, v_2)$ indicates whether the segments that share v_1

and v_2 have a similar speed. This is computed with the average speed of these segments.

$$w_{g2}(a,b) = \frac{\sum^{v_{ua}, v_{ub} \in T} sim(v_{ua}, v_{ub})}{min(\cup_{i=a,b} \text{ number of user trips } i)} \tag{3}$$

$$sim(v_1, v_2) = \begin{cases} s_{routes}(v_1, v_2) \times \alpha, & \text{if } s_{speed}(v_1, v_2) > max \\ & \text{and } s_{time}(v_1, v_2) > max \\ s_{routes}(v_1, v_2) \times \beta, & \text{if } s_{speed}(v_1, v_2) > min \\ & \text{and } s_{time}(v_1, v_2) > min \\ s_{routes}(v_1, v_2), & \text{in any other case} \end{cases} \tag{4}$$

$$\alpha = \frac{1}{max(\cup_{i=0}^{n} w_{g2})} \tag{5}$$

$$\beta = 1 + (\frac{1-\alpha}{2}) \tag{6}$$

In extreme cases of malicious behaviors, the users that share temporality and space will be strongly connected. Honest users would have low weighted edges.

False Event Graph. The main goal of this graph is to identify user groups that vote on the same events. In this case, the weight of each edge $w_{g3}(a,b)$ that links the users a and b is the sum of the events that the users a and b have voted for the same event.

Malicious users that also vote for events that honest users have voted on may create a graph that is not fast mixing and hinder Sybil detection. However, they require the effort of creating strong links with other users. Figure 2 shows a random subgraph built with the experimental data. Each vertex represents a user and the links represent the interaction the users had in time. The weight of these edges is determined by the number of votes of the users on the same events.

3.4   Malicious Behavior Detection

The malicious behavior was detected by analyzing the graphs and applying a threshold based approach or a Sybil detection algorithm, according to the characteristics of the graph. We will tag a user as malicious when:

- In the first graph, the more connected regions will be the malicious areas. Honest users that do not collude with others should present a small number of connections.
- In the second graph, strong relations are given when users share their behavior, which can be honest or malicious. We have to start the process with a previously known honest user to identify the regions.
- The third graph is similar to the second; we assume that users do not vote in group for an event, so the number of connections between them are going to be smaller compared to malicious Sybil users.

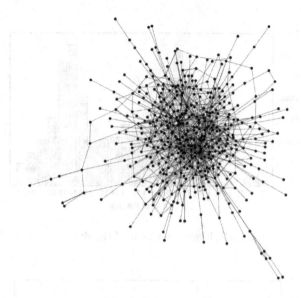

Fig. 2. Events graph

4   Experimentation

The data was crawled in a timespan of 6 months, from July 2015 until January 2016, with some data missing in October 2015 due to a server failure. We used the LiveMap API of Waze that was consulted every 1 min. The area consulted was around the city Santiago, Chile with the coordinates −33.2 North, −33.8 South, −70.87 East, −70.5 West.

In total, we considered 1,667,400 events, that where generated by 223,031 users. We captured 4,547,887 users with locations inside the coordinates, which is a large number, considering the size of the city of Santiago; however, Waze uses new identifiers for anonymous users, which explains the number of users.

In the data aggregation step, 30% of the events were fused. Figure 3 shows the distribution of the events per hour of the day. We are able to observe the peak time of the day in the figure, which is normal for a city like Santiago, at times when people go to work and when they return home.

In the data aggregation step, we have also obtained user trips with the trace we built from their locations that are close in time (maximum 7 min of difference between each subsequent pair). We consider trips that have at least 5 consecutive location points. These values were experimentally chosen, since most of the trips have an average of 1 min between consecutive points. The result is 192,248 trips of 184,992 users (mostly anonymous users). Figures 4 and 5 show the distribution of the duration and the distance traveled in each trip. Most trips are short in time and distance.

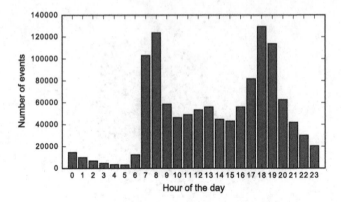

Fig. 3. Events per hour of the day

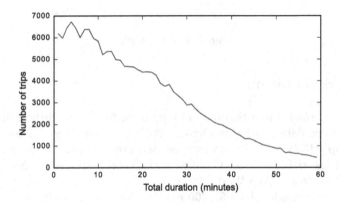

Fig. 4. Distribution of total trip time

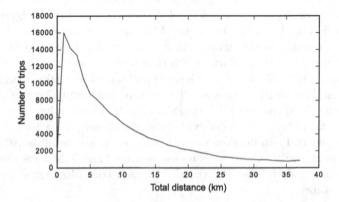

Fig. 5. Distribution of total distance of trips

4.1   False Event Graph

The obtained graph has 223,030 vertexes and 1,452,261 edges, with an average degree of 13. This is a non-connected graph, and has 59,815 components. In order to perform the experiments we selected the largest component of the graph that has 160,894 vertexes and 1,499,717 edges. The remaining graphs have a size that is negligible for this experiment.

In order to obtain a fast mixing graph, we removed vertexes with small degrees. Figure 6 shows how the mixing time changes with the minimum degree of the graph. This means that we can apply a Sybil detection mechanism when the graph is dense, with a minimum degree of 64. The resulting graph has 9,743 vertexes and 720,152 edges with an average degree of 73.

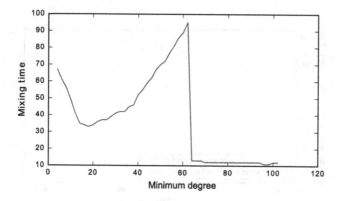

Fig. 6. Graph mixing time when vertex are removed

We connected a Sybil area to this graph in order to observe how the algorithm behaves. The Sybil area was created using the Erdős-Rényi model to create random and sparse graphs. This model is often invoked to capture the structure of social networks [5] and is defined as a set of N nodes connected by n edges chosen random from the $(N(N-1))/2$ possible edges. The Sybil area had 523 users and 1,080 edges, with a mixing time of 41. The number of vertexes corresponds to 0.03% of the number of honest nodes in the event graph. To connect both regions we created random attack edges between each region.

SybilDefender works mainly with two algorithms: the first identifies J judges from an honest known node. Then, from each judge, R random walks are computed of length L, counting how many nodes appear more than T times in the random walks. Then, the average and the standard deviation are computed for each element of the list L. In our case, we set the number of judges to $T = 50$, the number of random walks to $R = 100$, $L = 100, 200 \ldots 1000$ and $T = 5$, considering the size of the experiments presented in [14].

The second algorithm identifies if a node is Sybil or not, using the results of the first algorithm. This is done computing R random walks of length L from the suspicious node, counting how many nodes exceed T repetitions, which is called m. Then, a comparison is done to determine if the node is Sybil or not: $media - m > deviation \times \alpha$.

SybilDefender, with 20 attack edges joining the Sybil and honest areas, found a 99.1% of successfully detected Sybils and 100% successfully detected honest users using SybilDefender algorithms. However, if the number of attack edges grows to 40, then there is a 19% of successfully detected Sybil users and 100% of successfully detected honest users.

We modified the parameters of the algorithms, in order to observe the influence on the results. When using a $T = 7$ and changing the value α we obtained the results of Fig. 7. The best results are obtained when using $\alpha = 55$, when we obtained a 76% of Sybils detected and 96% of honest users.

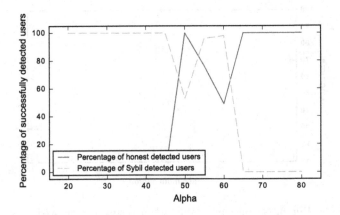

Fig. 7. Sybil defender results modifying α values

Furthermore, if we modify the length of the random walks, we obtain the results of Fig. 8. In this case, the algorithm always detects all the honest users and the best case for Sybils occurs at 350 maximum length where it finds 83% of Sybils.

4.2 Driving Speed Graph

This graph was built with parameters min and max set on 30 and 70, respectively. The resulting graph has 149,492 vertex and 7,048 edges. This is a non-connected graph with 142,582 components. Unlike the previous graph, this one has 138,810 components with one vertex, 2,479 with two vertexes and 1,293 with three or more vertex, with the largest component with 24 vertexes. The size of the graph is too small to apply Sybil defender.

Figure 9 shows the value of the edges in the largest component. Analyzing the edges values, we located an edge with a similarity value of 44,51. This is because they had a very different speed in the shared segments of the trip.

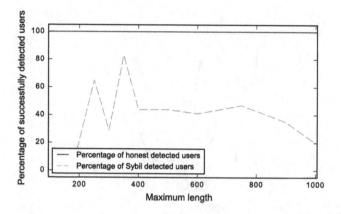

Fig. 8. Sybil defender results modifying maximum length

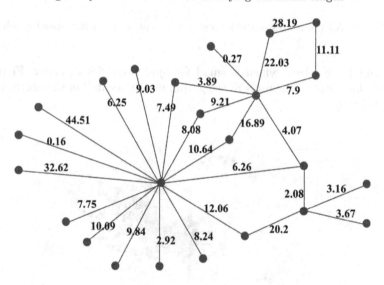

Fig. 9. Largest component of driver speed graphs

We have drawn all the travels involved in the generation of the graph, and obtained Fig. 10. It is clear that the graph show honest users that have similarities in the highways of the city.

4.3 Traffic Jam Graph

In this case, the parameter d was set to 1 km and t equals to 30 min. With this parameters we obtained a graph for this case has 38,455 vertex and 8,592 edges, with an average degree of 0.44 (maximum degree 14). This is a non-connected disperse graph that has 31,967 connected components. The largest part has 711

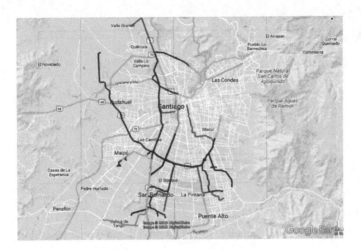

Fig. 10. All the routes of the largest component of the driver speed graph

vertex and 1,448 edges, which is small for applying Sybil defender. Figure 11 shows the locations of the users of the graph, mostly located in the northeastern area of Santiago.

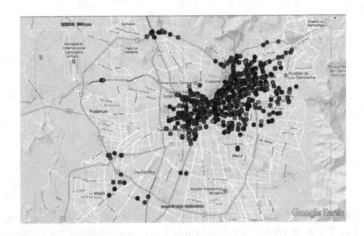

Fig. 11. Location of users of traffic jam graph

We analyzed the distribution of the edges weight and found that from 711 users, there are 643 that have only one stand still trip, 58 have only two stand still trips, 9 have between 3 and 8 trips and only one user have 27 stand still trips. Thus, we conclude that colluded users may be detected by their degree in the graph, which in our case can be set around 10 to consider a user as suspicious.

5   Conclusion

In this work, we have proposed a model to process Waze traces and detect Sybil behaviors. The model consists of five steps, standing out the modeling of targeted behaviors on an interaction graph. We provide three of these models that characterize the three different behaviors which we focus on in our study: (1) Collusion for traffic jam, where people collude in standing still to simulate a traffic jam and divert traffic; (2) Driver speed attack, where a coordinated group of Sybils simulate slow driving to trick the application into assuming a traffic jam; and (3) False event attacks, where a coordinated group of Sybils vote for a false event that obscures the honest users.

The general model was tested with real Waze traces and our results that show that malicious behaviors can be detected using a state-of-the-art Sybil attack detection mechanism and a threshold-based mechanism. In our experiment, we have exploited SybilDefender [14] and a threshold-based mechanism to detect abnormal behaviors. The former is applied on large interaction graphs and the latter, over small ones where the application of a large-scale detection mechanism is not necessary.

Our results show that it is complex to use the large-scale Sybil attack detection techniques due to the parameter tuning. However, good success rates can be achieved to tag users as honest and malicious, if the number of interactions between those groups of users is small. On the other hand, for small graphs, a straightforward analysis can be performed since the graphs are sparse and the users have a small number of connections between each other, making clear the presence of unusual behaviors.

Acknowledgment. This work is partially supported by the University of Santiago research project PMI-USA 1204 and FONDEF Idea ID15I10560, CONICYT, Chile.

References

1. Carney, M.: Angry LA residents are trying to sabotage Waze data to stop side-street congestion (2014). https://pando.com/2014/11/17/angry-la-residents-try-to-sabotage-waze-data-to-stop-side-street-congestion/
2. Chang, S.H., Chen, Z.R.: Protecting mobile crowd sensing against Sybil attacks using cloud based trust management system. In: Mobile Information Systems 2016, p. 10 (2016)
3. Chinchore, A., Jiang, F., Xu, G.: Intelligent Sybil attack detection on abnormal connectivity behavior in mobile social networks. In: Uden, L., Heričko, M., Ting, I.-H. (eds.) KMO 2015. LNBIP, vol. 224, pp. 602–617. Springer, Cham (2015). https://doi.org/10.1007/978-3-319-21009-4_45
4. Danezis, G., Mittal, P.: SybilInfer: detecting Sybil nodes using social networks. Technical report MSR-TR-2009-6, Microsoft, January 2009
5. Dobrescu, R., Ionescu, F.: Large Scale Networks: Modeling and Simulation, 1st edn. CRC Press, Boca Raton (2016)
6. Douceur, J.R.: The Sybil attack. In: Druschel, P., Kaashoek, F., Rowstron, A. (eds.) IPTPS 2002. LNCS, vol. 2429, pp. 251–260. Springer, Heidelberg (2002). https://doi.org/10.1007/3-540-45748-8_24

7. Feng, X., Li, C.y., Chen, D.x., Tang, J.: A method for defensing against multisource Sybil attacks in VANET. Peer-to-Peer Netw. Appl. **10**(2), 305–314 (2017)

8. Fire, M., Goldschmidt, R., Elovici, Y.: Online social networks: threats and solutions. IEEE Commun. Surv. Tutor. **16**(4), 2019–2036 (2014, Fourthquarter)

9. Friedman, E.J., Resnick, P.: The social cost of cheap pseudonyms. J. Econ. Manag. Strateg. **10**(2), 173–199 (2001)

10. Goel, V.: Maps that Live and Breathe with Data (2013). http://www.nytimes.com/2013/06/11/technology/mobile-companies-crave-maps-that-live-and-breathe.html

11. Gu, P., Khatoun, R., Begriche, Y., Serhrouchni, A.: Vehicle driving pattern based Sybil attack detection. In: 2016 IEEE 18th International Conference on High Performance Computing and Communications; IEEE 14th International Conference on Smart City; IEEE 2nd International Conference on Data Science and Systems (HPCC/SmartCity/DSS), pp. 1282–1288, December 2016

12. Gu, P., Khatoun, R., Begriche, Y., Serhrouchni, A.: Support vector machine (SVM) based Sybil attack detection in vehicular networks. In: 2017 IEEE Wireless Communications and Networking Conference (WCNC), pp. 1–6, March 2017

13. Sinai, M.B., Partush, N., Yadid, S., Yahav, E.: Exploiting Social Navigation, October 2014. arXiv:1410.0151 [cs]

14. Wei, W., Xu, F., Tan, C., Li, Q.: SybilDefender: defend against Sybil attacks in large social networks. In: 2012 Proceedings IEEE INFOCOM, pp. 1951–1959, March 2012

15. Xu, Z., Chen, B., Meng, X., Liu, L.: Towards efficient detection of Sybil attacks in location-based social networks. In: 2017 IEEE Symposium Series on Computational Intelligence (SSCI), pp. 1–7, November 2017

16. Yu, H., Kaminsky, M., Gibbons, P.B., Flaxman, A.: Sybilguard: defending against Sybil attacks via social networks. In. ACM SIGCOMM 2006, pp. 267–278. ACM Press (2006)

17. Zhang, X., Zheng, H., Li, X., Du, S., Zhu, H.: You are where you have been: Sybil detection via geo-location analysis in OSNs. In: 2014 IEEE Global Communications Conference (GLOBECOM), pp. 698–703, December 2014

From Knowledge to Trust: A Logical Framework for Pre-trust Computations

Mirko Tagliaferri$^{(\boxtimes)}$ and Alessandro Aldini$^{(\boxtimes)}$

Urbino University, Urbino, PU, Italy

Abstract. Computational trust is the digital counterpart of the human notion of trust as applied in social systems. Its main purpose is to improve the reliability of interactions in online communities and of knowledge transfer in information management systems. Trust models are typically composed of two parts: a trust computing part and a trust manipulation part. The former serves the purpose of gathering relevant information and then use it to compute initial trust values; the latter takes the initial trust values as granted and manipulates them for specific purposes, like, e.g., aggregation and propagation of trust, which are at the base of a notion of reputation. While trust manipulation is widely studied, very little attention is paid to the trust computing part. In this paper, we propose a formal language with which we can reason about knowledge, trust and their interaction. Specifically, in this setting it is possible to put into direct dependence possessed knowledge with values estimating trust, distrust, and uncertainty, which can then be used to feed any trust manipulation component of computational trust models.

Keywords: Computational trust · Trust logic · Subjective Logic

1 Introduction

Given the growing number of interactions in online communities and of information exchanges in information management systems, it's becoming increasingly important to have security mechanisms that can prevent fraudulent behaviors. However, implementing hard security mechanisms for every possible interaction, e.g. authentication methods or access controls, can be costly and a failure of such mechanisms might put the whole system in jeopardy. For this reason, it is necessary to include other soft security mechanisms in the design of those environments where transactions and exchanges take place [10, 19]. Trust is one form of soft security that can be implemented into a system: trust is a social control mechanism that brings an undoubtedly positive impact on cooperative operations, both by increasing the chances of performing an interaction and by decreasing the chances of having malevolent behaviors during those interactions [1, 18]. Therefore, trust has both a proactive and a control effect over interactions. Computational trust is the digital counterpart of trust as applied in ordinary social communities and computational trust models are soft security mechanisms that implement the notion of trust in digital environments to increase the quantity and quality of interactions[1]. Computational trust models are typically

---

[1] See [2, 3, 5, 14–16, 20] for surveys on computational trust models.

© IFIP International Federation for Information Processing 2018
Published by Springer International Publishing AG 2018. All Rights Reserved
N. Gal-Oz and P. R. Lewis (Eds.): IFIPTM 2018, IFIP AICT 528, pp. 107–123, 2018.
https://doi.org/10.1007/978-3-319-95276-5_8

composed of two parts: a trust computing part and a trust manipulation part. While trust manipulation is widely studied, very little attention is paid to the trust computing part. In this paper, we propose a formal language with which it is possible to reason about how knowledge[2] and trust interact. Specifically, in this setting it is possible to put into direct dependence possessed knowledge with values estimating trust, distrust, and uncertainty, which can then be used to feed the trust manipulation component of any computational trust models. The paper will proceed as follows: in Sect. 2, we discuss the distinction between trust computation and trust manipulation by providing some examples of both components as implemented in computational trust models; in Sect. 3, following on the discussion of Sect. 2, we will show how one well-known model for trust manipulation, i.e. Jøsang's Subjective Logic [11], struggles when dealing with the trust computing component; in Sect. 4, we provide the syntax and semantics of what we will call trust logic. In this logic, we will show how we can talk about the notion of trust and we will then show how the semantical structure in which the logic is interpreted helps in compute trust values that can be fed into Subjective Logic's trust manipulation component; finally, in Sect. 5, we conclude the paper with some general remarks.

2 Trust Computing and Trust Manipulation

A good formalization of the notion of trust must accomplish two goals. The first goal is that of explaining how trust is generated: while it is possible to take trust as a primitive and unexplained notion, it is often preferable to provide a reduction of the notion of trust to more basic concepts, aiding our comprehension of the phenomenon of trust in various contexts. The second goal is that of explaining the dynamics of trust, i.e. how trust evolves under different circumstances: this should help in determining how dynamics in an environment (e.g. a group of friends or a multinational company) influence trust. To each goal corresponds a different component of trust models. Specifically, it is possible to identify a trust computing and a trust manipulation component. The former serves the purpose of gathering relevant information, which is considered basic, and then use it to compute trust values; the latter takes trust values as granted and manipulates them for specific purposes using different operators.

Even though both components are important, authors often concentrate on one or the other: models that concentrate on the trust computing component rely on the fact that when an environment changes, it is possible to repeatedly compute new trust values, therefore no trust manipulation component is needed; models that concentrate on the trust manipulation component can rely on conceptions of trust that take the concept as a primitive or depend for their initial values on other models, therefore neglecting the trust computing component. To highlight the distinction between trust

---

[2] It is important to note that, even though we employ the word 'knowledge', we do not commit to any specific epistemological notion of knowledge. In fact, our term might refer to very different conceptions of knowledge and, in some cases, also to beliefs. Although important from a philosophical point of view, this fact does not influence the formal framework we are presenting in the paper.

computing and trust manipulation, we will now provide three examples of trust models and show how each component behaves in those models. To those three models we will then add a fourth one, which will be used as a target for the reflections of the rest of the paper. Note that the models presented were selected for explanatory purposes (i.e. to make clearer the distinction between the two components). No important or specific facts are derived from the models and, therefore, no results of this paper depend on the choices made.

2.1 Marsh's Trust Model

In [13], Stephen Marsh presented the first example of a thorough and detailed analysis of the notion of trust in a computational setting. His system was designed for possible implementations in distributed artificial intelligence and multi-agent systems: the main purpose of his thesis was that of using a formal variant of common-sense trust to increase the quality of the evaluation an autonomous agent should perform to decide whether to collaborate or not with other agents. In this model, it is possible to identify three different forms of trust:

(1) Basic trust;
(2) General trust;
(3) Situational trust.

Basic trust represents the general attitude of an agent, when all his experiences in life are considered; general trust is the overall trust a trustor has in a trustee; situational trust is the specific trust a trustor has in a trustee when a specific collaborative task should take place. Basic trust and general trust are taken as primitives, while situational trust is reduced to more basic concepts.

In Marsh's model, the trust computing component is arrived at through a conceptual analysis of the notion of trust, which either classify trust as a primitive notion or helps in identifying the basic elements that form specific versions of trust (i.e. situational trust). We will now briefly explain how situational trust is analyzed, since this form of trust is at the core of Marsh's model. Specifically, situational trust is computed starting from three basic parameters: $U_x(\alpha)$, the amount of utility agent x gains if situation α occurs; $I_x(\alpha)$, the importance of situation α for agent x; $\widehat{T_x(y)}$, the general trusting disposition of agent x towards agent y. To obtain the situational trust, those three components are multiplied together.

The trust computing component of Marsh's model is straightforward. Once some basic information is gathered and expressed with numerical values, those values are multiplied to obtain a specific trust value.

What is limited in Marsh's model is the trust manipulation component. This is because the model relies on repeated computations of the trust values, rather than a manipulation of already obtained values. We will show in later sections (Sect. 3) that this is a very severe limiting factor in computational trust models, since it makes it hard to provide evaluations for trust in different scenarios, e.g. when trust is obtained through referrals from one agent to another.

2.2   Yu and Singh's Trust Model

In [21], the authors present a formal framework in which to evaluate the reputation of agents based on witnesses. The model also provides tools to avoid deception in rating provision. Yu and Singh's model is based on Dempster-Shafer theory of evidence and favors the trust manipulation component over the trust computing one. The trust computing component is based on past interactions between agents, where an agent x trusts another agent y if the percentage of positive past experiences over the whole number of recent experiences is superior to a given threshold. The trust computing component of this model is extremely simple and is lacking a proper analysis of trust. Moreover, it relies on the fact that the amount of data on past interactions is big, otherwise the values computed might be misleading. This is troublesome, since in digital environments interactions between the same agents are scarce. However, the strength of the model is associated with its trust manipulation component. In this model, it is possible to aggregate together ratings from different agents. Given a trust net, which is a directed graph representing the referral chains produced by an agent x's query about the trustworthiness of another agent y, x might obtain a value of the trustworthiness of y by combining the various ratings given to y by all close acquaintances of x in the trust net. The operation is based on Dempster rule of combination and the result is that of combining as a weighted sum all the trust values of other agents into one for the trustor.

2.3   BDI + Repage

In [17], the authors present a sophisticated model for trust and reputation evaluation and propagation. This model has both a simple trust computing and a good trust manipulation component. First, in BDI Rapage, there is a clear distinction between a trust and a reputation evaluation, where the former (called image) is interpreted as the trustor's belief in the trustworthiness of the trustee, while the latter is interpreted as the trustor's meta-belief on the beliefs about the trustee of other agents. The trust computing part is based, like in [21], on past experiences, which can be categorized under five different labels (Very Bad, Bad, Neutral, Good, Very Good). Past experiences influence the weight of each label, providing a specific numerical value for each. Those numerical values are then used to generate an image (what we call trust evaluation) of the trustee for the given trustor. This trust evaluation, coupled with the desires, the beliefs and the intentions of the trustor, leads to the decision of collaborating or not. As in [21], the trust computing component suffers from the requirement of having many past interactions and the real strength of the model lies in its trust manipulation component. For such component, this model includes a full logical language that can help reasoning about trust and reputation. The logical framework is that of a hierarchical multi-sorted first-order language. In such language is easy to express formulas that describe, over and above simple properties of objects, the desires, beliefs, intentions and the trust evaluations of a given agent and then, using various logical connectives (e.g. conjunction and disjunction), it is possible to specify different conditions for the presence or absence of trust by the trustor.

2.4 Summing up

We saw three computational trust models and their respective trust computing and trust manipulation components. It has been shown that none of the model can deal perfectly with both components. We will now present a fourth model, which will be the starting point for the reflection made in this paper. This model, i.e. Audun Jøsang's Subjective Logic [11], is extremely well-suited to manipulate trust values using different algebraic operators, but suffers from a poor trust computing component. We will show how the logical language we present in this paper, can be used to implement a good trust computing component in Subjective Logic.

3 Subjective Logic

We described in Sect. 2 the two main components of computational trust models and provided some examples of the role those two components have in such models. In this section, we will introduce a further computational trust model, i.e. Audun Jøsang's Subjective Logic. We will explain why we choose this model as the starting point of our work and why we believe the model requires some improvements.

In Subjective Logic trust is represented as the opinion of agent x about a given proposition p. An opinion has three major components, and a fourth added component which completes the trust evaluation and helps in computing an expected value for trust. The three major components are, respectively, a belief component, a disbelief component and an uncertainty component[3], while the fourth added component is labelled as base rate and indicates the prior probability associated with the truth of a proposition when no initial relevant information is available. The belief, disbelief and uncertainty components are additive to one, leading to the fact that Subjective Logic is effectively an extension of traditional probability logics. The additivity principle of the three major components allow also for a nice visualization of opinions through a triangle, which we will call the opinion triangle (Fig. 1). It is possible to observe in the figure that an opinion ω_x is identified through the three major components of belief, disbelief and uncertainty and, after the generic opinion is obtained, it is possible to compute the expected trust value $E(\omega_i)$ using the base rate (indicated in the figure with the letter a): the base rate determines the slope of the projection of the opinion on the base of the triangle and allows to compute an expected value when no uncertainty is taken into account in the valuation of the opinion.

Subjective Logic is a widely employed model to manipulate trust, but is rather ill-suited when it comes to compute initial trust values to be used as inputs to the model. The reason is that the only source of information that Subjective Logic allows to compute trust values is reputation scores based on past interactions. Once it is noticed that different agents might evaluate interaction differently and that reputation scores in

---

[3] Uncertainty plays a crucial role in the formalization of trust. There are many ways this concept has been described formally (see e.g. [6] for a survey). Dealing with trust in a formal way can thus help also understand how uncertainty can be modelled, providing useful insight also for fields other than computer science, e.g. economics.

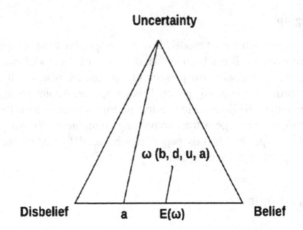

Fig. 1. Opinion triangle where all components used to compute trust are represented.

one context are not easily transferable to other context, the fact that Subjective Logic has no other means to compute initial trust values becomes a big drawback. This is also noted by Jøsang himself:

"The major difficulty with applying subjective logic is to find a way to consistently determine opinions to be used as input parameters. People may find the opinion model unfamiliar, and different individuals may produce conflicting opinions when faced with the same evidence." [8].

The aim of this paper is specifically to implement a trust computing component that can produce initial trust values which can then be plugged into Subjective Logic.

4   A Language for Trust

We will now introduce the syntax and semantics of a formal language that will allow us to reason about knowledge and trust and, furthermore, to provide a trust computing mechanism that can produce values to be fed into Subjective Logic's trust manipulation component. This, we believe, is an improvement to Subjective Logic. The leading idea of the framework comes from an insight given by Jøsang:

"...[T]rust ultimately is a personal and subjective phenomenon that is based on various factors or evidence, and that some of those carry more weight than others. Personal experience typically carries more weight than second hand trust referrals or reputation..." [9].

The idea is therefore that of using the expressive power of a formal language to describe the information possessed by an agent and then transform this knowledge into an opinion value about a given proposition with all the three major components of Subjective Logic made explicit.

4.1   Syntax

In our language $\mathcal{L}$, we start with two sets. The two initial sets are a finite set Ag of agents and a finite set At of atomic propositional constant. Given $p \in At$, $i \in Ag$ and b a rational number in the interval $[0, 1]$ (with 0 and 1 included), the grammar for our language is given by the following BNF:

$$\varphi := p | \neg \varphi | \varphi \wedge \varphi | K_i(\varphi) | \omega_i(\varphi) \geq b$$

All other connectives and operators are defined in the standard way:

(i) $\varphi \vee \psi := \neg(\neg \varphi \wedge \neg \psi)$;
(ii) $\varphi \rightarrow \psi := \neg \varphi \vee \psi$;
(iii) $\varphi \leftrightarrow \psi := (\varphi \rightarrow \psi) \wedge (\psi \rightarrow \varphi)$;
(iv) $F_i(\varphi) := \neg K_i(\neg \varphi)$;
(v) $\omega_i(\varphi) \leq b := -\omega_i(\varphi) \geq -b$;
(vi) $\omega_i(\varphi) < b := \neg(\omega_i(\varphi) \geq b)$;
(vii) $\omega_i(\varphi) = b := (\omega_i(\varphi) \geq b) \wedge (\omega_i(\varphi) \leq b)$.

$K_i(\varphi)$ should be intuitively read as "agent i knows that φ"; we will call such formulas *knowledge formulas*. $\omega_i(\varphi) \geq b$ should be intuitively read as "agent i trusts formula φ to degree at least b"; we will call such formulas *trust formulas*. The degree to which an agent can trust goes from 0, complete distrust, to 1, complete trust.

4.2   Semantics

The semantics we will provide in this paper is in truth theoretical form and depends on a structure that is a combination of traditional relational structures for modal logics with added components to interpret trust formulas [4, 7, 12]. We will interpret the above presented language in the following structure $M = (S, Cntx, \pi, R_{i1}, \ldots, R_{in}, T)$, where S is a finite set of possible states of the system; $Cntx$ is a finite set of contexts, i.e. scenarios in which to evaluate trust; π is a valuation function over the set At, assigning to each atomic proposition in At a set of possible worlds, i.e. $\pi : At \rightarrow \wp(S)$; R_i, one for each agent $i \in Ag$, is an accessibility relation defined over S, i.e. $R_i \subseteq S \times S$; finally, $T = (X_{(i,c)}, \mu_{(i,c,\varphi)})$ is a trust relevance space which determines, for each formula of the language, which propositional constants are relevant and how relevant they are. T has two distinct components: a qualitative relevance component $X_{(i,c)}$ and a quantitative relevance component $\mu_{(i,c,\varphi)}$.

The qualitative relevance component $X_{(i,c)}$, one for each couple of elements $i \in Ag$ and $c \in Cntx$, takes formulas of the language as arguments and returns as values subsets of At, i.e. $X_{(i,c)} : \mathcal{L} \rightarrow \wp(At)$; the quantitative relevance component $\mu_{(i,c,\varphi)}$, which is a family of functions, one for each formula of the language and defined over the same couple of $i \in Ag$ and $c \in Cntx$ of $X_{(i,c)}$, assigns to each relevant atomic proposition p member of the subset of At selected by $X_{(i,c)}$, a rational number in the range $(0, 1]$, i.e. $\mu_{(i,c,\varphi)} : X_{(i,c)}(\varphi) \to (0, 1]^4$. The weights assigned must be additive to 1. Since the set of agents and the set of contexts are finite, there is a finite number of trust relevance spaces.

A possible state $s \in S$ represent a way in which the system can be specified; two states differ from one another by what propositions hold in such states. For example, in one state it might hold that it is sunny in San Francisco, while in another state it might hold that it is raining in San Francisco and therefore it is not sunny. If no non-standard conditions[5] are placed on the description of a system (i.e. proscriptions on propositions that can or can't hold together), there will be exactly $2^{|At|}$ states in S, where $|At|$ is the cardinality of the set of propositional constants.

The valuation function π assigns to each proposition $p \in At$ a set of states; a state is included in the set if, and only if, the proposition holds in the given state.

The accessibility relations R_i connect possible states according to the epistemic status of the agent to whom the accessibility relation is associated. Two states are therefore connected if they are epistemically indistinguishable for the agent (i.e. according to what the agent knows, he can't determine which of two states is the actual one). For example, if an agent only knows the weather of Rome, he can't determine which is the actual state between the state in which it is sunny in San Francisco and the one in which it is raining in San Francisco; therefore, the two states would be connected by an accessibility relation; for the current paper, we are assuming that the accessibility relations are equivalence relations, i.e. reflexive, symmetric and transitive relations.

Finally, the trust relevance space T provides both a qualitative and a quantitative evaluation of the information that will help in determining the exact trust value an agent places in a formula. The qualitative relevance function $X_{(i,c)}$, specifies, for an evaluating agent (the trustor) and an evaluation scenario (the context), which information (under the form of propositional constants) is relevant to compute an actual trust value. The relevance weight assigning functions $\mu_{(i,c,\varphi)}$ provide a quantitative assessment of relevance of a given proposition to trust, assigning specific weights to all propositional constants that are selected by applying $X_{(i,c)}$ to φ. The additivity condition on $\mu_{(i,c,\varphi)}$ is in place to guarantee that in the best-case scenario (the one in which all relevant propositional constants do hold in the state and the agent is aware of all of them) there is full trust on the part of the trustor and moreover, it is never possible, in the system, to exceed full trust.

Once the basic components of the model are given, it is possible to extend the functions π and $\mu_{(i,c,\varphi)}$ to consider other formulas over and above the ones on which those functions are defined. This is fundamental to provide proper satisfiability conditions for the language. We will proceed to give the extensions explicitly: we will label the extension of π with π^{ext} and the extension of $\mu_{(i,c,\varphi)}$ with $\mu^{ext}_{(i,c,\varphi)}$. Intuitively, the

---

[4] It is important to stress that $\mu_{(i,c,\varphi)}$ is not a single function, but a family of functions. Therefore, each member of $\mu_{(i,c,\varphi)}$ assigns a value to the relevant atomic propositions according to the specific formula on which the function depends.

[5] With standard conditions we refer to conditions such as the principle of non-contradiction, for which a proposition and its negation can't both hold in the same state. An example of a non-standard condition is the fact that one proposition always implies a second one, therefore proscribing states in which the former holds while the latter doesn't.

function π^{ext} assigns to each formula of the language the set of states in which the formula holds, i.e. $\pi^{\text{ext}} : \mathcal{L} \to \wp(S)$. Put another way, π^{ext} returns, for each formula of the language, the states that are compatible with the truth of such formula. This means that if an agent knows a given formula (i.e. he/she thinks that the formula is true), he/she will consider possible only the states contained in the set identified by π^{ext}. For now, it is only possible to extend π to negations, conjunctions and knowledge formulas, we will then extend it also to trust formulas. The function π^{ext} is defined recursively as follows:

$$\pi^{\text{ext}}(p) = \pi(p) \tag{1}$$

$$\pi^{\text{ext}}(\neg\varphi) = S \backslash \pi^{\text{ext}}(\varphi) \tag{2}$$

here $S \backslash \pi^{\text{ext}}(\varphi)$ is the set-theoretic complement of $\pi^{\text{ext}}(\varphi)$ with respect to the whole set of possible states S.

$$\pi^{\text{ext}}(\varphi \wedge \psi) = \pi^{\text{ext}}(\varphi) \cap \pi^{\text{ext}}(\psi) \tag{3}$$

$$\pi^{\text{ext}}(K_i(\varphi)) = \{s \in S \,|\, \forall t \in S \text{ s.t. } sR_it,\, t \in \pi^{\text{ext}}(\varphi)\} \tag{4}$$

The valuation of knowledge formulas should be read intuitively as follows: to check if a given state s is a member of the valuation set of the formula $K_i(\varphi)$, take all states t of the system that are accessible from the state s; if all those states t are members of the valuation set of the formula φ, then the state s is a member of the valuation set of the formula $K_i(\varphi)$; repeat the process for every state of the system (since the set of states S is finite, the process will eventually end). Before extending π^{ext} also to trust formulas, we are required to extend the family of functions $\mu_{(i,c,\varphi)}$. To obtain such an extension, we define another family of functions $\tau_{(i,c,\varphi)}$. The $\tau_{(i,c,\varphi)}$, one for each formula φ of the language, are defined over the possible states of the system and associate with every state $s \in S$ a rational number in the interval $[0, 1]$, i.e. $\tau_{(i,c,\varphi)} : S \to [0, 1]$. The family $\tau_{(i,c,\varphi)}$ depends on a trust relevance space T and the members of such family sum up all the relevance weights of the propositional constants that hold in the state s taken as argument. This sum represents the upper bound of trust in φ for each state. Intuitively, a function $\tau_{(i,c,\varphi)}$ indicates how much trust an agent has in the formula φ in each state, if he/she is aware, in the state, of all the relevant information related to that φ (i.e. he/she knows what relevant propositions are true in that state). Another way to put it is the following: if an agent knows exactly which is the current state, $\tau_{(i,c,\varphi)}$ indicates the amount of trust he/she has in φ. Thus, $\tau_{(i,c,\varphi)}$ is an ideal measurement of trust. The function is defined explicitly as follows:

$$\tau_{(i,c,\varphi)}(s) = \sum \mu_{(i,c,\varphi)}(p), \text{ s.t. } s \in \pi^{\text{ext}}(p) \tag{5}$$

Note that since $\mu_{(i,c,\varphi)}$ is additive to 1, we are guaranteed that $\tau_{(i,c,\varphi)}$ itself never exceeds 1. We assume that if the state to which $\tau_{(i,c,\varphi)}$ is applied is not contained in any $\pi^{\text{ext}}(p)$, then $\tau_{(i,c,\varphi)}$ assigns to it the value 0:

$$\text{If there is no } \pi^{\text{ext}}(p) \text{ s.t. } s \in \pi^{\text{ext}}(p), \text{ then } \tau_{(i,c,\varphi)}(s) = 0 \tag{6}$$

We can now define $\mu^{\text{ext}}_{(i,c,\varphi)}$ for all formulas. Intuitively, the function $\mu^{\text{ext}}_{(i,c,\varphi)}$ assigns a trust relevance weight to all formulas of the language, i.e. $\mu^{\text{ext}}_{(i,c,\varphi)} : \mathcal{L} \to [0, 1]$. Note that $\mu^{\text{ext}}_{(i,c,\varphi)}$ also depends on all the elements on which $\mu^{\text{ext}}_{(i,c,\varphi)}$ depend. This allows for the possibility of taking φ both as parameter and as argument of the function. $\mu^{\text{ext}}_{(i,c,\varphi)}$ takes the sum of the relevance weights of all worlds in which a formula holds, i.e. the members of the valuation of the formula, and then divides the result for the cardinality of the valuation of the formula. It is extremely important to understand the behavior of $\mu^{\text{ext}}_{(i,c,\varphi)}$, because this function is the one properly defining trust in our formal language. The explicit definition of $\mu^{\text{ext}}_{(i,c,\varphi)}$ is the following:

$$\mu^{\text{ext}}_{i,c,\varphi}(\psi) = \left(\sum \tau_{(i,c,\varphi)}(s), \text{ s.t. } s \in \pi^{\text{ext}}(\psi) \right) / |\pi^{\text{ext}}(\psi)| \qquad (7)$$

Two remarks must be made about (7): first, it should be noted that the $\mu^{\text{ext}}_{(i,c,\varphi)}$ of a formula, again, never exceeds 1; furthermore, the reader should note that $\pi^{\text{ext}}(\psi)$ is yet to be defined for trust formulas and, therefore, the function $\mu^{\text{ext}}_{(i,c,\varphi)}$ is undefined for this typology of formulas. The reason is that, in our language to obtain the valuation of a trust formula, we need to be able to apply the function $\mu^{\text{ext}}_{(i,c,\varphi)}$ to knowledge formulas first. This should be expected, since the main intuition behind the language presented in the paper is that trust depends on the knowledge of agents.

To properly define $\mu^{\text{ext}}_{(i,c,\varphi)}$ for all formulas, we must return first to the function π^{ext} and see how this function can be fully extended to include in its domain trust formulas. To obtain the valuation π^{ext} for trust formulas, we now present a complete procedure. This procedure indicates what are the step necessary to obtain the set of states in which a given trust formula hold and a by-product of the procedure will be that of understanding how to compute the value of a trust formula in each state.

The procedure has 6 steps:

1. We start with the trust formula $\omega_i(\varphi) \geq b$ that we want to evaluate. We consider the trust relevance space T of the formula φ. Note that the set $X_{i,c}$ of any formula will only contain propositional constants and, particularly, it will not contain any occurrence of trust formulas[6].

---

[6] This is an extremely important point, since it avoids infinite regresses in the procedure and, consequently, in the evaluation process of trust formulas. If we allow arbitrary formulas in the qualitative relevance set, then an infinite regress might happen, for example, if the trust formula we are evaluating $(\omega_i(\varphi) \geq b)$ appears in the qualitative relevance set of the formula for which we are trying to determine trust (φ). In such case, when we apply the recursive procedure and try to determine the valuation of $\omega_i(\varphi) \geq b$, the same formula will appear again in the qualitative relevance set of φ, ab infinitum.

2. Given a state $s \in S$, we take the formulas ψ s.t. $s \in \pi^{\text{ext}}(K_i(\psi))$ and ψ does not contain occurrences of trust formulas (i.e. no subformula of the formula is a trust formula)[7].

3. We take the conjunction of the formulas identified in step 2 and we manipulate it to transform it in the equivalent simplified Conjunctive Normal Form (CNF), i.e. a CNF on which redundant formulas are eliminated and the annihilation and absorption law have been applied[8].

4. We compute the $\mu^{\text{ext}}_{(i,c,\varphi)}$ of the formula obtained in step 3. This is a rational number in the range $[0, 1]$. Note that, given our conditions during the procedure, we are guaranteed that $\mu^{\text{ext}}_{(i,c,\varphi)}$ is properly defined for such a formula, since there is no occurrence of trust formulas at this point.

5. We compare the value obtained in step 4 with the value b that appears in the trust formula we are evaluating. If the value is more than or equal to b, we say that $\omega_i(\varphi) \geq b$ holds in the state $s \in S$ and we therefore add it to the set $\pi^{\text{ext}}(\omega_i(\varphi) \geq b)$.

6. We return to step 2 and repeat the process for another state of the system. Note that, since the set S of states is finite, the procedure will eventually end.

When the procedure ends, the result is the valuation set of the formula $\omega_i(\varphi) \geq b$, i.e. $\pi^{\text{ext}}(\omega_i(\varphi) \geq b)$. Even if not strictly necessary for the evaluation of the formulas of our language, we also complete the extension of function $\mu^{\text{ext}}_{(i,c,\varphi)}$ to all formulas by giving the valuation function of trust formulas.

We will now provide truth-theoretical conditions for the satisfiability of a formula. Given a model M, a state $s \in S$, a context $c \in Cntx$ and a rational number b in the range $[0, 1]$, the satisfiability conditions are defined as follows:

- $(M, s, c) \vDash p$ iff $s \in \pi^{\text{ext}}(p)$;
- $(M, s, c) \vDash \neg\varphi$ iff $s \in \pi^{\text{ext}}(\neg\varphi)$;
- $(M, s, c) \vDash \varphi \wedge \psi$ iff $s \in \pi^{\text{ext}}(\varphi \wedge \psi)$;
- $(M, s, c) \vDash K_i(\varphi)$ iff $s \in \pi^{\text{ext}}(K_i(\varphi))$;
- $(M, s, c) \vDash \omega_i(\varphi) \geq b$ iff $s \in \pi^{\text{ext}}(\omega_i(\varphi) \geq b)$.

Given the above satisfiability conditions, we define four concepts of validity. A formula is *context-valid* with respect to a structure if, and only if, it is satisfied by every state of the system, once a specific context is given. A formula is *state-valid* with respect to a structure if, and only if, it is satisfied in every context, once a specific state is given. A formula is *model-valid* if, and only if, it is both *context-valid* and *state-valid*. A formula is *fully-valid* if, and only if, it is *model-valid* for all possible models. This structure is sufficient to be able to reason about knowledge and trust.

---

[7] This condition is similar in spirit to the one we impose on the qualitative relevance set. See note 3 for further explanations.

[8] Note that in our language a tautology is the neutral element for conjunction and the destructive element for disjunction, while a contradiction is the neutral element for disjunction and the destructive element for conjunction.

The above presented language is sufficient to reason about knowledge and trust and their interrelationship. The language provides a good way to compute pre-trust values and therefore can be employed as a trust-computing component of a computational trust model. We will now show how it is possible to use this language to feed the trust manipulation component of Jøsang's Subjective Logic.

4.3   From Knowledge to Trust: Pre-trust Computations

The aim of our pre-trust computation is to obtain the three distinct components of Subjective Logic's opinions. Such components are respectively, belief, disbelief and uncertainty. We will now show that obtaining those three components is straightforward in our system, once our semantical structure is given. We start by specifying the three opinion components: "agent i believes in proposition p" (symbolically $b_i(p)$) means that agent i, the trustor, believes, to a given degree, in the truth of proposition p; "agent i disbelieves in proposition p" (symbolically $d_i(p)$) means that agent i disbelieves, to a given degree, in the truth of proposition p; finally, "agent i is uncertain about proposition p" (symbolically $u_i(p)$) means that agent i does not possess any relevant information on whether to trust or not the proposition p. In our case, it is possible to connect the amount of information with the cardinality of the set attributed by π^{ext} to the simplified CNF of the known formulas. Specifically, the smaller the cardinality, the higher the amount of information possessed and viceversa.

The three components are obtained in the following way:

1. We start by considering the trust relevance space T corresponding to a given context and a given agent for the formula p.
2. Assuming the actual state is $s \in S$, we take the formulas ψ s.t. $s \in \pi^{ext}(K_i(\psi))$ and ψ does not contain occurrences of trust formulas.
3. We take the conjunction of the formulas identified in step 2 and we manipulate it to transform it in the equivalent simplified Conjunctive Normal Form (CNF). We label this formula with Φ.
4. We compute $\pi^{ext}(\Phi)$.
5. For each state $s \in \pi^{ext}(\Phi)$, compute $\tau_{(i,c,p)}(s)$.
6. Identify the maximum and the minimum value among the results of step 6.
7. $b_i(p)$ is equal to the minimum value identified; $d_i(p)$ is equal to 1 minus the maximum value identified; $u_i(p)$ is equal to the difference between the maximum and the minimum values.

The three components so defined form the basis of subjective logic's opinions and they can therefore be manipulated by Jøsang's model to obtain further trust values. We believe that augmenting subjective logic with the trust computing component that comes from the application of the interpretational structure of the language we proposed is an improvement of the original model presented by Jøsang.

4.4   Summing Up

We will explain the intuitive idea behind the semantical structure we just presented and explain why we believe this structure is able to capture formally the traditional notion of trust. We will do so by describing how each component of the system contributes to the generation of trust values.

In our language, we take propositions as pieces of information. Each proposition tells us something about the system and, doing so, it helps us in determining the state of the system. The set S of possible states includes, initially, all the possible combinations of propositional constants: this is equivalent to a setting where there is complete ignorance, i.e. the system can be in every possible state. On top of this initial setting we start constructing ideal settings. To do so we first identify which information is relevant for trust in a formula in each context (i.e. evaluation scenario): this role is fulfilled by the structure T, which takes formulas of the language and returns the relevant information for such formulas. Obviously, this step is subjective in nature and this is the reason the X set depends both on agents and contexts. Each agent might consider different information as relevant in different contexts and therefore there is a different X set for each couple (i, c). However, determining what is relevant isn't sufficient. We are dealing with a formal version of trust and this makes it necessary that trust is somehow measurable. For this reason, we have the μ function, that assigns measures to the relevant information, telling us how much each piece of information is relevant to the trust in a given proposition. Again, this measure is subjective in nature and therefore must depend both on agents and contexts. Once obtained the T structure, we can now compute trust values for ideal situations. This is the role of the τ function. What a τ function does is to take states and determine the trust value in the formula in such a state, if an agent can determine univocally that that state is the only possible one. To this extent, the value of the τ function and that of the μ^{ext} function is the same, if the formula to which μ^{ext} is applied univocally identifies the state to which τ is applied. As we said, though, this is an ideal situation and often, in the real world, agents do not possess enough information to univocally determine a state over the others. For this reason, we introduce the function μ^{ext}, which tells us how much trust must be placed into a given formula, when that formula identifies a subset of S. This is the reason μ^{ext} depends on the function π^{ext} (i.e. the function that identifies the states compatible with the information carried by a given formula). One possible critique is that we take the average of the ideal trust values of the remaining possible states and this is not justified, since we might want to take the minimum or the maximum value among the ones available. To justify our choices, we rely on the principle of sufficient reason. For the principle of sufficient reason, if an agent has no sufficient reasons for preferring a state to another, he should attribute to each state the same probability. Since we are assuming that agents can't determine which is the actual state among all the ones compatible with his/her information (if he/she could determine the actual state, we would again return to the reflections on ideal settings), he/she has no way of preferring one trust value over the others. Note that this might lead, in some scenarios, to trust a formula in a situation where there shouldn't be trust and distrusting a formula in a situation where there should be trust. We believe that this is not fully problematic, since the traditional concept of trust is open to the same issues and therefore it might be that the problem is inherently connected with trust and not specifically with our formalism. Nonetheless, it is possible to change the computation of μ^{ext} to consider optimistic and pessimistic attitudes in the part of the agent. Note, however, that this would only avoid one part of the problem of misplaced trust by enhancing the other part (e.g. an optimistic approach would avoid the possibility of not trusting when trust should be warranted, at the expense of having many more scenarios in which the agent trusts when trust shouldn't be warranted). For those reasons, at least at the theoretical level of this work, we prefer using the average.

This exhaust the intuitive description of our formal language. We will now include a concrete example, to show a practical application of our language to a real scenario.

4.5   Example

In this section we build a concrete example and show how our formal language (especially the semantical structure) helps in analyzing the example.

Assume we have 2 agents (Anne and Bob) and 2 contexts (Fixing_the_car and Preparing_dinner). Imagine we have a third agent, Charlie, Anne's father and a car mechanic. What we are trying to evaluate in this example is the trust Anne and Bob place in the proposition "Charlie will help me". We will call the agents A and B, the contexts with F and P and the proposition "Charlie will help me" with φ. Imagine the world is completely described by 4 propositional constants: p_1: Charlie has a master degree in engineering; p_2: Charlie has taken cooking classes; p_3: Charlie offers a guarantee when he repairs a car; p_4: Charlie is a meticulous person.

Given the fours propositional constants, we have 16 possible states of the world, representing all the possible combinations of the four propositions. We will label the states with the letter s, with subscripts. The initial valuation π of the propositional constants is the following: $\pi(p_1) = \{s_1, s_2, s_3, s_4, s_5, s_6, s_7, s_8\}$; $\pi(p_2) = \{s_1, s_2, s_3, s_4, s_9, s_{10}, s_{11}, s_{12}\}$; $\pi(p_3) = \{s_1, s_2, s_5, s_6, s_9, s_{10}, s_{13}, s_{14}\}$; $\pi(p_4) = \{s_1, s_3, s_5, s_7, s_9, s_{11}, s_{13}, s_{15}\}$.

The R for each agent are the following: $R_A = \{(s_1, s_3), (s_3, s_5), (s_5, s_7), (s_2, s_4), (s_4, s_6), (s_6, s_8), (s_9, s_{11}), (s_{11}, s_{13}), (s_{13}, s_{15}), (s_{15}, s_{17}), (s_{10}, s_{12}), (s_{12}, s_{14}), (s_{14}, s_{16})\}$; $R_B = \{(s_1, s_2), (s_2, s_5), (s_5, s_6), (s_6, s_9), (s_9, s_{10}), (s_{10}, s_{13}), (s_{13}, s_{14}), (s_3, s_4), (s_4, s_7), (s_7, s_8), (s_8, s_{11}), (s_{11}, s_{12}), (s_{12}, s_{15}), (s_{15}, s_{16})\}$[9].

We will now specify the trust relevance space for the three couples (A, F), (B, F) and (A, P) and the proposition φ. We start with the X sets: $X_{(A,F)}(\varphi) = \{p_4\}$; $X_{(B,F)}(\varphi) = \{p_1, p_3, p_4\}$; $X_{(A,P)}(\varphi) = \{p_2, p_4\}$.

We now apply μ : $\mu_{(A,F,\varphi)}(p_4) = 1$; $\mu_{(B,F,\varphi)}(p_1) = 0.5$, $\mu_{(B,F,\varphi)}(p_3) = 0.4$, $\mu_{(B,F,\varphi)}(p_3) = 0.4$; $\mu_{(A,P,\varphi)}(p_2) = 0.6$, $\mu_{(A,P,\varphi)}(p_4) = 0.4$.

We now have all the elements to assess how much trust an agent has in the proposition φ in each possible scenario. Let's imagine we want to evaluate the two formulas $\omega_A(\varphi) \geq 0.5$ and $\omega_B(\varphi) \geq 0.8$. We will evaluate the first formula for two contexts in the same state, i.e. the contexts Fixing_the_car and Preparing_dinner in the

---

[9] For this example, we are assuming that the R relations are equivalence relations; however, we omit the couples generated by the reflexive, symmetric and transitive closure of the relations specified in the example. The reader should consider them present.

state s_7. We will evaluate the second formula for the same context in two different states, i.e. the context Fixing_the_car in the states s_2 and s_8.

Let's try to determine first whether $(M, s_7, F) \vDash \omega_A(\varphi) \geq 0.5$. Given the structure we presented above, it is possible to derive that in every state Anne knows whether or not her father has a master degree in engineering and whether or not he is meticulous. Therefore, she knows those facts also in s_7, meaning that s_7 is contained both in the set $\pi^{ext}(K_A(p_1))$ and $\pi^{ext}(K_A(p_4))^{10}$. We therefore identified the two propositions p_1 and p_4. The simplified CNF of the conjunction of those two propositions is just their conjunction $p_1 \wedge p_4$. We now compute the $\mu^{ext}_{(A,F,\varphi)}$ function of this proposition:

- $\mu^{ext}_{(A,F,\varphi)}(p_1 \wedge p_4) = \left(\sum \tau_{(A,F,\varphi)}(s), \text{ s.t. } s \in \pi^{ext}(p_1 \wedge p_4) \right) / |\pi^{ext}(p_1 \wedge p_4)|$

Note that $\pi^{ext}(p_1 \wedge p_4) = \{s_1, s_3, s_5, s_7\}$ and therefore $|\pi^{ext}(p_1 \wedge p_4)| = 4$. The $\tau_{(A,F,\varphi)}(s)$ are: $\tau_{(A,F,\varphi)}(s_1) = \tau_{(A,F,\varphi)}(s_3) = \tau_{(A,F,\varphi)}(s_5) = \tau_{(A,F,\varphi)}(s_7) = 1$. This means that $\mu^{ext}_{(i,c,\varphi)}(p_1 \wedge p_4) = 4/4 = 1$. Therefore, $(M, s_7, F) \vDash \omega_A(\varphi) \geq 0.5$ holds. This should be expected, because for Anne to trust that Charlie will help in the context of fixing the car the only relevant fact is that Charlie is meticulous. Since she knows in s_7 that Charlie is meticulous, she has full trust in the fact that Charlie will help.

Let's now check $(M, s_7, P) \vDash \omega_A(\varphi) \geq 0.5$. Given that the knowledge Anne has in state s_7 is not affected by the context, part of the procedure is like the previous one, we therefore must compute:

- $\mu^{ext}_{(A,P,\varphi)}(p_1 \wedge p_4) = \left(\sum \tau_{(A,P,\varphi)}(s), \text{ s.t. } s \in \pi^{ext}(p_1 \wedge p_4) \right) / |\pi^{ext}(p_1 \wedge p_4)|$

The $\tau_{(A,P,\varphi)}(s)$ are: $\tau_{(A,P,\varphi)}(s_1) = \tau_{(A,P,\varphi)}(s_3) = 1$ and $\tau_{(A,P,\varphi)}(s_5) = \tau_{(A,P,\varphi)}(s_7) = 0.4$. This means that $\mu^{ext}_{(A,P,\varphi)}(p_1 \wedge p_4) = 2.8/4 = 0.7$. Therefore $(M, s_7, P) \vDash \omega_A(\varphi) \geq 0.5$ holds. This result should be expected, because for Anne to trust that Charlie will help in the context of preparing the dinner the relevant facts are that Charlie tool cooking classes and that he is meticulous. Since Anne knows that Charlie is meticulous, her trust increases slightly above the indifference threshold. We now check both $(M, s_2, F) \vDash \omega_B(\varphi) \geq 0.8$ and $(M, s_8, F) \vDash \omega_B(\varphi) \geq 0.8$.

Note that in our structure, Bob knows whether p_3 holds each state (i.e. if it holds he knows it and if it doesn't hold he knows the negation of it). Again, we will only compute the values, without giving discursive explanations. The reader can check autonomously that the computations are correct. Since p_3 holds in s_2 Bob knows it. We will therefore compute $\mu^{ext}_{(B,F,\varphi)}(p_3) = \left(\sum \tau_{(B,F,\varphi)}(s), \text{s.t. } s \in \pi^{ext}(p_3) \right) / |\pi^{ext}(p_3)| = 0.7$.

---

[10] Strictly speaking she also knows the conjunction of the two facts, but we won't consider it, since the conjunction of the two propositions corresponding to our fact would be eliminated during the simplification of the CNF.

Therefore $(M, s_2, F) \vDash \omega_B(\varphi) \geq 0.8$ does not hold. Finally, in s_2, p_3 does not hold and therefore Bob knows $\neg p_3$. We then must compute $\mu^{ext}_{(B,F,\varphi)}(\neg p_3) = (\sum \tau_{(B,F,\varphi)}(s)$, s.t. $s \in \pi^{ext}(\neg p_3))/|\pi^{ext}(\neg p_3)| = 0.3$. Therefore, $(M, s_8, F) \vDash \omega_B(\varphi) \geq 0.8$ does not hold.

When evaluating the $\omega_A(\varphi)$ opinion in the context fixing_the_car and assuming the actual state is s_7, we first determine Φ, which is $p_1 \wedge p_4$. We then compute $\pi^{ext}(p_1 \wedge p_4)$, which is $\{s_1, s_3, s_5, s_7\}$. The next step is that of computing the various $\tau_{(A,F,\varphi)}(s)$, i.e. $\tau_{(A,F,\varphi)}(s_1) = \tau_{(A,F,\varphi)}(s_3) = \tau_{(A,F,\varphi)}(s_5) = \tau_{(A,F,\varphi)}(s_7) = 1$. We can finally determine the various components of the opinion $\omega_A(\varphi)$: $b_A(\varphi)$ is equal to 1, i.e. the minimum among the values of the $\tau_{(A,F,\varphi)}(s)$; $d_A(\varphi)$ is equal to 0, i.e. 1 minus the maximum among the values of the $\tau_{(A,F,\varphi)}(s)$; $u_A(\varphi)$ is equal to 0, i.e. the maximum minus the minimum. We now give the result for the other three examples we examined, without providing the computations. For the opinion $\omega_A(\varphi)$ in the context preparing_dinner and assuming the actual state is s_7: $b_A(\varphi)$ is equal to 0.4; $d_A(\varphi)$ is equal to 0; $u_A(\varphi)$ is equal to 0.6. For the opinion $\omega_B(\varphi)$ in the context fixing_the_car and assuming the actual state is s_2: $b_B(\varphi)$ is equal to 0.4; $d_B(\varphi)$ is equal to 0; $u_B(\varphi)$ is equal to 0.6. For the opinion $\omega_B(\varphi)$ in the context fixing_the_car and assuming the actual state is s_8: $b_B(\varphi)$ is equal to 0; $d_B(\varphi)$ is equal to 0.4; $u_B(\varphi)$ is equal to 0.6. This last computation exhausts our example.

5   Conclusion and Future Work

In this paper, we first discussed the distinction between the trust computing component and the trust manipulation component of computational trust models. We then showed that classical computational models are often focused only on one of the two components. Specifically, we showed that Audun Jøsang's Subjective Logic, one of the best-suited models for trust manipulation, is lacking a proper trust computing mechanism. To overcome this downside of Subjective Logic, we proposed a logical language that can be employed to reason about knowledge and trust. Moreover, we showed how to move from our logical language to Subjective Logic. This, we believe, is an improvement for Subjective Logic and, generally, for the understanding of computational trust. In the future, the aim is to provide an actual implementation of the language and the ideas contained in this paper. Moreover, we believe it is possible to provide dynamic version of the language, which can take into consideration flow of information and time-related concerns. A final and interesting research direction is that of comparing the language proposed with others formal structures employed to represent uncertainty.

References

1. Arrow, K.: Gifts and exchanges. Philos. Public Aff. **1**(4), 343–362 (1972)
2. Artz, D., Gil, Y.: A survey of trust in computer science and the semantic web. Web Semant.: Sci. Serv. Agents World Wide Web **5**, 58–71 (2007)

3. Cho, J.H., Chan, K., Adali, S.: A survey on trust modeling. ACM Comput. Surv. **48**(2), 1–40 (2015)
4. Fagin, R., Halpern, J.Y.: Reasoning about knowledge and probabilities. J. ACM **41**(2), 340–367 (1994)
5. Grandison, T., Sloman, M.: A survey of trust in internet applications. IEEE Commun. Surv. Tutor. **3**(4), 2–16 (2000)
6. Halpern, J.Y.: Reasoning about Uncertainty. The MIT Press, Cambridge (2003)
7. Hughes, G., Cresswell, M.: A New Introduction to Modal Logic. Routledge, Abingdon (1996)
8. Jøsang, A., Knapskog, S.J.: A Metric for trusted systems. In: Reinhard, P. (ed.) Proceedings of the 15th IFIP/SEC International Information Security Conference, IFIP (1998)
9. Jøsang, A.: Trust and reputation systems. In: Aldini, A., Gorrieri, R. (eds.) FOSAD 2006-2007. LNCS, vol. 4677, pp. 209–245. Springer, Heidelberg (2007). https://doi.org/10.1007/978-3-540-74810-6_8
10. Jøsang, A., Ismail, R., Boyd, C.: A survey of trust and reputation systems for online service provision. Decis. Support Syst. **43**(2), 618–644 (2007)
11. Jøsang, A.: Subjective Logic. Springer, Cham (2016). https://doi.org/10.1007/978-3-319-42337-1
12. Kripke, S.: Semantical considerations on modal logic. Acta Philosophica Fennica **16**, 83–94 (1963)
13. Marsh, S.: Formalising trust as a computational concept. Ph.D. thesis (1994)
14. Mui, L., Halberstadt, A., Mohtashemi, M.: Notions of reputation in multi-agent systems: a review. In: Proceedings of AAMAS 2002, pp. 280–287 (2002)
15. Pinyol, I., Sabat-Mir, J.: Computational trust and reputation models for open multi-agent systems: a review. Artif. Intell. Rev. **40**, 1–25 (2013)
16. Pinyol, I., Sabater-Mir, J., Dellunde, P., Paolucci, M.: Reputation-based decisions for logic-based cognitive agents. Auton. Agents Multi-Agents Syst. **24**(1), 175–216 (2012)
17. Putnam, R.: Making Democracy Work. Princeton University Press, Princeton (1993)
18. Rasmusson, L., Jansson, S.: Simulated social control for secure internet commerce. In: NSPW Proceedings of the 1996 Workshop on New Security Paradigms, pp. 18–25 (1996)
19. Sabater-Mir, J., Sierra, C.: Review on computational trust and reputation models. Artif. Intell. Rev. **24**(1), 33–60 (2005)
20. Tagliaferri, M., Aldini, A.: A Taxonomy of Computational Models for Trust Computing in Decision-Making Procedures (forthcoming)
21. Yu, B., Singh, M.P.: Detecting deception in reputation management. In: Proceedings of AAMAS 2003, pp. 73–80 (2003)

Towards a Computational Model
of Information Trust

Tosan Atele-Williams[(⊠)] and Stephen Marsh

Faculty of Business and Information Technology,
University of Ontario Institute of Technology, Oshawa, ON L1H 7K4, Canada
{ftosan.atele-williamsg, fstephen.marshg}@uoit.ca

Abstract. Information has been an essential element in the development of collaborative and cooperative models. From decision making to the attainment of varying goals, people have been relatively adept at making judgments about the trustworthiness of information, based on knowledge and understanding of a normative model of information. However, recent events, for example in elections and referenda, have stretched the ability of people to be able to measure the veracity and trustworthiness of information online. The result has been an erosion of trust in information online, its source, its value and the ability to objectively determine the trustworthiness of a piece of information, a situation made more complex by social networks, since social media have made the spread of (potentially untrustworthy) information easier and faster. We believe that this exacerbated the need for assisting humans in their judgment of the trustworthiness of information. We have begun working on a social cognitive construct: a trust model for information. In this paper we outline the problems and the beginnings of our trust model and highlight future work.

Keywords: Computational trust · Information trustworthiness
Decision support · Trust properties · Information value

1 Introduction

Information does not exist in a vacuum, how it is perceived and used is influenced by a number of social, cultural, and historical factors. Moreover, information is of no value or worth the investment of time and money, for example in making business decisions, or decisions in elections, if it is not relevant, does not have the right amount of detail, cannot be easily stored in a way that it can be accessed effortlessly, or easily understood by the end user [13, 17, 29].

But we have a problem, not necessarily new but increasingly challenging, since we are seeing 'information only subsistence,' which focuses on an issue by simply offering more information [8]. This has resulted in a need to share information, even when the validity of the information cannot be vouched for, or when the person sharing such information does not believe it. Regardless of the validity of information, people still go ahead to share because it serves a narrative, a means to manipulate rather than to inform, as a source of social influence [4]. This situation is aptly demonstrated by the recent political and business climate in the west that have added relatively new lexicons like "fake news" and "alternate facts."

The consequences of deceptive and misleading information can be far-reaching for governments, citizens, business institutions, data professionals, and designers. It can create an atmosphere of mistrust, distrust, confusion or panic. It can influence decisions and damage reputations. Information agents or brokers may find it difficult to use information, or seek alternate and less reliable sources of information because of the air of uncertainty. The result is an erosion of trust in information and potentially a fragmentation of, and polarisation of, societies.

What is needed is a way to measure the veracity and trustworthiness of information. As a first step, we propose an information trustworthiness model based on computational trust [16].

The paper is organized as follows; in Sect. 2 we examine related work, before presenting our proposed model in Sect. 3, and worked examples in Sect. 4. We conclude with limitations, and ongoing and future work in Sect. 5.

2 Background

2.1 Information is Social

Information and by extension misinformation has a social undertone, because it is seen as an observation of individuals or groups formed through cultural and social observance, as Tuominen and Savolainen put it "a communicative construct produced in a social context" [33]. To understand what construe information, it is imperative to explore information behavior in a social context; that is conversations among a social group that such individuals or groups use as an index to construct some semblance of reality [8]. People by nature are drawn to misinformation and tend to share such information even if the belief in it is nonexistent, partly due to the promise it holds as well as due to any psychological predetermination. As social beings we adopt a collective approach to order, collaboration, cooperation and knowledge [8, 13, 29]. Hence the need to look at the social side of trust in tackling the social undertone associated with misinformation.

2.2 So, Why Use Trust?

Technological advances have made communication seamless, connectivity and information sharing an essential part in the proper functioning of many systems. Technology trends require openness and interaction between systems, which are continuously increasing in number, complexity, and functionality, giving rise to management, privacy and security challenges [15].

Trust management has evolved over the years, with some computational trust models focusing on different application and propagation areas. Computational trust and its related associations have drawn from social, cultural, psychological and many more aspects of relationships, trying to model the best in these relationships computationally. Trust as a computational concept is essential in understanding the thought process about choice, options and decision-making process in human-computer inter-actions, especially in situations where there is a measure of risk [16].

Privacy and security are at the vanguard of many information systems, compromise and abuse of these systems bring about distrust. Trust research extends over a wide range of concepts and computational environments; focusing not just on trust for-malization and management but also trust siblings like mistrust, distrust, regret, and forgiveness [16].

2.3   Information Behavior and Trustworthiness

Various information behavior models, suggest a normative model of information as true, complete, valid, able to be relied on as being correct and from a trusted source [13]. For instance, census data from Statistics Canada (or indeed any governmental statistics agency) can be regarded as valid and from a trusted source which can be reliably used for planning purposes [27, 34]. As an economic tool, such data should carry more trusted weight than information sourced from a third party sources or social media platforms [6, 13, 27, 29]. Other normative information behavior prescribes trusted information as timely in the sense that it should be from a precise time period [13, 29], for example when analyzing census data for planning and developmental purposes it is paramount to look at current or the most recent figures.

Other factors that add value and trustworthiness to information include its accuracy, consistency, and completeness. Despite the best effort of information scientists on the nature of information [13], and work on information literacy behaviour, misinformation and disinformation still permeate social networks [13, 17], social media platforms like Twitter and Facebook have helped in the spread of inaccurate information [13, 29].

Computational Trust [11, 21] is important in understanding the thought process with regard to choice, options and decision-making process in human and computer interactions, especially in situations where there is a measure of risk [12, 16] (which is all trusting decisions [22].

There is the need for an inclusive and context-aware information literacy behavior [13]. Our goal is to incorporate the characteristics of information: reliability, validity and importance, into a trust model. Depending on the context, the model will also factor in the reputation of a source, the value of the information, its provenance, and cues to credibility and deception. The aim is to enable agents to make judgments and situational decisions about the trustworthiness of information.

2.4   Significant Prior Research

The problem of trust in information has been around for a while, in many prehistoric civilizations, the information conveyed by an emissary of an authoritative figure on behalf of the principal could be trusted completely because the outcome of any omission will leave the conveyor at the mercy of his principal. Such measures well beyond borderline extreme, in contemporary times worries about information trust, quality and problems associated with information are usually addressed by offering more, an approach which supports the narrow focus design paradigm. This situation has only been exasperated with the speed of information outpacing the speed of human travel, having a life of its own, constantly evolving with technology, now at a stage where the information lifecycle is becoming independent of human intervention [8].

People are adept at dealing with conflicting information to an extent based on judgment derived from knowledge, either based on what was known before or most current knowledge [17]. Humans are social. The information DNA architecture takes advantage of this trait by integrating social knowledge into distinct parts of information. To link the divide between what is possible with information by agents and people, by doing this it gives importantly added meta-information. Marshs InfoDNA paradigm follows the information as an agent paradigm of ACORN [19], where agents deliver data, as well as meta-data relating to the information. The infoDNA architecture added a society's estimate of trustworthiness, to an extent. A dual trust rating and a ranking system geared towards people, arguably first of its kind that is interested in the value of information based on feedback even if it is contrary, using the trust to foster collaboration and cooperation [17, 19].

Other approaches have looked at the problem of misinformation, computationally regarding trust. Much research on information trustworthiness does not put a great deal of emphasis on the factors that lead to hoaxes, misinformation and deviant information behavior. Silverman [29] looks at the problem from a journalistic perspective – the role not just news organizations but also technology companies play in driving the narrative in a bid to boost traffic and social engagement – as well as possible solutions. Among the 'bad practices' identified are the tendency of news sites to offer little or no rudimentary proof to claims but rather engaging in relating such claims to other media reports which in turn did the same thing. Hence the origin of an assertion which they transmitted is buried amongst chains of links, and on proper examination, the original story might have originated from an unreliable entity or social media platform, whose initial goal might have been to gain traction (clicks) by getting mainstream media outlets to refer to their content.

Information, as technology, does not occur in a vacuum, and is often socially influenced or constructed. [8] highlights this and proposes the adoption of not just balance and perspective in making sense of information but breath and vision, to feature the cues that lie at the periphery of information.

The world of information is complex. This is exacerbated by technology. Clues and cues, adopted to restrain deviant information behavior, are insufficient and lacking in some instances. Hence the need for a trust model that not only considers the physical environment which precipitates information but also incorporates the social context of information.

3   Information Trust: The Model

It is widely assumed that technology, and to a greater extent information occurs in a vacuum [8], often overlooked is the milieu like tradition, environment, and judgment embedded in information, which acts as an important variable in the successful dissemination of information [8, 13, 29]. The success of information as an integral part of social relations can be attributed to the wide-ranging support of strong communities and institutions [8]. The human factor in the alternate information behavior can be overstated, and squarely blamed for the recent upsurge in the misinformation paradigm, but often overlooked is the in-escapable intertwining of information, and individuals as part of a copious social matrix. Often enough, proffered solutions often assume that the best approach in tackling misinformation, and by extension the challenges of technology lies in more technology, using Moores approach [8, 10], forgetting or deliberately neglecting the need for balance, perspective, and clarity by failing to look beyond the edge, at context, social cognition, and resources [8, 13, 29]. That is focusing on the pebble and the ripples but not on the lake [8].

The social context [8] surrounding information is important in understanding information behavior, and should be factored in the design process of information technology solutions. But this is often neglected, the environment, human habits, and judgment play an important role in the successful acceptance of a solution. Information is inevitably embedded in social relation, information does not work unless supported by viable communities and institutions [8, 13, 29]. In as much as the support, the social context of information provide in forming a shared disposition, a community of trust, there has to be a way for information agents to express their comfort level based on trust ratings. Here lies the concept of Device Comfort, earlier introduced in this work, a paradigm that aims to empower the device to better reason about its owner, the environment [18, 20, 30], by factoring context and relationship. The focus here is on the device - human relationship, which is aptly represented in device customization from selecting screen savers to ring tones and even the use of various third party applications. The methodology builds on an augmented notion of trust between the device and its owner, to better enable the device to advice, encourage as well as potentially act for its owner in everyday interactions [16–18, 20, 30], from information management, in this context how to relate trust rating on a piece of information by expressing comfort or discomfort, to personal security.

Theres usually a larger context to the different information delivery methods, as social beings we look for meaning, and understanding in clues and cues, gaining insight from unexpressed meaning [8]. Unfortunately, contemporary Information paradigm is so narrowly construed, leaving us with very little insight, hence the need for an information model that takes into consideration, the resources at the edge of information, not limited to physical constraints. But embraces the social context of information, the institutions, and communities that shape human societies, and our understanding of the challenges of deviant information behaviour, not getting caught up in the noise, hence avoid addressing the problem by simply offering more [8, 10, 13, 29].

In using mathematical notations to formalize a social cognitive construct like information behavior, and trust. we trying to allow for tractability, capturing the cost and benefit of information - the value to an organization or entity, acting or making decisions based on misleading data, which is considerable taking account of the effort and resources that go into such decisions be it emotional and or physical, which could be simulated mathematically. Since a lot of resources go into the decision-making process, great opportunities are expected, and when they are not met, the cost is high. Hence trust is affected [3, 16, 21]. Our approach is not new; there has been a long-established tradition of trying to formalize social concepts using mathematical methods, Birkhoff [7, 26] an eminent mathematician in the early 19th century formalized aesthetic measure, which has been built upon by Bense and Moles [5, 24] in developing information theoretic aesthetic. Scha and Bod took it further by postulating the integration of other ideas from psychology, and computational linguistics to form a foundation for the development of robust formal models [28].

Our model builds on elements of Birkhoffs model [7], drawing parallels by integrating aspects of context, author, and observer, in this case recipient, in information. We see value of information stemming from a symmetry of the elements that helps shape information, the social context - environment, tradition, communities, background, history, shared knowledge, social resources, institutions. These items are not irrelevant; they provide valuable balance and perspective - the amount of content; deviant information behavior is often characterized by lack of crucial information, and a combination of information characteristics, importance, and utility [6, 8, 13, 29]. Information does not happen spontaneously on its own; it is a process of selection and reflection, it is made and shaped by some factors, a weaving and shaping process in concordance with space and priorities, in the context of the medium of its audience, which requires harmony [23]. This harmony (H), is introduced as the quotient of the amount, and quality of content and it's order (o), and the number of element that help shape the information, or complexity. Drawing parallel with Birkhoffs equation [7].

Information wants to be free, having a life of its own and used for a variety of purposes, from a business decision to storage and retrieval. It is paramount that the information is useful and helps in the decision making process. Society has the challenge of speaking for itself about its credibility as do information, resulting to Moores law in the face of distrust, more information in an attempt to address this problem. Ironic since we do not add to our standing by averring to our trustworthiness, but we let our character speak for us. The qualities of good information should speak for itself [8, 13, 29]. X represents the characteristics of useful information, currency, relevance, authority, accuracy, and purpose. A measure often referred to as the CRAAP test developed by librarians at CSU for evaluating web resources [1]. Description of these characteristics is in order, to highlight their importance.

- Currency: places value on the timeliness of the information, when it was published, updates or revisions. If there are links or references to the information, their credential, and significance like shares, likes, repost in the case of social media platforms. These chains add context, details to the story or information.
- Relevance: Relates the information to the recipient needs, it relays the intended audience, the significance of the information to the recipient topic of interest or questions. Is the level of information suitable for needs? Is the source reliable and compared to other sources is there confidence in its use?
- Authority: looks at the information source, the author or publisher, their reputation and credentials, any affiliations, qualifications, contact information an if there exist any revelation about author or source.
- Accuracy: Deals with the correctness of the information content, evidence supporting it, reviews, references. Where it comes from, and independent corroboration either from an independent source or personal knowledge. Any obvious biases and tone and structure of the content.

– Purpose: Looks at why the information exists, its justification: to inform, teach, persuade. Are its intentions obvious, objective? An opinion? Fact, or propaganda? And are there biases based on a worldview, political leaning, institutional or personal view.

Each characteristic is scored on a scale of $[-1, +1]$, -1 distrust, $+1$ trust. Each information object is graded on a trust continuum, with the average signifying the trust rating. While many of the CRAAP elements were designed with online media in mind, they hold true for a cross-section of information media.

Knowledge is an important parameter in the decision-making process, its not enough to know how, but to know when to apply what is known. We introduce the quantity Knowledge (K), which is a combination of tacit and explicit knowledge.

$K = (Kt + Ke)$. Ke explicit knowledge, the knowledge that could be drawn upon is not enough, but when to use this knowledge Kt is equally essential. Value is further enhanced with a combination of these two knowledge domains. The thinking is not to treat knowledge as a collection of discrete parts, but a mosaic made up of a blend of different elements all contributing to create the image [9, 25, 32].

Knowledge flows with ease in an ecology - a community of shared interest-it produces a synergy of collective wisdom and experience, a narrative of a sort, a sequential presentation of causes, effects, and events. Individuals and groups give different forms of narratives, a scientist in experiments, researchers in their research, an economist in models, all an important aspect of learning and education [2, 8] with the aim of delivering information and principles which apply to different situations, times and places. It is not the common narrative per se that brings people together to form an ecology of collaborative information sharing, but collective interpretation, a basis for elucidation. Herein we introduce a network of shared interest, an Ecology (E) in the model. A knowledge base of representatives insights, collective pool of knowledge and insight which allows the sharing of knowledge. The concept of a world view of related information, that is consistent and around the same topic [2, 8]. Here in, it is worthy to note that Knowledge resides less in its structures but in people [8] and it is harder to isolate, unlike information, learning like knowledge is much more than information, or search and retrieval. As exemplified, when expertise is lost. We learn by repetition and practice shapes assimilation, hence the need to pull from a collaborative pool of learning and knowledge not to simply get information but to allow to allow for sagacity and use the information to predicate divergent information behavior.

$E = h + v$ Cluster or Ecology (E) comprises of horizontal view (h) and a vertical view (v), the horizontal view (h), a community of practice draws on the collective pool of knowledge from a community or an ecology of complementary practice. Bound by proximity, similar ethics, and culture but inhibit the flow of knowledge outside the cluster. To address this pitfall, we combine it with a vertical view of clusters that are not bound to these communities by geography or ethics or by a shared practice to allow them to share knowledge, which might have been bound within these structures by processes. The goal is to capture interchange required to preserve these resilient and informal relations needed to allow the flow of knowledge. Lastly, time factor (t) is introduced to preserve and deliver information across space and time. It is vital since information structures society and trends dazzle which lexicons like fake news or information currently do, in order not lose sight of what is essential and preserve its value for reuse. It also frames the way information is presented and much more, giving context to how we read, and interpret, were to read, meaning and importance.

For simplicity, a metric that takes in values [−1, 1] is used. Where −1 represents trust in the negative, or no confidence, distrust. 0 depicts a state of uncertainty or ignorance, not enough information to decide to trust an information object and +1 a point in the continuum where we have enough to trust.

To estimate the value of Information, we have:

$$V(i) = 1/n[(\sum_{x=1}^{n} X) + I + U]H$$

The $(\sum_{x=1}^{n} X)$, emphasizes the characteristic of information (a + b + c ... n), which include, currency, relevance, authority, accuracy and purpose. The value of the Importance and Utility in context is added to the Information Characteristics. For balance and perspective the H factor, elements that help in molding information is factored in as a product.

Reputation, $(R) = \left[\frac{s + \delta L}{K}\right] E$, with δL signifying captured changes as a result of links the information has passed through.

Trust in Information T(i) is then seen as a quotient of the cumulative of the product of Value and reputation with time, for fixity or immutability.

$$T(i) = \frac{V + R}{T}$$

4 Worked Example

Scenario. In this section, the model is put through a use case example taking into consideration context, environment, applications and possibly "personalities" of agents, this vital considering in a cooperative, collaborative and decision-making processes, a lot of factors come into play.

Alice and Bob are high-frequency traders, they both have agents that help manage their busy lives, including personal and professional matters. Alices and bobs agent belong to the same trusted circle. Bob is away on a remote retreat somewhere in the Amazon. Alices agent comes across an unverified report suggesting a product lunch in one of the upcoming tech companies is about to be canceled due to a security flaw in their groundbreaking. Alices agent does not have the mechanism to verify the viability of this report and passes the information to Bobs since they both belong to the same trusted cycle, and Bob has an interest in this company. Bobs agent acts on this information and sells short, hoping to avert any loss from the expected gloom, which turns out to be false, company Xs stocks rebound and Bobs portfolio is left at a loss. Bs (Bob) agent gets hold of Bob and explains the situation, which leaves a bitter taste. The cost could be more if some other agent in the cycle decides to let this information out in the open, which could potentially have broader economic reverberations. The trust rating for As (Alice) agent is reduced, and the need to upgrade the information trustworthiness mechanisms of both agents is realized. Agent A could have avoided this scenario if its value assigned to information was based on a social aware trust model, using an objective state of information, its source, reputation, behavior and the social context surrounding it.

We have two agents A and B, after receiving the information A will require more insight before deciding to act, the trust threshold to respond positively or negatively depends on some factors; the importance and the utility attached to this scenario, which will be considerably high based on the cost-benefit ratio. It is safe to say the benefit and importance attributed to information directly affects the pressure to act, in a different context say agent A passes information regarding ongoing sales of a required household item available at a particular outlet; agent B can decide not to purchase this item from the proposed store. Though the item may be needed and the value placed on this information is high considering all available parameters, the importance in this context does not require the agent to act. In this context, B's threshold is high; A has provided information without content, hence factoring all the elements connected to the model, the metric attributed to $V(i)$ will be low. The only components that work in her favor is being a member of A's trusted cycle. Though δL presently her reputation may be high based on previous behavior, there is little content regarding the information either from A, or other similar links represented by L.

Because of this lack of content, the value attributed to $X = (\sum_{x=1}^{n} X)$, - elements constituting the quality of information like justification, purpose-, will be low, invariably having a negative impact on Harmony (H) factor = o/c because of lack of balance and perspective. Depending on circumstances the weights attributed to some elements varies, B might decide to revise its threshold to invest based on positive metrics assigned to the cluster $(E = h + v)$, and knowledge $(K = ke + kt)$ values. Because it has tried to glean insight from experience and looking at ideas drawn from a collective pool of insight within B's trusted cycle, while not neglecting related communities who might share joint membership or agents who interact and are linked together by complementary practice but separated proximity, ethics and probably culture. Agent A might adjust its threshold based on its updated knowledge of the situation.

4.1   Mathematical Analysis

I and U play an essential part in trust decisions, and they are a measure of the cost, benefit, and risk ratio involved in a decision and varies depending on context. Agents could adjust their decision based on their value, though trust might be low, the risk of not acting could be high. For simplicity, we have chosen the values $[-1, +1]$. For the first scenario $T(i) = V + R/t$ for Alice and Bob, to calculate trust in the information, we first look at the values for the characteristics of information (Table 1):

Table 1. Notations and value

Description	Representation	Value
Importance	I	0.4
Utility	U	0.8
Information source(s)	S	0.6
Traversed links	δL	0
Order	O	−0.1
Complexity	C	−0.2
Horizontal view	h	0.2
Vertical view	v	−0.1
Explicit K	ke	0
Tacit K	kt	0
Currency	x_1	−0.1
Relevance	x_2	0.3
Authority	x_3	0.2
Accuracy	x_4	−0.1
Purpose	x_5	−0.1

$$X = 1/n(\sum_{x=1}^{n} X) = (x_1 + x_2 + \cdots x_n)/n \tag{1}$$
$$x = (-0.1 + 0.3 + 0.2 - 1 - 0.1)/5 = 0.04$$

$$H = O/C \tag{2}$$
$$H = -0.1/-0.2 = 0.5$$

$$V(i) = 1/n[(\sum_{x=1}^{n} X) + I + U]H \tag{3}$$
$$V(i) = [0.04 + 0.4 + 0.8]0.5 = 1.24$$

$$E = h + v \ldots (4) \tag{4}$$
$$E = 0.2 - 0.1 = 0.1$$

$$K = Ke + Kt \tag{5}$$
$$K = 0$$

$$R = \left[\frac{s + \delta L}{K}\right]E \tag{6}$$
$$R = [(0.6 + 0)/0]0.1 = 0.06$$
$$T(i) = 1.24 + 0.06/1 = 1.3$$

Time (t) is constant. Considering the values of I and U are higher than the trust value in the information, and taking into consideration its lack of content, Bob's agent, will be better off ignoring the information from Alice's agent. We have aimed for simplicity in our model to aid in understanding and make it easy to relate to, in a bid to help people think more, have a second thought, before sharing information.

5   Future Work

The concept of trust and information is not novel; there have been several studies on the idea of reliability in information, and it's source cutting across disciplines [4, 6, 8, 13, 29]. Recent events in social, economic and political spheres have given rise to continued interest, proposing solutions ranging from experiments, technical solutions, policy, law, journalism, and other social sciences endeavors. The inference drawn so far from this work suggest technology tends to outpace policy and law [14, 31], a trend not different in the fake news situation. There are various arguments on where the focus should lie in tackling the challenges raised [13, 14, 29, 31]. In the course of our research these questions, whether policy, law, or technology should be at the forefront in efforts to address the situation, has also come to our attention.

This work presents an overview of the trustworthiness of information, and it's source from different perspectives, thereby proposing an information trust model based on a multidisciplinary approach. We believe there is no one perfect solution, and a multidisciplinary approach encompasses the strengths of the various disciplines. The model in this work is based on such an idea, presenting information trustworthiness as a social phenomenon, which requires a social context in tackling some of the ills associated with deviant information behavior.

Our approach is not novel in that, we set about trust in information, in a computational environment, its propagation and representation [16, 21]. With the focus on enabling agents to interact with, or factor in the "noise", and background of information, in making decisions with trust playing an integral role. Further refining is needed to incorporate decision support and justification trough comfort, AMI interface, information sharing, and management systems.

So far we have focused on the following areas:

- The nature of information
- Information Characteristics
- Information ecosystem and anomalies (Misinformation, disinformation, rumors, fake news...)
- History and Dynamics of rumors
- Trust
- Device Comfort
- Information Theory.

In the course of our research, we have looked at the nature of information, information behavior, and literacy. The inference drawn indicates the problem of misinformation, disinformation, hoaxes, rumors, and unverified claims is a persistent challenge which appeals to our social cognitive existence, and there are few signs it will just go away by highlighting the problem. It is a narrative that requires a multi-disciplinary approach because the contributing factors as discussed earlier are not only driven by technology alone, but there are sociological, psychological and economic undertone [13, 29]. Modelling these factors is not straightforward because of the consideration of inherent biases among groups in society. Another particularly exciting challenge is the communication of information trust metrics to nonartificial agents in a way that will enhance value and trustworthiness of information an essential property in an increasingly interconnected and data-driven world. The next phase of the research is the model implementation, using game theory; a well-recognized methodology often employed in many scientific as well as social science disciplines for performing research, experimenting with agents and enhancing strategies. The simplicity of the Optional Prisoner Dilemma games makes it an ideal tool estimating the value, cost, and benefit of the model as well as measure the performance of the agents, and the society. Finally, model evaluation to gauge performance, compare results and explore the possibilities of incorporating the model into agents in an IOT and media platforms, towards the goal achieving a verifiable and trustworthy information model.

References

1. Is this source or information good?
2. Agrafiotis, I., Creese, S., Goldsmith, M., Nurse, J.: Information trustworthiness as a solution to the misinformation problems in social media (2015)
3. Bacharach, M., Gambetta, D.: Trust in signs. Trust Soc. **2**, 148–184 (2001)
4. Barber, K.S., Kim, J.: Belief revision process based on trust: agents evaluating reputation of information sources. In: Falcone, R., Singh, M., Tan, Y.-H. (eds.) Trust in Cyber-societies. LNCS (LNAI), vol. 2246, pp. 73–82. Springer, Heidelberg (2001). https://doi.org/10.1007/3-540-45547-7_5
5. Bense, M.: Introduction to theoretical aesthetics fundamentals and application in text theory (1969)
6. Berger, J., Milkman, K.L.: What makes online content viral? J. Mark. Res. **49**(2), 192–205 (2012)
7. Birkho, G.D.: Aesthetic Measure, vol. 38. Harvard University Press, Cambridge (1933)
8. Brown, J.S., Duguid, P.: The Social Life of Information: Updated, with a New Preface. Harvard Business Review Press, Watertown (2017)
9. Carayannis, E.G., Campbell, D.F.J.: Knowledge Creation, Diffusion, and Use in Innovation Networks and Knowledge Clusters: A Comparative Systems Approach Across the United States, Europe, and Asia. Greenwood Publishing Group, Westport (2006)
10. Coffman, K.G., Odlyzko, A.M.: Internet growth: is there a "Moores Law" for data traffic? In: Abello, J., Pardalos, P.M., Resende, M.G.C. (eds.) Handbook of Massive Data Sets, pp. 47–93. Springer, Boston (2002). https://doi.org/10.1007/978-1-4615-0005-6_3
11. Dwyer, N., Marsh, S.: Self-trust, self-efficacy and digital learning. In: Steghöfer, J.-P., Esfandiari, B. (eds.) IFIPTM 2017. IAICT, vol. 505, pp. 110–115. Springer, Cham (2017). https://doi.org/10.1007/978-3-319-59171-1_9
12. Golbeck, J. (ed.): Computing with Social Trust. HumanComputer Interaction Series. Springer, London (2009). https://doi.org/10.1007/978-1-84800-356-9
13. Karlova, N.A., Fisher, K.E.: Plz RT: a social diffusion model of misinformation and disinformation for understanding human information behaviour. Inf. Res. **18**(1), 1–17 (2013)

14. Koops, B.J., Prins, C., Hijmans, H.: ICT Law and Internationalisation: A Survey of Government Views. Kluwer Law International, Alphen aan den Rijn (2000)
15. Liu, X., Datta, A., Lim, E.P.: Computational Trust Models and Machine Learning. CRC Press, Boca Raton (2014)
16. Marsh, S., Briggs, P.: Examining trust, forgiveness and regret as computational concepts. In: Golbeck, J. (ed.) Computing with Social Trust. Springer, London (2009). https://doi.org/10.1007/978-1-84800-356-9_2
17. Marsh, S.: InfoDNA (version 2) agent enhanced trustworthy distributed information. In: PST, pp. 149–153 (2004)
18. Marsh, S., Briggs, P., El-Khatib, K., Esfandiari, B., Stewart, J.A.: Defining and investigating device comfort. J. Inf. Process. 19(7), 231–252 (2011)
19. Marsh, S., Ghorbani, A.A., Bhavsar, V.C.: The ACORN multi-agent system. Int. J. Web Intell. Agent Syst. 1(1), 65–86 (2003)
20. Marsh, S., Wang, Y., Noel, S., Robart, L., Stewart, J.: Device comfort for mobile health information accessibility. In: 2013 Eleventh Annual Conference on Privacy, Security and Trust, pp. 377–380. IEEE, July 2013
21. Marsh, S.P.: Formalising trust as a computational concept (1994)
22. McKnight, D.H., Chervany, N.L.: The meanings of trust (1996)
23. McLuhan, M., Fiore, Q.: The medium is the message. New York 123, 126–128 (1967)
24. Moles, A.: Information Theory and Esthetic Perception. University of Illinois Press, Urbana (1968)
25. Pinch, S., Henry, N., Jenkins, M., Tallman, S.: From industrial districts to knowledge clusters: a model of knowledge dissemination and competitive advantage in industrial agglomerations. J. Econ. Geogr. 3(4), 373–388 (2003)
26. Rigau, J., Feixas, M., Sbert, M.: Informational aesthetics measures. IEEE Comput. Graph. Appl. 28(2) (2008)
27. Ross, N.A., Wolfson, M.C., Dunn, J.R., Berthelot, J.-M., Kaplan, G.A., Lynch, J.W.: Relation between income inequality and mortality in Canada and in the United States: cross sectional assessment using census data and vital statistics. BMJ 320(7239), 898–902 (2000)
28. Scha, R., Bod, R.: Computationele esthetica. Informatie en Informatiebeleid 11(1), 54–63 (1993)
29. Silverman, C.: Lies, damn lies and viral content (2015)
30. Storer, T., Marsh, S., Noel, S., Esfandiari, B., El-Khatib, K., Briggs, P., Renaud, K., Bicakci, M.V.: Encouraging second thoughts: obstructive user interfaces for raising security awareness. In: 2013 Eleventh Annual Conference on Privacy, Security and Trust, pp. 366–368. IEEE, July 2013
31. Takach, G.S.: Computer Law. Irwin Law, Toronto (1997). (Reviewed by D. Johnston, Chair of the Highway Advisory Council (1998). CB LJ., 30:314)
32. Tallman, S., Jenkins, M., Henry, N., Pinch, S.: Knowledge, clusters, and competitive advantage. Acad. Manag. Rev. 29(2), 258–271 (2004)
33. Tuominen, K., Savolainen, R.: A social constructionist approach to the study of information use as discursive action. In: Proceedings of an International Conference on Information Seeking in Context, pp. 81–96. Taylor Graham Publishing (1997)
34. Witkowski, M., Artikis, A., Pitt, J.: Experiments in building experiential trust in a society of objective-trust based agents. In: Falcone, R., Singh, M., Tan, Y.-H. (eds.) Trust in Cyber-societies. LNCS (LNAI), vol. 2246, pp. 111–132. Springer, Heidelberg (2001). https://doi.org/10.1007/3-540-45547-7_7

Public Privacy and Brick Houses Made of Glass

Stephen Marsh[1]([✉]), Ada Diaconescu[2], David Evans[3], Tracy Ann Kosa[4],
Peter R. Lewis[3], and Sheikh Mahbub Habib[5]

[1] University of Ontario Institute of Technology, Oshawa, Canada
stephen.marsh@uoit.ca
[2] Telecom ParisTech, Paris, France
ada.diaconescu@telecom-paristech.fr
[3] Aston University, Birmingham, UK
{d.j.evans,p.lewis}@aston.ac.uk
[4] Stanford University, Stanford, USA
[5] Technische Universitaet Darmstadt, Darmstadt, Germany
sheikh@tk.tu-darmstadt.de

Abstract. In this work in progress paper, we present a description of a new view of privacy in public, examining how it is possible to ascertain the privacy levels of individuals in context and in groups, and different ways of visualising these Public Privacy levels. We examine how awareness of one's Public Privacy may have an impact on behaviour and privacy protection in general, and propose future work to examine the concept in more detail.

1 Introduction: Privacy and the Privacy Paradox

Most people shut their curtains, and don't live in glass houses – at least, not without the aforementioned curtains. We might like to watch Big Brother, but that doesn't mean we all want to participate. And yet, for various reasons – time, efficiency, lack of choice, lack of awareness, and so on – we intentionally sometimes and unintentionally oftentimes leak or broadcast information to whomever might be listening. Certainly, it's possible to adjust our privacy settings on social networks and so forth, but in reality, the tools we use and the environments, such as smart cities, we exist in, thrive on sharing data around and, crucially, *about* us.

A perhaps more pernicious problem is that the people around us may well be either unaware or uncaring about the effects that their own behaviour with respect to privacy and sharing can have on the world around them. These effects can range from inadvertently exposing private information that can be used against others to deliberately sharing pictures or movies that include others in them, with similar potentially bad results.

Privacy, then, is a social problem, with social ramifications, even when there are people who care about it.

© IFIP International Federation for Information Processing 2018
Published by Springer International Publishing AG 2018. All Rights Reserved
N. Gal-Oz and P. R. Lewis (Eds.): IFIPTM 2018, IFIP AICT 528, pp. 137–148, 2018.
https://doi.org/10.1007/978-3-319-95276-5_10

The effect is that whilst we might believe that we live in brick houses with the curtains closed, those around us may well just be turning those houses into glass, and no amount of effort on our part can put curtains around the whole building.

Recent work on Privacy Awareness [5] acknowledges that, whilst information is 'out there', it is no bad thing to help people become more aware of both where it is and how it might be linked to other extant information to provide fuller pictures of people (profiles).

Other work in the realm of Device Comfort [2,3,11] focuses on the ability of the very technology that causes the problems to ameliorate these problems when the technology's sensing (and reasoning) capabilities are combined with human social norms as expressive tools. That is, trust, comfort, regret and so forth are useful tools to assist people to better *understand* the way in which their actions, in context, can effect, reveal, or damage their security and privacy postures.

In this paper we propose *Public Privacy* as a toolset to address some of the problems associated with the social aspect of privacy, within the context of Privacy Awareness. In the Public Privacy paradigm, we assign privacy states [6] to group spaces, which we intend will have the result of making more public the privacy sensitivity and actions of the members of that space. Additionally, we conjecture that it then can provide suggestions, tools, and societal pressure in different contexts to raise more awareness and potentially initiate or support behaviour changes.

2   On Privacy, Problems, What Has Come Before, and What It Means

This work falls generally in the arena of Privacy Awareness, although with a significant twist. It is also firmly situated in boundary regulation (see for example [7]), but again from the point of view of physical space. In this, the work is directly related to Altman's [1] dialectical conception of privacy in which boundaries are used and negotiated. In our work, the boundaries may already be established but the individual in the shared space can choose to participate or indeed exercise forms of control, thus, the idea of Public Privacy support in technical tools allows for boundary and personal privacy negotiations in a sociotechnical setting. It is similar to Petronio's communication privacy management [14] theory in that it allows this negotiation but the toolset is paramount here. Boundary regulation is also a feature in [7] but once again, the emphasis is on online networks, where physical social boundaries may not be present.

As well, [13] discusses privacy in a sociotechnical situation, in particular unpacking how privacy is determined and considered in sociotechnical systems, but uses Altman's theory to examine how privacy could be understood in digital systems.

Here, we are bringing the model back to shared social spaces in which technology is an adjunct: people do stuff with it, but it's not the technology that enables people to work together, in the sense, for example, of [15] and other similar CSCW-related work. That is, we don't care so much about the stuff, we care about providing awareness so that people can negotiate boundaries together so that they can work and play together in comfort and safety. To achieve this effectively, it might also be necessary or beneficial to design the awareness-raising and mediation system such that it explicitly considers the awareness of users, and its role in promoting and being sensitive to it, in decision-making. Thus, we draw on and further develop work on computational self-awareness, particularly, public self-awareness [8] and social self-awareness [4].

Further, the work in this paper differs from related work in that, whilst it certainly is about 'digital' privacy, its concern in things like boundary regulation is in the physical world. As well, whilst in some cases examining the content of messages is used to determine if privacy is about to be violated or harmed, such invasive methods are not necessary here: we are focused on behaviour in society where privacy is respected, not the online aspect of how much information is 'out there' in social networking sites, for instance. The end results may be similar: increased awareness, better management of information and boundaries, and so forth, but the methods differ.

3 Public Privacy

In the Public Privacy paradigm, we focus on privacy as two[1] things in a group space (a meeting room or a coffee shop, for example):

- A goal to be worked towards (at some level[2] or state)
- A state, in a space, in context, that can be expressed to everyone in that space.

In the former, everyone in the space has their own 'desired' level of privacy and sets up their own devices or behaviours toward that end, whilst when in a space that desire may conflict with that of the space itself, and so the latter expresses how the two (individual and public) may differ, with attendant possibilities we will discuss further below.

Following Kosa [6] we place privacy as an abstract notion within a set of states, or levels, which are shown in Table 1.

One option is to represent these states as numbers, since we need to be able to compute the state of a space from that of the people in it (amongst other things). The most basic aspect of public privacy is that any space within which there are people (and devices) has an inherent privacy state, which we can compute and display in a public form (and forum). For simplicity, we have added numbers to the states here. The higher the number, the less 'private' the state.

---

[1] It can definitely be both at the same time.

[2] Kosa [6] talks about privacy states, which we think is a reasonable way to express the level of privacy at a suitable concrete level, and has the associate benefits of understandability and computational tractability of sorts. In this work we interchange level and state because different states obviously have different achievable privacy, or levels of privacy.

Table 1. Privacy states (from [6]) with Sn (State Number) added

Sn	State	Physical self	Digital self	Example
1	Private	Existence is unknown	Existence is unknown	A child hiding
2	Unidentified	Existence is known	No identity data	A shadow
3	Masked	Existence is visible	Limited identity information	An organ donor
4	De-identified	Existence is unconnected	Non-specific identity information is known	Unpublished identity information is available about a patient in a study
5	Pseudonymous	Existence is connected but accuracy is unreliable	Identity data could apply to multiple persons	Reference to common characteristic, e.g., female person such as Jane Doe
6	Confidential	Existence is connected but limited distribution	Limited identity data available to defined person in a certain role	A doctor with access to her patient's records
7	Identified	Existence is connected with unlimited distribution	Data is available with few or no controls	Social networking sites
8	Public	Existence is completely transparent	Digital self is livecast, online and cross-referenced	Babies or small children (limited control)

3.1 Formalising the Public Privacy State of a Space

The Public Privacy State of a shared space S is a function of:

- the Context, Con of the space;
- The Privacy States of the individuals in that space (including that of their devices present), which we represent as $P_S = f(\rho_{S,1} \ldots \rho_{S,i})$, where i is the number of individuals in the space, and $\rho_{S,n}$ is the Privacy State of individual n);
- Privacy 'requirements' of the individuals in the space, which we represent as $\Lambda(S, \text{Con}) = f(\lambda_1(S, \text{Con}_1) \ldots \lambda_i(S, \text{Con}_i))$ with again $\lambda_n(S, \text{Con}_n)$ that of individual n.

Each of these can be calculated, as we discuss in this section. Note also that the Public Privacy state of a space is highly dynamic based on the individuals joining and leaving the space, as well as its context (which may change from time to time). For example, a meeting room may be in a context of *Business Meeting* or *Legal Meeting* or *Interview*, *Presentation*, and so forth, whilst a coffee shop would usually be in the context of *Public Space*, but this also might change in different circumstances.

In this instance, we consider that the Context of a space is obtainable in some fashion, and that the Context is the same for every individual in the space (see Sect. 4 for a further discussion on this).

The Context of a Space. Spaces are used to *do* things. What this means is that it should be possible to determine from moment to moment what the space is purposed for. This context may change over time for a given space, or the space may indeed be designed in a way that ensures its context (but even that may be subverted: the best parties usually end up in the kitchen).

For our purposes, it is sufficient to split the context in a relatively rough manner. The contexts available to a space are:

1. Private-Meeting: A closed session where attendees are potentially invited.
2. Public-Meeting: A session where anyone can potentially attend, but which is dedicated to a specific task. For example, a workshop or conference session.
3. Public-Static: A space, such as coffee shop, restaurant, where people can enter and leave freely. Can also include spaces like supermarkets, malls, etc.
4. Public-Transient: Slightly different from Public-Static, the Public-Transient space is one which is used as a place through which people move. For instance, railway stations, airports, etc.

Without getting into a discussion about the language of architecture, consider that in general some spaces are designed to facilitate certain contexts. Lecture theatres are designed for Private-Meeting or Public-Meeting contexts, for example. However, it's entirely possible to convert such spaces into, say, Public-Static spaces at need. Other spaces, such as railway stations, are much more difficult to turn into certain contexts.

Contexts advise behaviours. Each context has specific expectations associated with it. These are expectations of behaviour (how many people are talking at once, how many listening, who pays attention to whom, and so on) which naturally impact privacy expectations for the space. It's unusual to for instance tweet about what is happening in a private meeting, but more acceptable from a public meeting such as a workshop or a press briefing.

Regardless of space, to an extent, the context is what is important to us here since it sets its own expectations. We would suggest that the privacy expectations of the contexts listed above decrease as we move down the list.

It is a matter for future work to determine different other contexts and sub-contexts for spaces.

Private Privacy: The Privacy State of Individuals. In the functions above, $P_S = f(\rho_{S,1} \ldots \rho_{S,i})$, where i is the number of individuals in the space. How do we determine ρ for any individual, since this is perhaps the most important aspect of the problem?

Ironically, more information is of great utility in this computation, but let us gloss over that for a moment. What is needed is something akin to that calculated by the Device Comfort methodology [11]. However, in and of itself, that may prove troublesome, since by its nature the concept can be seen as privacy-invasive on an individual level.

In general, then, there are two different aspects here:

- What is currently being done by the individual;
- The history of the individual.

In the first, we can determine something about what is being done at a specific time by observation, which includes the status of their devices, if any: what apps are being run, what OS is installed, and what patches, for instance, all of which have an impact on the potential for the device to be used in privacy invasive ways either intentionally or not.

For the purpose of the current work, we can place a value on the status and action being taken. More privacy problematic behaviours (such as texting or using social networks, using cameras and so forth) have a higher 'risk' score.

For the latter, we use Kosa's states [6]. To determine the state of the individual based on past history, privacy awareness tools can be used (see e.g. [5]).

At this point, we can combine the two aspects to make sense of the person in the moment. What usually takes precedence in a situation where there is a conflict (wildly differing states for each of the two aspects) is perhaps a matter of preference, although we would argue, much as with trust, that historical behaviour is a relatively good predictor of what immediate future behaviour might be. This being the case, the history aspect is usually the one which is chosen. That said, conflict should be acknowledged and so here we can put certainty values on the result.

How Do You Feel About Privacy? The second aspect of the computation is what we call a privacy 'requirement' for an individual. In this, we agree with [12] with regard to context. In order to compute the context and requirements within it, we need but ask. [2,3], used a simple method to determine both how people felt about sharing information, to whom, and also what for, with the context being indicated by purpose of information sharing. Another method for eliciting what we might call privacy stance is in using labels such as those identified in [16]. Note that there are also certainly tools for expressing privacy preferences, including for instance the Platform for Privacy Preferences, and these can also be used readily in the calculations here, but the approach taken is one that aims explicitly for simplicity (we just don't need to make it harder than it has to be [10]).

3.2   Expressing the Privacy State of a Space

Ironically, the privacy state of a public space is both a public and a private notion. As a public measure, it is available to everyone in that space to show

how everyone's tools and behaviours come together. As a private measure it is affected by the context of the individual as well as the space. In both it becomes a warning, a guide, a queryable service, a political statement, and a suggestion, as we will see.

Publicly... A public expression of the privacy level of a space is just that: something of which everyone in the space is or can be aware. We can express it on a shared display in the space (in our development we are using Apple TV apps on shared screens as well as other shared devices - the key here is that the displays are social and shared). The value can be expressed in different ways. Currently we are working with colours, icons and numbers, potentially in combinations. We are planning experiments to determine how these may be received and understood, and as such they are in flux.

Privately... We envisage that Public Privacy in private (sic) can be a tool for the individual in various ways.

To begin with, the expression of the privacy state of the space can be shown on a personal screen (when, for instance a public shared screen is unavailable or unsuitable for a particular use, for reasons of different ability or requirements) and thus available to all.

Moreover, Public Privacy, when discussed in the context of the individual, becomes even more interesting because it can be changed from that individual point of view. To illustrate what is meant here, consider a brief scenario, where there is a group of strangers in a shared space (say an ice cream parlour), and a new individual (our subject) enters. The privacy state of the space, as calculated, is shown to the subject. For the sake of argument, let's say the state is one that reflects a low level of privacy, a low level of privacy awareness, and a social (in this space) acceptance of sharing as 'okay.' Our subject is, for one reason or another, a person who values their privacy in special ways - pictures aren't okay, for example - and the calculated level of privacy is, in ordinary circumstances, outside of their comfort zone (to put it another way, it's way too low to make them happy). However, in context, that makes sense. Plus, no-one in the place is taking pictures (they're all enjoying the ice cream instead) and so the privacy level in that context is reasonable for our subject because their own context is specific to pictures. That given, two things may happen: firstly, the contextual privacy view of public privacy state is that it is reasonable, but also the public view of privacy within other individual devices is updated to reflect that context. In other words, the 'requirement' that pictures of other people in the space not be taken can be added to individual contexts whilst the public view may not change (unless cameras start to be pulled out).

3.3 And, How Do We Use This Knowledge?

Public Privacy is a Privacy Awareness tool, but it is one with something of a twist: we are not concerned here with online privacy *per se*. We are concerned with potential actions in a contextual physical space, populated by others, with their own goals, devices and behaviours, that may have an impact on an individual's privacy. This could be because personal or shared information might be further shared outside the group, inadvertently or purposely, images could be shared, videos might be taken, and so on. Each of these things has an impact on our privacy state as individuals. Public Privacy makes the potential for these things known and to some extent we hope understood.

This has different possibilities in various contexts, some of which we illustrate here. Before entering into these discussions, a few words about trust and associated topics are in order. As we note in e.g., [9], trusting behaviour is the answer to two questions: how much does one have, and how much does one need (and the obvious happy result is that if you have more than you need, you can say you 'trust' the other). In many circumstances, we can use artificial tools, often legal or social ones, to increase one or decrease the other, with the effect that some form of relationship might be entered into. We will use this observation in some of our scenarios below.[3]

- In a situation where for example business discussions around a private topic might be ongoing, the members of the discussion have different options, including Non-Disclosure Agreements (NDAs). These tools have an effect on trust that may or may not be beneficial - the act of asking people to sign a legal document may decrease the amount of trust needed, but it doesn't always match the circumstances, and it doesn't always encourage others to feel comfortable in a given situation. However, if everyone was made aware of the Privacy state of the room in which the meeting was taking place, based in this instance on past history and potentially trust in the members of the discussion, a level of comfort may be achieved which allows discussion to take place without the legal niceties.
- Related to this, there may be circumstances where the members of the discussion simply don't want to have their names on such documents, and the ability to discuss privacy in such a space, aided by the Public Privacy model at the time, is a powerful social aid.
- Entering into a space with a specific Privacy State allows a participant in that space to better protect themselves with more technical privacy and security tools as needed, since forewarned may well be forearmed in this case. The Privacy State is additionally valuable for tools that use Device Comfort [11] since it provides information that such tools can use to automatically adjust their security posture.
- The members of a space which has a certain Privacy State can observe changes to that state as others enter ands behave accordingly (for more discussion of this, see below in Sect. 5).

---

[3] We are sure other scenarios exist!

4   Current Status, Future Work

Public Privacy is a work in progress. We are currently implementing the system using both 'public' and 'personal' tools, include Apple TV apps to be able to display the Public Privacy state on shared screens, iOS and Android apps for displays on personal screens, and a cloud-based approach which allows a multi-platform approach with web browsers.

More importantly, we are using the scenarios above, amongst others, to design experiments that will illustrate the usefulness of the idea in physical spaces and for different cultures.

There are some other limitations to the model thus far. For instance, the context of an individual in a space might not in fact be that of the space itself. It is entirely possible to be a small group of people within a coffee shop having an at least semi-private meeting. In this case, the contexts of the individuals in the meeting form something of a *sub* space for that group of people. In other words, some spaces can encompass multiple contexts at the same time. We leave the calculation and implementation of this for future work.

A further avenue to explore in operationalising Public Privacy, could be to represent privacy states not as scalar values but as logical propositions. An individual's *logical privacy labels* could represent different expectations and preferences over their behaviour and the behaviour of others. Then, upon entering a social situation, the individuals' propositions could be combined, and 'solved' for contradictions, which are then used to prompt or otherwise raise awareness with the respective users. For example, the person walking into the ice cream parlour can realise that their own propositions (expectations and preferences) are entirely compatible with the prevailing ones (no contradictions), or can be prompted that there are existing contradictions, that the group may wish to address. We therefore arrive at a form of computer-mediated privacy agreement. In general, one advantage of this approach would be to enable us to capture, reason about, and attempt to reconcile a more qualitative, multi-dimensional trust, and hence facilitate decisions based on a richer set of human expectations.

Having operationalized the Privacy State of a space we introduce the idea of Alliance States as a method for aligning and codifying individual and group's intentions in space.

This is extended from the idea of a designed alliance, a social ritual where a group of people designs the emotional atmosphere it wants in a space and context, and, its conflict protocol, how the group wants to be when things get difficult between them. We propose that we codify a 'digital-alliance' between systems.

Often, what comes up in the emotional-atmosphere part of the Designed Alliance are concepts like - trust, safety, and confidentiality. Building on Kosas Privacy States, we create Alliance States, that codify levels of trust, safety and confidentiality. Alliance States could have some quantitate assessment of their quality - i.e. a system could have trust as 2/10, i.e. low, safety 8/10 i.e. high, confidentiality 1/10 i.e. low or unknown.

A 'public' space would quantify its Alliance State, and a 'personal' device entering a pubic space could read the Alliance State of the space. Systems could negotiate Alliance States, before sharing information. The comparison between a Public and Private alliance states and only interact when certain criteria are met between the Alliance States - and, if they are different, then the systems work to adjust their states so that there is a match before they interact.

5   Discussion: How Societies, or at Least Outlooks, Might Change

One goal of Public Privacy is to change minds. How might this work? It is our view that much social change happens because society makes it clear that the change is needed. This can happen in various ways - laws, for example, are in many cases expressions of societal expectations, and social pressures are also expressed in interpersonal encounters. Consider, for instance, smoking or driving under the influence. In many cases, since expectations change, so have the ways in which people are influenced in these circumstances (people in many countries don't smoke in different spaces not just because the law says they can't (the law says nothing about smoking in your home), but also because often if they try they are told (asked!) not to). And so, slowly, opinions and potentially behaviours change.

Right now, we have a privacy problem. It is seen, at least in part, as a socially acceptable thing to take pictures, and share them and other information, regardless of other peoples' opinion, wants or needs. The potential effects are not always beneficial, as has been pointed out elsewhere, including in initiatives such as the Privacy Awareness Weeks of several territories.

In part, we see Public Privacy as a tool to raise social awareness within individuals of the consequences of their actions. If one enters a space and sees the privacy state change, and behaviours change with it, this is the first step to this awareness. A second step comes when people take the public awareness tool and use it to *ask* others for change - instead of 'please don't smoke' the refrain becomes 'I'd rather you didn't tweet about this' or 'please don't share that picture', or even 'you really shouldn't be sharing all this stufff.' Once privacy instead of profligate sharing becomes an acceptable stance, we believe[4] change can happen.

6   Conclusions

Public Privacy is a tool, an awareness raising mechanism, and a method of social change (and as such a political stance). It uses a technical methodology to estimate the Privacy State of shared spaces - that is, spaces where more than one person and their devices are present. This shared Public Privacy State can be used in a variety of different ways:

---

[4] Granted, perhaps naïvely!.

- To help people in the space better protect their own information (or private selves) either automatically or with human input;
- To raise awareness of issues to help change behaviours or at least educate, and not least
- To help people get things done in contextual shared spaces.

The Public Privacy tool is currently being developed based on the technical discussion in this paper. Experiments for both correct behaviour and acceptance are planned.

References

1. Altman, I.: Environment and Social Behaviour. Brooks/Cole Publishing, Pacific Grove (1976)
2. Behrooz, S.: Trust-based framework for information sharing in health care. Master's thesis, University of Ontario Institute of Technology (2016)
3. Behrooz, S., Marsh, S.: A trust-based framework for information sharing between mobile health care applications. In: Habib, S., Vassileva, J., Mauw, S., Mühlhäuser, M. (eds.) IFIPTM 2016. IAICT, vol. 473, pp. 79–95. Springer, Cham (2016). https://doi.org/10.1007/978-3-319-41354-9_6
4. Bellman, K., Botev, J., Hildmann, H., Lewis, P.R., Marsh, S., Pitt, J., Scholtes, I., Tomforde, S.: Socially-sensitive systems design: exploring social potential. IEEE Technol. Soc. Mag. **36**(3), 72–80 (2017)
5. Fischer-Hübner, S., Angulo, J., Karegar, F., Pulls, T.: Transparency, privacy and trust – technology for tracking and controlling my data disclosures: does this work? In: Habib, S., Vassileva, J., Mauw, S., Mühlhäuser, M. (eds.) IFIPTM 2016. IAICT, vol. 473, pp. 3–14. Springer, Cham (2016). https://doi.org/10.1007/978-3-319-41354-9_1
6. Kosa, T.A.: Towards measuring privacy. Ph.D. thesis, University of Ontario Institute of Technology (2015)
7. Lampinen, A., Lehtinen, V., Lehmuskallio, A., Tamminen, S.: We're in it together: interpersonal management of disclosure in social network services. In: Proceedings of the SIGCHI Conference on Human Factors in Computing Systems, CHI 2011, pp. 3217–3226. ACM, New York (2011)
8. Lewis, P.R., Platzner, M., Rinner, B., Torresen, J., Yao, X. (eds.) Self-Aware Computing Systems: An Engineering Approach. Springer, Heidelberg (2016). https://doi.org/10.1007/978-3-319-39675-0
9. Marsh, S.: Formalising trust as a computational concept. Ph.D. thesis, Department of Computing Science, University of Stirling (1994). http://www.stephenmarsh.ca/Files/pubs/Trust-thesis.pdf
10. Marsh, S., Basu, A., Dwyer, N.: Rendering unto Cæsar the things that are Cæsar's: complex trust and human understanding. In: Dimitrakos, T., Moona, R., Patel, D., McKnight, D.H. (eds.) Proceedings IFIPTM 2012: Trust Management VI, Surat India. AICT, vol. 374, pp. 191–200. Springer, Heidelberg (2012). https://doi.org/10.1007/978-3-642-29852-3_13
11. Marsh, S., Briggs, P., El-Khatib, K., Esfandiari, B., Stewart, J.A.: Defining and investigating device comfort. J. Inf. Process. **19**, 231–252 (2011)
12. Nissenbaum, H.: Privacy in Context. Stanford Law Books, Redwood City (2009)

13. Palen, L., Dourish, P.: Unpacking "privacy" for a networked world. In: Proceedings of the SIGCHI Conference on Human Factors in Computing Systems, CHI 2003, pp. 129–136. ACM, New York (2003)
14. Petronio, S., Durham, W.T.: Communication privacy management theory. In: Baxter, L.A., Braithwaite, D.O. (eds.) Engaging Theories in Interpersonal Communication: Multiple Perspectives, pp. 309–322. Sage, Thousand Oaks (2008)
15. Salimian, M.H., Reilly, D., Brooks, S., MacKay, B.: Physical-digital privacy interfaces for mixed reality collaboration: an exploratory study. In: Proceedings of the 2016 ACM International Conference on Interactive Surfaces and Spaces, ISS 2016, pp. 261–270. ACM, New York (2016)
16. Wisniewski, P.J., Knijnenburg, B.P., Lipford, H.R.: Making privacy personal. Int. J. Hum.-Comput. Stud. **98**(C), 95–108 (2017)

The Social Construction of "Shared Reality" in Socio-Technical Systems

Kristina Milanović(✉) and Jeremy Pitt

Imperial College London, Exhibition Road, London SW7 2BT, UK
{kristina.milanovic08,j.pitt}@imperial.ac.uk

Abstract. As the size, complexity and ubiquity of socio-technical systems increases, there is a concomitant expectation that humans will have to establish and maintain long-lasting 'relationships' with many types of digital artefact: for example with humanoid robots, driverless cars or software agents running on 'smart' devices. Rather than being limited to one-off interactions, these relationships will continue over longer time frames, correspondingly increasing the likelihood of errors occurring from numerous causes. When digital errors occur, often complete human mistrust and distrust is the outcome. The situation is exacerbated when the computer can make no act of reparation and no avenue of forgiveness is open to the human. In the pursuit of designing long-lasting socio-technical systems that are fit-for purpose, this position paper reviews past work in relevant social concepts and, based on the sociological theory of social constructivism, proposes a new approach to the joint human-computer construction of a "shared reality".

Keywords: Trust · Forgiveness · Norms · Socio-technical systems
Social constructivism

1 Introduction

In a world of increasing interconnectivity, socio-technical systems, which are defined as any multi-agent system where there is a mix of human and computational agents working together to achieve a common goal [1], are becoming increasingly prevalent in every day life. Agents can be human, physical computers (including robots) or digital (software). The digital or computational agents can be working with the human agents in any combination. This includes facilitating human-human communication/interaction via smart devices, a number of computational agents and human overseers such as a network of driverless cars or smart meters being monitored remotely and a human agent interacting with multiple digital agents in the form of digital home assistants in a smart home.

The 'relationships' here between the various computer, digital and human agents will not be one-off interactions, such as the purchase of an item on the internet with the help of a digital shopping assistant, where a single task needs

© IFIP International Federation for Information Processing 2018
Published by Springer International Publishing AG 2018. All Rights Reserved
N. Gal-Oz and P. R. Lewis (Eds.): IFIPTM 2018, IFIP AICT 528, pp. 149–159, 2018.
https://doi.org/10.1007/978-3-319-95276-5_11

to be accomplished and the agents either do not interact again, or do not interact until a long time period has passed. They will need to be maintained through multiple interactions in order for the goal of the system to be achieved. Continuing with the preceding examples, this includes optimal energy pricing for neighbouring households in a smart energy network, safe operation of smart cars in traffic flow and efficient operation of devices within the home.

Like any device these computational and digital agents inherently have some level of error and humans occasionally make mistakes too. As the longevity and size of the system of agents increases, the likelihood of errors occurring also increases. This can be in the form of system faults or misunderstandings between the human and computational or digital agents. Since the agents in the system will need to interact over long time periods, agents will need to have mechanisms to enable these relationships to last over time in the face of these errors. One method of doing this is to apply concepts of trust and forgiveness which have enabled human society to maintain long-term relationships, to systems which include computational and digital agents. In order to use socio-cognitive theories, where trust is a mental state of a social cognitive agent (i.e.: an agent with goals and beliefs) [2], the non-human agents need to interact with the human agents in a manner akin to other humans.

In this position paper past work in computational models of trust, forgiveness, norms and values is reviewed. A new theory for how these concepts can be combined together addressing and how, specifically, the effect of system errors may be mitigated is proposed. The paper is split into two parts, the first section covers previous work on human relationship building mechanisms in computing while the second section outlines how the proposed new theory fits within this already established framework.

Pulling from sociology to apply utilise the trust and forgiveness mechanisms already well established in human society, the new proposal follows on from the theory of social constructivism. An artificial form of social constructivism is suggested which can be applied to socio-technical systems to created a "shared reality" based on shared experiences [3], in this case shared social norms and values. This will allow for the creation of more fit-for purpose models of socio-technical systems which should enable long-lasting 'relationships' between agents.

2   Social Concepts in Socio-Technical Systems

Socio-technical systems in particular are useful for their ability to model inherent human attributes which can have profound effects on the system. Concepts of trust, forgiveness and social norms have long been studied in sociology, psychology and evolutionary biology and their adaptation into the field of computing, to analyse network behaviour, has an advantage over simpler Game theoretic approaches as they are better able to take into account human attributes such as deception. Game theoretic models tend to simplify observed behaviour in order to model it, for example, they reduce the trust decision to a probability [2]. This form of modelling is insufficient when attempting to create a model that accurately represents human decision making, thus socio-cognitive approaches are better suited to it. This section covers previous work key human traits which may be applied to socio-technical systems to assist with modelling and analysis and how they fit into the overarching framework of social capital.

2.1 Social Capital

Social capital encompasses concepts which are established as part of institutions of individuals such as trust, forgiveness and social norms and values. It was defined by Ostrom as "*an attribute of individuals that enhances their ability to solve collective action problems*" [4], where a collective action problem is one that requires the cooperation of multiple individuals to achieve a shared goal. Trust is the method, or "glue", which enables the solving of these collective action problems [5].

Social capital can broken down into three general categories: trustworthiness, social networks and institutions. The definition of institutions here is synonymous with the most generic of social norm definitions. According to Ostrom, institutions outline allowed and forbidden actions, or "*collections of conventional rules by which people mutually agree to regulate their behaviour*" [6]. Recent developments in the field have include the theory of electronic social capital [7], and upholds the idea that it can be used to solve collective action problems in a digital environment [6].

Trust. The concept of trust has been defined many times. From sociology, one often cited definition is that trust "*is the subjective probability by which an individual, A, expects that another individual, B, performs a given action on which its welfare depends*" [8]. Another definition, also from sociology, is that trust can be used to reduce complexity of social interactions [9]. Applying this definition to computational networks can used to simplify behaviour in complex networks and it is this aspect in particular that is relevant to the proposal outlined here.

Computational trust has been a topic of increasing research over the past two decades since one of the first models was presented by Marsh in 1994 [10]. Marsh proposed that incorporating trust into artificial intelligence would assist with social decision making by the agents. Following on from this, one of the earliest cognitive trust models [11] was outlined by Castelfranchi and Falcone [2] in 2001. They proposed that only agents with goals and beliefs, in other words cognitive agents, are capable of trust. Another proposal from Jones in 2002 suggested that trust has two components, a belief in another agent and the expectation that the agent would perform some action, or attain a desired goal [12].

Since then there have been a proliferation of trust models in multiple fields [13] where the concept of trust has which have been expanded to include extended definitions and situations. Concepts of mistrust (misplaced trust), distrust (how much the truster believes the trustee will consciously work against them in a given situation) and untrust (the truster does not believe the trustee will work with them in a given situation) have been postulated [14]. Specific models for use in areas as diverse as ecommerce systems [15] and multi-agent systems have developed. These models have been compared and contrasted at length in recent years [11,16]. Overall the key concept these models have in common is that there is a need for systems which mimic human social interactions, so that the agents are able to make decisions about who and how much to trust, without external input from human operators.

In terms of modelling, in large socio-technical systems, cognitive models of trust have advantages over more simplistic game theoretic models [11]. Game theory tends to assume that all system agents are rational, however this may not be the case in a system involving humans, where the agents may deceive each other or act in a (seemingly) irrational manner [1]. Models such as those proposed by Axelrod in the 1980's [17], are less able to represent the complicated relationships between agents when humans are involved.

This is particularly relevant when errors in the system occur. Errors can come in broadly two categories, malfunctions and mistakes. Malfunctions are where there is a bug in the code or a physical breakdown of some sort leading to agents not behaving in the expected manner. Mistakes occur where there has been some kind of misunderstanding between what the agent was expected to do and what they actually did. One way this has been addressed previously is through reputation mechanisms which aggregate past behaviour over time [18] or trusted third parties which act as a guarantee of trustworthiness [19]. The most visible application of this is in ecommerce, for example the in the form of ratings and reviews for online buyers and sellers.

Forgiveness. When there has been a trust breakdown in human relationships, forgiveness is often used as a mechanism for rebuilding trust after a breakdown has occurred. It is not unconditional and is governed by a number of motivating factors. These factors include offence severity and frequency, as well as the offender's previous behaviour towards the victim, and the offender's intent (was there deliberate or accidental error) and subsequent efforts to reconcile or repair the relationship [20]. Forgiveness is a mechanism which allows the victim to replace their formerly negative feelings towards the offender with positive ones which would allow them to reconcile and maintain their relationship [21]. In fact, it may have evolved specifically in humans to allow valued social relationships to be maintained over time [22].

A socio-cognitive model, where social agents have cognisant goals and objectives, therefore may provide the basis for agents which are able to repair relationships, through forgiveness, when there has been a breakdown. This is something which can be seen even using game theoretic approaches. Axelrod found that in a series of iterated prisoner's dilemmas forgiving strategies were the most robust over time [23]. Additionally, in games where the structure of the agents was fixed, where agents had the same neighbours throughout the iterations, cooperative strategies dominated and agents were more forgiving and friendlier to their neighbours [24].

Mechanisms for facilitating forgiveness have been proposed which allow offenders not only to apologise but also to validate their apology with some kind of reparation action [25]. Without reparations, it has been found that victims in online interactions took revenge against the offender where their apology was not seen as costly enough by the victim [25]. Apologies need to be costly to the offender in order to facilitate forgiveness [26]. This serves two purposes as it punishes the offender for their offence and makes reparations towards the victim.

Another part of the forgiveness process is that the offender admits that they are guilty of a transgression. The victim is more likely to forgive the offender if they believe the offender is less likely to repeat the transgression in future interactions [22]. The acknowledgement of guilt itself is an intangible cost for breaking a social norm [27] and in face to face interactions, humans have emotional and physical reactions which who the victim if they are regretting, or feeling ashamed or embarrassed by their actions, for example by blushing [28]. Since physical cues are difficult to transmit in socio-technical systems mechanisms enabling apology, admission of guilt and suitable reparations to the victim are key in order to facilitate forgiveness.

Social Norms and Values. Although social norms and social values tend to be used interchangeably, social norms are specific guidelines which members of a society are expected to uphold in given situations, whereas social values are much broader [29]. They are the general ideas which a society holds true and include concepts such as trusting and forgiving each other [30].

Human interactions are governed by many social norms of behaviour which are learnt in childhood [31] and dictate what is and is not acceptable in society. It is so ingrained in human society, that is has been shown that humans unconsciously and automatically apply them to computer agents in social situations [32]. Examples of this include following politeness norms when interacting with a computer agent [33], showing empathy to virtual characters [34] and considering the computer agent as part of a team despite the agent showing no physical human attributes [33]. In the context of building relationships with agents, it has been found that in situations where there errors have occurred, humans are friendlier and more positive to robots who blame themselves rather than their human counterparts, even if the blame should be equally distributed [35].

In multi-agent systems norms are usually set up as a series of permissions and sanctions [36]. Over time, two issues can emerge. Firstly, how to enforce the current norms and secondly how to allow the norms to evolve (to create new norms or modify existing ones) as the system evolves [37]. There have been a number of suggestions for resolving these issues. One proposal is to establish leader and follower behaviour amongst agents to enable new joiners to the system to know who to look to for guidance [38]. Another method is to enable agents to log histories of interactions and identify "special events" which they then confirm with the rest of the system to see if other agents also exhibit the same behaviour [39]. Machine learning, leadership, imitation and data mining have all been used in multi-agent normative systems to study the creation, identification and propagation of norms [40,41].

3   Constructing a Social Socio-Technical System

Increasingly generalised norms, or values, are being used to assist with designing technology and systems. The concept of value sensitive design [42] is becoming increasingly relevant as society shapes technology and vice versa and the threat of breakdown or malicious attacks of systems increases. One way in which systems breakdowns may be combated is to create a socio-technical system which encompasses key social norms and educates the agents in it to create values which correspond to similar values in human society, thus establishing a "shared reality" between agents.

Before considering how to imbue social values in a socio-technical system, it must first be considered how social values are created in human society. Sociology allows analysis of how human society develops. It also considers how to create a society based on social interactions. One theory in particular which is useful when considering this, is the concept of social constructivism.

3.1   Social Constructivism

The starting point of the proposal is the theory of social constructivism. Social constructivism was initially proposed in the 1960's by the sociologists Berger and Luckmann in their book "The Social Construction of Reality" [43]. It remains a key work in sociology and has inspired a number of diverging theories in the social sciences [44].

Berger and Luckmann proposed that it is *"knowledge that guides conduct in everyday life"* [43, p. 33]. One of the main ways in which humans communicate is through language. How we define the objects around us is part of our reality, the very action of talking to one another allows humans to pass on key ideas which then form part of their reality. Our use of language is therefore how knowledge is transferred over time, between generations and cultures. Since we need to communicate to other members in our society to pass on this knowledge, this means that our reality is actually a social construct which we have developed over time. They proposed that reality is composed of two parts, the objective and the subjective. The objective part of reality is the part external to us, the part that as a society we have defined and we all understand to be true. The subjective part of reality is each person's individual experience of this reality.

To give an example of this, in a global context the term "father" is given to the male parent of a child, every individual reading a newspaper article about a father understands this to be true. The definition of father might have pre-existed them, but as part of their objective reality they nevertheless understand what it means. The subjective reality is that the individual understands that the article is not about *their* father. The link between these two realities is the knowledge that all individuals have the same understanding of the term.

Knowledge is key to being able to function within a socially constructed reality. Individuals need to know current norms of behaviour but also the definitions of objects and ideas which already exist in society. Berger and Luckmann proposed that institutions (or norms) are created through a process called habitualisation- *"all human activity is subject to habitualisation. Any action that is repeated frequently becomes cast into a pattern, which can then be performed again in the future in the same manner and with the same economical effort"* [43, pp. 70–71]. These repeated patterns of actions introduces institutions, or norms, into society which *"control human conduct by setting up predetermined patterns of conduct"* [43, p. 72]. According to this theory institutions are not created instantaneously but over time and it is this continual repetition of human actions and interactions which is passed on through language that builds human society.

This concept of habitualisation, learning from patterns over time and then using it to inform future behaviour, is also something which is already extensively used in computing in the form of machine learning.

3.2 Artificial Social Constructivism

Since it is possible to create a shared reality based on social interaction between humans, it is proposed that by imbuing socio-technical systems with human social concepts it is possible to create a shared social reality between the human, computational and digital agents in the network. This could be done by enabling the computational and digital agents access to digitised versions of trust and forgiveness mechanisms seen in human society and by allowing them to learn from each other to establish norms of behaviour which, over time, would develop into values. Although this is more complicated than building up a model of the user and programming it into agents, this method allows the agents to interpret human behaviour more accurately and react accordingly.

Using sociological theories is advantageous in this situation since sociology, which is based on real observed human behaviour, would allow computational and digital agents in the network to better interpret the behaviour of the most irrational agents, humans. This would allow the computational and digital agents to more accurately react and conform to expected human norms. This is particularly important in the occurrence of errors which lead to relationship breakdown.

It is proposed that a computational form of social constructivism, termed artificial social constructivism, is required which encompasses both human, computational and digital agents in a socio-technical system. Artificial social constructivism has three core principles: norms, education and values. The agents will first need to establish norms over time. Then they will need to pass on these established, or changing, norms to both existing and new agents in the system, so that all agents learn how to behave when interacting with one anther. Similar to the same way a child brought up in a certain manner comes to view the system's successes and failures as its own [45] it is posited that through learning, maintaining and enforcing the norms of the system, the agents become invested in it and thus more motivated to uphold it as a whole. In this way the agents will establish key values (generalised norms) which the whole system will adhere to, effectively establishing what in human terms we would call a society.

4   Conclusion

By applying sociological theory to the network in this way, the computational or digital agents should behave as the human agents would expect other humans to behave. The resulting interactions between humans and computers may then be the same as interactions between humans themselves. This has multiple advantages, for example better understanding by agents of other agents' behaviour increases the likelihood of system longevity, but in this position paper we specifically considered the benefit in overcoming relationship breakdowns which occur as a result of errors. As humans automatically respond to computers if they exhibit the same social cues as a human would [33], shared values between agents should lead to a more predictable system from the agents perspectives. The computational and digital agents should be able to better anticipate how the human agents will respond in interactions, while, from the point of view of the human agents, the computer or digital agents will better conform to expected behavioural patterns as part of the human's own social network. The creation of a "shared reality", based on shared experience of social norms and values between the agents in the system, should therefore allow the system to more easily overcome errors by using human traits like trust and forgiveness to repair 'relationships' after faults or misunderstandings between agents occur.

This position paper put forward a review of the relevant literature in trust, forgiveness, norms, values and social capital in socio-technical systems and put forward for a theory which ties these concepts together. Social constructivism introduces a method by which reality is created by human social interactions. Artificial social constructivism, proposed here, is a way of applying this concept to a socio-technical system which uses digital versions of trust, forgiveness, norms, values to create a "shared reality" between humans and computers. The theory aims to address the question of how we can ensure that relationships with, and mediated by, computers are the same as those with other humans. This will in turn allow for the creation of long-lasting socio-technical systems which are better at overcoming errors, and maintaining 'relationships' between the agents, by using already established relationship management mechanisms from sociology.

Acknowledgements. The authors would like to thank the reviewers for their valuable insights and suggestions.

References

1. Nallur, V., Monteil, J., Sammons, T., Bouroche, M., Clarke, S.: Increasing information in socio-technical MAS considered contentious. In: 2015 IEEE International Conference on Self-Adaptive & Self-Organizing Systems Workshops, pp. 25–30. IEEE, September 2015

2. Castelfranchi, C., Falcone, R.: Social trust: a cognitive approach. In: Castelfranchi, C., Tan, Y.H. (eds.) Trust and Deception in Virtual Societies, pp. 55–90. Springer, Dordrecht (2001). https://doi.org/10.1007/978-94-017-3614-5_3

3. Hardin, C.D., Higgins, E.T.: Shared reality: how social verification makes the subjective objective. In: Sorrentino, R.M., Higgins, E.T. (eds.) Handbook of Motivation and Cognition. Guilford Press, New York (1996)

4. Ostrom, E., Ahn, T.: Foundations of Social Capital. Edward Elgar Pub, Cheltenham (2003)

5. Pitt, J., Nowak, A.: The reinvention of social capital for socio-technical systems. IEEE Technol. Soc. Mag. 33(1), 27–34 (2014)

6. Petruzzi, P.E., Busquets, D., Pitt, J.: Experiments with social capital in multi-agent systems. In: Dam, H.K., Pitt, J., Xu, Y., Governatori, G., Ito, T. (eds.) PRIMA 2014. LNCS (LNAI), vol. 8861, pp. 18–33. Springer, Cham (2014). https://doi.org/10.1007/978-3-319-13191-7_2

7. Petruzzi, P.E., Pitt, J., Busquets, D.: Electronic social capital for self-organising multi-agent systems. ACM Trans. Auton. Adapt. Syst. 12(3), 1–25 (2017)

8. Gambetta, D. (ed.): Trust. Basil Blackwell, Oxford (1990)

9. Luhmann, N.: Trust and Power. Wiley, Chichester (1979)

10. Marsh, S.: Formalising trust as a computational concept. PhD thesis, University of Stirling (1994)

11. Pinyol, I., Sabater-Mir, J.: Computational trust and reputation models for open multi-agent systems: a review. Artif. Intell. Rev. 40(1), 1–25 (2013)

12. Jones, A.J.I.: On the concept of trust. Decis. Support Syst. 33, 29–78 (2002)

13. Cho, J.H., Chan, K., Adali, S.: A survey on trust modeling. ACM Comput. Surv. 48(2), 40 (2015)

14. Marsh, S., Dibben, M.R.: Trust, untrust, distrust and mistrust – an exploration of the Dark(er) side. In: Herrmann, P., Issarny, V., Shiu, S. (eds.) iTrust 2005. LNCS, vol. 3477, pp. 17–33. Springer, Heidelberg (2005). https://doi.org/10.1007/11429760_2

15. Mcknight, D.H., Choudhury, V., Kacmar, C.: The impact of initial consumer trust on intentions to transact with a web site: a trust building model. J. Strateg. Inform. Syst. 11, 297–323 (2002)

16. Han, Y., Shen, Z., Leung, C., Miao, C., Lesser, V.R.: A survey of multi-agent trust management systems. IEEE Access 1, 35–50 (2013)

17. Axelrod, R.: An evolutionary approach to norms. Amer. Polit. Sci. Rev. 80(4), 1095–1111 (1986)

18. Pinyol, I., Sabater-Mir, J., Dellunde, P., Paolucci, M.: Reputation-based decisions for logic-based cognitive agents. Auton. Agents Multi-Agent Syst. 24(1), 175–216 (2012)

19. Rea, T.: Engendering trust in electronic environments. In: Castelfranchi, C., Tan, Y.H. (eds.) Trust Deception in Virtual Societies. Springer, Dordrecht (2001). https://doi.org/10.1007/978-94-017-3614-5_11

20. Vasalou, A., Hopfensitz, A., Pitt, J.: In praise of forgiveness: ways for repairing trust breakdowns in one-off online interactions. Int. J. Hum Comput Stud. 66(6), 466–480 (2008)

21. McCullough, M.E.: Forgiveness: who does it and how do they do it? Curr. Dir. Psychol. Sci. 10(6), 194–197 (2001)

22. McCullough, M.: Beyond Revenge The Evolution of the Forgiveness Instinct, 1st edn. Jossey-Bass, San Francisco (2008)

23. Axelrod, R., Wu, J.: How to cope with noise in the iterated Prisoner's Dilemma. J. Confl. Resolut. 39(1), 183–189 (1995)

24. Cohen, M.D., Riolo, R.L., Axelrod, R.: The role of social structure in the maintenance of cooperative regimes. Ration. Soc. **13**(1), 5–32 (2001)
25. Vasalou, A., Hopfensitz, A., Pitt, J.: Is an apology enough? How to resolve trust breakdowns in episodic online interactions. In: 21st BCS HCI, vol. 2, pp. 119–122 (2007)
26. Lenaerts, T., Martinez-Vaquero, L.A., Han, T.A., Pereira, L.M.: Conditions for the evolution of apology and forgiveness in populations of autonomous agents. In: AAAI Spring 2016 Symposium on Ethical and Moral, pp. 242–248 (2016)
27. Ostrom, E.: Collective action and the evolution of social norms. J. Econ. Perspect. **14**(3), 137–158 (2000)
28. Pitt, J.: Digital blush: towards shame and embarrassment in multi-agent information trading applications. Cogn. Technol. Work **6**(1), 23–36 (2004)
29. Mondal, P.: Difference Between Norms and Values of Society (2017)
30. Pitt, J.: From trust and forgiveness to social capital and justice. In: Reif, W., et al. (eds.) Trustworthy Open Self-Organising Systems, pp. 185–208. Springer, Cham (2016). https://doi.org/10.1007/978-3-319-29201-4_7
31. Binmore, K.: Social norms or social preferences? Mind Soc. **9**(2), 139–157 (2010)
32. Nass, C., Steuer, J., Tauber, E.R.: Computers are social actors. In: Conference on Companion on Human Factors in Computing Systems, p. 204 (1994)
33. Reeves, B., Nass, C.: The Media Equation. Cambridge University Press, Cambridge (1996)
34. Paiva, A., et al.: Caring for agents and agents that care: building empathic relations with synthetic agents. In: 3rd International Joint Conference on Autonomous Agents & Multiagent Systems, pp. 194–201 (2004)
35. Groom, V., Chen, J., Johnson, T., Kara, F.A., Nass, C.: Critic, compatriot, or chump?: responses to robot blame attribution. In: 2010 5th ACM/IEEE Internationl Conference on Human-Robot Interaction (HRI), pp. 211–218. IEEE (2010)
36. Artikis, A., Sergot, M., Pitt, J.: Specifying norm-governed computational societies. ACM Trans. Comput. Logic **10**(1), 1–42 (2009)
37. Posner, R.A., Rasmusen, E.B.: Creating and enforcing norms, with special reference to sanctions. Int. Rev. Law Econ. **19**(3), 369–382 (1999)
38. Savarimuthu, B.T.R., Cranefield, S., Purvis, M., Purvis, M.: Role model based mechanism for norm emergence in artificial agent societies. In: Sichman, J.S., Padget, J., Ossowski, S., Noriega, P. (eds.) COIN -2007. LNCS (LNAI), vol. 4870, pp. 203–217. Springer, Heidelberg (2008). https://doi.org/10.1007/978-3-540-79003-7_15
39. Savarimuthu, T., Cranefield, S., Purvis, M.A., Purvis, M.K.: Obligation norm identification in agent societies. J. Artif. Soc. Soc. Simul. **13**(4), 3 (2010)
40. Savarimuthu, B.T.R., Cranefield, S.: Norm creation, spreading and emergence: a survey of simulation models of norms in multi-agent systems. Multiagent Grid Syst. **7**(1), 21–54 (2011)
41. Savarimuthu, B.T.R., Arulanandam, R., Purvis, M.: Aspects of active norm learning and the effect of lying on norm emergence in agent societies. In: Kinny, D., Hsu, J.Y., Governatori, G., Ghose, A.K. (eds.) PRIMA 2011. LNCS (LNAI), vol. 7047, pp. 36–50. Springer, Heidelberg (2011). https://doi.org/10.1007/978-3-642-25044-6_6
42. Friedman, B., Kahn, P.: Value sensitive design: theory and methods. Technical report, University of Washington, pp. 1–8, December 2002

43. Berger, P., Luckmann, T.: The Social Construction of Reality. Penguin Books, London (1966)
44. Knoblauch, H., Wilke, R.: The common denominator: the reception and impact of Berger and Luckmann's the social construction of reality. Hum. Stud. **39**, 51–69 (2016)
45. Dewey, J.: Democracy and Education. Simon & Brown, California (2011)

Author Index